THE UNDERCOVER ECONOMIST

THE UNDERCOVER ECONOMIST

Exposing Why The Rich Are Rich,
The Poor Are Poor—
And Why You Can Never Buy
A Decent Used Car!

Tim Harford

OXFORD
UNIVERSITY PRESS

2006

OXFORD
UNIVERSITY PRESS

Oxford University Press, Inc., publishes works that
further Oxford University's objective of excellence
in research, scholarship, and education.

Oxford New York
Auckland Cape Town Dar es Salaam Hong Kong Karachi
Kuala Lumpur Madrid Melbourne Mexico City Nairobi
New Delhi Shanghai Taipei Toronto

With offices in
Argentina Austria Brazil Chile Czech Republic France Greece
Guatemala Hungary Italy Japan Poland Portugal Singapore
South Korea Switzerland Thailand Turkey Ukraine Vietnam

Copyright © 2006 by Tim Harford

Published by Oxford University Press, Inc.
198 Madison Avenue, New York, New York, 10016
www.oup.com

Oxford is a registered trademark of Oxford University Press

Library of Congress Cataloging-in-Publication Data
Harford, Tim, 1973–
The undercover economist / Tim Harford.
p. cm.
ISBN-13: 978-0-19-518977-3
ISBN-10: 0-19-518977-9
1. Economic history, 1990–
2. Economics.
3. Consumer education.
I. Title.
HC59.15.H35 2005 330.9'0511—dc22
2005010297

5 7 9 8 6
Printed in the United States of America
on acid-free paper

To Deborah Harford, Fran Monks, and Stella Harford—family
. . . past, present, and future.

Acknowledgments

Peter Sinclair got me into economics; Tony Courakis, Simon Cowan, Stan Fischer, Bob Garhart, Paul Klemperer, Brendan McElroy, Elinor Ostrom, Hyun Shin, Bill Sjostrom, and many others helped me along the way. I am grateful to them all.

At Shell, Ged Davis let me work part-time while I produced the first draft of the book. I was flattered by his reluctance and grateful for his support. Other colleagues at Shell were inspirational, especially Betty-Sue Flowers, Anupam Khanna, Cho Khong, Michael Klein, Doug McKay, and John Robinson.

At the *Financial Times*, Pilita Clark, Andy Davis, Chris Giles, Andrew Gowers, John Kay, John Willman, and Martin Wolf gave me opportunities and then made sure I didn't waste them.

At the World Bank, Michael Klein and Suzanne Smith are wonderful colleagues and every day with them is an education.

David Bodanis, Felicity Bryan, Penny Dablin, Moore Flannery, Juri Gabriel, Mark Henstridge, Diana Jackson, Oliver Johnson, John Kay, Cho Khong, Paul Klemperer, Stephen McGroarty, Doug McKay, Fran Monks, Dave Morris, Rafael Ramirez, Jillian Reilly, John Robinson, Tim Savin, Martin Wolf, and Andrew Wright improved the book with their comments.

Sally Holloway, my agent, has been superb. Tim Bartlett and Kate Hamill at Oxford University Press infuriated me with their precision and insight—I have been very lucky to work with them.

Most importantly, emotional support came from Diana Jackson, my wife Fran Monks, "Uncle" Dave Morris, and Jillian Reilly. Above all I have to thank Andrew Wright, a genius, without whom the book could never have been finished, and David Bodanis, an inspiration, without whom it would never have been started.

Contents

CONTENTS

THE UNDERCOVER ECONOMIST

Introduction

I would like to thank you for buying this book, but if you're anything like me you haven't bought it at all. Instead, you've carried it into the bookstore café and even now are sipping a cappuccino in comfort while you decide whether it's worth your money.

This is a book about how economists view the world. In fact, there might be an economist sitting near you right now. You might not spot him—a normal person looking at an economist wouldn't notice anything remarkable. But normal people look remarkable in the eyes of economists. What is the economist seeing? What could he tell you, if you cared to ask? And why *should* you care?

You may think you're enjoying a frothy cappuccino, but the economist sees you—and the cappuccino—as players in an intricate game of signals and negotiations, contests of strength and battles of wits. The game is for high stakes: some of the people who worked to get that coffee in front of you made a lot of money, some of them made very little, and some of them are after the money in your pocket right now. The economist can tell you who will get what, how, and why. My hope is that by the time you finish this book, you'll be able to see the same things. But please buy it first, before the store manager throws you out.

Your coffee is intriguing to the economist for another reason: he doesn't know how to make a cappuccino, and he knows that

nobody else does either. Who, after all, could boast of being able to grow, pick, roast, and blend coffee, raise and milk cows, roll steel and mold plastics and assemble them into an espresso machine, and, finally, shape ceramics into a cute mug? Your cappuccino reflects the outcome of a system of staggering complexity. There isn't a single person in the world who could produce what it takes to make a cappuccino.

The economist knows that the cappuccino is the product of an incredible team effort. Not only that, there is nobody in charge of the team. Economist Paul Seabright reminds us of the pleas of the Soviet official trying to comprehend the western system: "Tell me . . . who is in charge of the supply of bread to the population of London?" The question is comical, but the answer—nobody—is dizzying.

When the economist drags his attention away from your coffee and looks around the bookstore, the organizational challenges are even greater. The complexity of the system that made the store possible defies easy description: think of the accumulated centuries of design and development, from the paper upon which the books are printed to the spotlights that illuminate the shelves to the software that keeps track of the stock, not to mention the everyday miracles of organization through which the books are printed, bound, stored, delivered, stacked, and sold.

The system works remarkably well. When you bought this book—you have bought this book by now, haven't you?—you probably did so without having to give instructions to the bookstore to order it for you. Perhaps you did not even know when you left your home this morning that you were going to buy it. Yet by some magic, dozens of people took the actions necessary to fulfill your unpredictable desires: me, my editors, marketers, proofreaders, printers, paper manufacturers, ink suppliers, and many others. The economist can explain how such a system works, how companies will try to exploit it, and what you as a customer can do to fight back.

Now the Undercover Economist is gazing out of the window at the traffic jam outside. To some people, the jam is merely an

irritating fact of life. To the economist, there is a story to tell about the contrast between the chaos of the traffic and the smooth running of the bookshop. We can learn something from the bookstore that will help us avoid traffic jams.

While economists are constantly thinking about the things going on around them, they are not limited to discussing local matters. If you cared to engage one in conversation you might talk about the difference between bookshops in the developed world and libraries in Cameroon, which have eager readers but no books. You might point out that the gap between the world's rich countries and the world's poor countries is huge and appalling. The economist would share your sense of injustice—but he could also tell you why rich countries are rich and poor countries are poor, and what might be done about it.

Perhaps the Undercover Economist seems like a know-it-all, but he reflects the broad ambition of economics to understand people: as individuals, as partners, as competitors, and as members of the vast social organizations we call "economies."

This breadth of interest is reflected in the eclectic tastes of the Nobel Prize committee. Since 1990, the Nobel Prize in Economics has only occasionally been awarded for advances in the obviously "economic" things, such as the theory of exchange rates or business cycles. More often, it has been awarded for insights less obviously connected with what you might have thought was economics: human development, psychology, history, voting, law, and even esoteric discoveries such as why you can't buy a decent secondhand car.

My aim in this book is to help you see the world like an economist. I will tell you nothing about exchange rates or business cycles, but I will unlock the mystery of secondhand cars. We'll look at the big issues, such as how China is lifting a million people a month out of poverty, and the little ones, such as how to avoid paying too much money in the supermarket. It's detective work all the way, but I'll teach you how to use the investigative tools of the economist. I hope that by the end of the book, you'll be a more savvy consumer—and a more savvy voter too, able to see

the truth behind the stories that politicians try to sell you. Everyday life is full of puzzles that many people do not even realize are puzzles, so above all, I hope that you will be able to see the fun behind these everyday secrets. So let's start on familiar territory by asking, who pays for your coffee?

ONE

Who Pays for Your Coffee?

The long commute on public transportation is a commonplace experience of life in major cities around the world, whether you live in New York, Tokyo, Antwerp, or Prague. Commuting dispiritingly combines the universal and the particular. The particular, because each commuter is a rat in his own unique maze: timing the run from the shower to the station turnstiles; learning the timetables and the correct end of the platform to speed up the transfer between different trains; trading off the disadvantages of standing room only on the first train home against a seat on the last one. Yet commutes also produce common patterns—bottlenecks and rush hours—that are exploited by entrepreneurs the world over. My commute in Washington DC is not the same as yours in London, New York, or Hong Kong, but it will look surprisingly familiar.

Farragut West is the Metro station ideally positioned to serve the World Bank, International Monetary Fund, and even the White House. Every morning, sleep-deprived, irritable travelers surface from Farragut West into the International Square plaza, and they are not easily turned aside from their paths. They want to get out of the noise and bustle, around the shuffling tourists, and to their desks just slightly before their bosses. They do not welcome detours. But there is a place of peace and bounty that can tempt them to tarry for a couple of minutes. In this oasis,

rare delights are served with smiles by attractive and exotic men and women—today, a charming barista whose name badge reads "Maria." I am thinking, of course, of Starbucks. The café is placed, inescapably, at the exit to International Square. This is no quirk of Farragut West: the first storefront you will pass on your way out of the nearby Farragut North Metro is—another Starbucks. You find such conveniently located coffee shops all over the planet and catering to the same desperate commuters. The coffee shop within ten yards of the exit from Washington's Dupont Circle Metro station is called Cosi. New York's Penn Station boasts Seattle Coffee Roasters just by the exit to Eighth Avenue. Commuters through Shinjuku Station, Tokyo, can enjoy a Starbucks without leaving the station concourse. In London's Waterloo station, it is the AMT kiosk that guards the exit onto the south bank of the Thames.

At $2.55 a tall cappuccino from Starbucks is hardly cheap. But of course, I can afford it. Like many of the people stopping at that café, I earn the price of that coffee every few minutes. None of us care to waste our time trying to save a few pennies by searching out a cheaper coffee at 8:30 in the morning. There is a huge demand for the most convenient coffee possible—in Waterloo Station, for example, seventy-four million people pass through each year. That makes the location of the coffee bar crucial.

The position of the Starbucks café at Farragut West is advantageous, not just because it's located on an efficient route from the platforms to the station exit, but because there are no other coffee bars on that route. It's hardly a surprise that they do a roaring trade.

If you buy as much coffee as I do you may have come to the conclusion that somebody is getting filthy rich out of all this. If the occasional gripes in the newspapers are correct, the coffee in that cappuccino costs pennies. Of course, the newspapers don't tell us the whole story: there's milk, electricity, cost of the paper cups—and the cost of paying Maria to smile at grouchy custom-

ers all day long. But after you add all that up you still get something a lot less than the price of a cup of coffee. According to economics professor Brian McManus, markups on coffee are around 150 percent—it costs forty cents to make a one-dollar cup of drip coffee and costs less than a dollar for a small latte, which sells for $2.55. So somebody is making a lot of money. Who?

You might think that the obvious candidate is Howard Schultz, the owner of Starbucks. But the answer isn't as simple as that. The main reason that Starbucks can ask $2.55 for a cappuccino is that there isn't a shop next door charging $2.00. So why is nobody next door undercutting Starbucks? Without wishing to dismiss the achievements of Mr. Schultz, cappuccinos are not in fact complicated products. There is no shortage of drinkable cappuccinos (sadly, there is no shortage of undrinkable cappuccinos either). It doesn't take much to buy some coffee machines and a counter, build up a brand with a bit of advertising and some free samples, and hire decent staff. Even Maria is replaceable.

The truth is that Starbucks' most significant advantage is its location on the desire line of thousands of commuters. There are a few sweet spots for coffee bars—by station exits or busy street corners. Starbucks and its rivals have snapped them up. If Starbucks really did have the hypnotic hold over its customers that critics complain about, it would hardly need to spend so much effort getting people to trip over its cafés. The nice margin that Starbucks makes on their cappuccinos is due neither to the quality of the coffee nor to the staff: it's location, location, location.

But who controls the location? Look ahead to the negotiations for the new rental agreement. The landlord at International Square will not only be talking to Starbucks but to other chains like Cosi and Caribou Coffee, and DC's local companies: Java House, Swing's, Capitol Grounds, and Teaism. The landlord can sign an agreement with each one of them or can sign an exclusive agreement with only one. She'll quickly find that nobody is very eager to pay much for a space next to ten other coffee bars, and so she will get the most advantage out of the exclusive agreement.

In trying to work out who is going to make all the money, simply remember that there are at least half a dozen competing companies on one side of the negotiating table and on the other side is a landlord who owns a single prime coffee-bar site. By playing them off against each other, the landlord should be able to dictate the terms and force one of them to pay rent, which consumes almost all their expected profits. The successful company will expect some profit but not much: if the rent looks low enough to leave a substantial profit, another coffee bar will be happy to pay a little extra for the site. There is an unlimited number of potential coffee bars and a limited number of attractive sites—and that means the landlords have the upper hand.

This is pure armchair reasoning. It's reasonable to ask if all of this is actually true. After I explained to a long-suffering friend (over coffee) all of the principles involved, she asked me whether I could prove it. I admitted that it was just a theory—as Sherlock Holmes might say, a piece of "observation and deduction," based on clues available to all of us. A couple of weeks later she sent me an article from the *Financial Times*, which relied on industry experts who had access to the accounts of coffee companies. The article began, "Few companies are making any money" and concluded that one of the main problems was "the high costs of running retail outlets in prime locations with significant passing trade." Reading accounts is dull; economic detective work is the easy way to get to the same conclusion.

Strength from scarcity

Browsing through the old economics books on the shelf at home, I dug out the first analysis of twenty-first-century coffee bars. Published in 1817, it explains not just the modern coffee bar but much of the modern world itself. Its author, David Ricardo, had already made himself a multimillionaire (in today's money) as a stockbroker, and was later to become a Member of Parliament. But Ricardo was also an enthusiastic economist, who longed to understand what had happened to Britain's economy during

the then-recent Napoleonic wars: the price of wheat had rock-eted, and so had rents on agricultural land. Ricardo wanted to know why.

The easiest way to understand Ricardo's analysis is to use one of his own examples. Imagine a wild frontier with few settlers but plenty of fertile meadow available for growing crops. One day an aspiring young farmer, Axel, walks into town and offers to pay rent for the right to grow crops on an acre of good meadow. Everyone agrees how much grain an acre of meadow will pro-duce, but they cannot decide how much rent Axel should pay. Because there is no shortage of land lying fallow, competing land-lords will not be able to charge a high rent . . . or any significant rent at all. Each landlord would rather collect a small rent than no rent at all, and so each will undercut his rivals until Axel is able to start farming for very little rent—just enough to compen-sate for the landlord's trouble.

The first lesson here is that the person in possession of the desired resource—the landlord in this case—does not always have as much power as one would assume. And the story doesn't specify whether Axel is very poor or has a roll of cash in the false heel of his walking boot, because it doesn't make any difference to the rent. Bargaining strength comes through scarcity: settlers are scarce and meadows are not, so landlords have no bargain-ing power.

That means that if relative scarcity shifts from one person to another, bargaining shifts as well. If over the years many immi-grants follow in Axel's footsteps, the amount of spare meadow-land will shrink until there is none left. As long as there is any, competition between landlords who have not attracted any ten-ants will keep rents very low. One day, however, an aspiring farmer will walk into town—let's call him Bob—and will find that there is no spare fertile land. The alternative, farming on inferior but abundant scrubland, is not attractive. So Bob will offer to pay good money to any landlord who will evict Axel, or any of the other farmers currently farming virtually rent-free, and let him

farm there instead. But just as Bob is willing to pay to rent meadowland rather than scrubland, all of the meadow farmers will also be willing to pay not to move. Everything has changed, and quickly: suddenly the landlords have acquired real bargaining power, because suddenly farmers are relatively common and meadows are relatively scarce.

That means the landowners will be able to raise their rents. By how much? It will have to be enough that farmers earn the same farming on meadows and paying rent, or farming on inferior scrubland rent free. If the difference in productiveness of the two types of land is five bushels of grain a year, then the rent will also be five bushels a year. If a landlord tries to charge more, his tenant will leave to farm scrubland. If the rent is any less, the scrub farmer would be willing to offer more.

It may seem odd that the rents changed so rapidly simply because one more man arrived to farm the area. This story doesn't seem to explain how the world really works. But there is more truth to it than you might think, even if it is oversimplified. Of course, in the real world, there are other elements to consider: laws about evicting people, long-term contracts, and even cultural norms, such as the fact that kicking one person out and installing a new tenant the next day is just "not done." In the real world there are more than two types of farmland, and Bob may have different options to being a farmer—he may be able to get a job as an accountant or driving a cab. All these facts complicate what happens in reality; they slow down the shift in bargaining power, alter the absolute numbers involved, and put a brake on sudden movements in rents.

Yet the complications of everyday life often hide the larger trends behind the scenes, as scarcity power shifts from one group to another. The economist's job is to shine a spotlight on the underlying process. We should not be surprised if, suddenly, the land market shifts against farmers; or if house prices go up dramatically; or if the world is covered by coffee bars over a period of just a few months. The simplicity of the story emphasizes one

part of the underlying reality—but the emphasis is helpful in revealing something important. Sometimes relative scarcity and bargaining strength really do change quickly, and with profound effects on people's lives. We often complain about symptoms— the high cost of buying a cup of coffee, or even a house. The symptoms cannot be treated successfully without understanding the patterns of scarcity which underlie them.

"Marginal" land is of central importance

The shifts in bargaining power don't have to stop there. While the farming story can be elaborated indefinitely, the basic principles remain the same. For example, if new farmers keep arriving, they will eventually cultivate not only the meadowland but also all of the scrubland. When a new settler, Cornelius, walks into town, the only land available will be the grassland, which is even less productive than scrubland. We can expect the same dance of negotiations: Cornelius will offer money to landlords to try to get onto scrubland, rents will quickly rise on scrubland, and the differential between scrubland and meadow will have to stay the same (or farmers would want to move), so the rent will rise on meadow too.

The rent on meadowland, therefore, will always be equal to the difference in grain yield between meadowland and whatever land is available rent-free to new farmers. Economists call this other land "marginal" land because it is at the margin between being cultivated and not being cultivated. (You will soon see that economists think about decisions at the margin quite a lot.) In the beginning, when meadowland was more plentiful than settlers, it was not only the best land, it was also the "marginal" land because new farmers could use it. Because the best land was the same as the marginal land, there was no rent, beyond the trivial sum needed to compensate the landlord for his trouble. Later, when there were so many farmers that there was no longer enough prime land to go around, scrubland became the marginal land, and rents on meadows rose to five bushels a year—the difference

in productivity between the meadowland and the marginal land (in this case, the scrubland). When Cornelius arrived, the grassland became the marginal land, meadows became yet more attractive relative to the marginal land, and so the landlords were able to raise the rent on meadows again. It's important to note here that there is no absolute value: everything is relative to that marginal land.

From meadows back to coffee kiosks

A nice story, but those of us who like Westerns may prefer the gritty cinematography of *Unforgiven* or the psychological isolation of *High Noon*. So, David Ricardo and I get no prizes for our screenwriting, but we might be excused, as long as our little fable actually tells us something useful about the modern world.

We can start with coffee kiosks. Why is coffee expensive in London, New York, Washington, or Tokyo? The commonsense view is that coffee is expensive because the coffee kiosks have to pay high rent. David Ricardo's model can show us that this is the wrong way to think about the issue, because "high rent" is not an arbitrary fact of life. It has a cause.

Ricardo's story illustrates that two things determine the rent on prime locations like meadowland: the difference in agricultural productivity between meadows and marginal land, and the importance of agricultural productivity itself. At a dollar a bushel, five bushels of grain is a five-dollar rent. At two hundred thousand dollars a bushel, five bushels of grain is a million-dollar rent. Meadows command high dollar rents only if the grain they help produce is also valuable.

Now apply Ricardo's theory to coffee bars. Just as meadowland will command high rents if the grain they produce is valuable, prime coffee-bar locations will command high rents only if customers will pay high prices for coffee. Rush-hour customers are so desperate for caffeine and in such a hurry that they are practically price-blind. The willingness to pay top dollar for convenient coffee sets the high rent, and not the other way around.

Spaces suitable for coffee kiosks are like meadows—they are the best quality property for the purpose, and they fill up quickly. The ground-floor corner units of Manhattan's Midtown are the preserve of Starbucks, Cosi, and their competitors. Near Washington DC's Dupont Circle, Cosi has the prime spot at the southern exit, and Starbucks has the northern one, not to mention staking out territory opposite the adjacent stations up and down the Metro line. In London, AMT has Waterloo, King's Cross, Marylebone, and Charing Cross stations, and indeed every London station hosts one of the big-name coffee chains. These spots could be used to sell secondhand cars or Chinese food, but they never are. This isn't because a train station is a bad place to sell a Chinese meal or a secondhand car, but because there is no shortage of other places with lower rents from which noodles or cars can be sold—customers are in less of a hurry, more willing to walk, or order a delivery. For coffee bars and similar establishments selling snacks or newspapers, cheaper rent is no compensation for the loss of a flood of price-blind customers.

Portable models

David Ricardo managed to write an analysis of cappuccino bars in train stations before either cappuccino bars or train stations existed. This is the kind of trick that makes people either hate or love economics. Those who hate it argue that if we want to understand how the modern coffee business works, we should not be reading an analysis of farming published in 1817.

But many of us love the fact that Ricardo was able, nearly two hundred years ago, to produce insights that illuminate our understanding today. It's easy to see the difference between nineteenth-century farming and twenty-first-century frothing, but not so easy to see the similarity before it is pointed out to us. Economics is partly about modeling, about articulating basic principles and patterns that operate behind seemingly complex subjects like the rent on farms or coffee bars.

There are other models of the coffee business, useful for different things. A model of the design and architecture of coffee bars could be useful as a case study for interior designers. A physics model could outline the salient features of the machine that generates the ten atmospheres of pressure required to brew espresso; the same model might be useful for talking about suction pumps or the internal combustion engine. Today we have models of the ecological impacts of different disposal methods for coffee grounds. Each model is useful for different things, but a "model" that tried to describe the design, the engineering, the ecology, and the economics would be no simpler than reality itself and so would add nothing to our understanding.

Ricardo's model is useful for discussing the relationship between scarcity and bargaining strength, which goes far beyond coffee or farming and ultimately explains much of the world around us. When economists see the world, they see hidden social patterns, patterns that become evident only when one focuses on the essential underlying processes. This focus leads critics to say that economics doesn't consider the whole story, the whole "system." How else, though, could a nineteenth-century analysis of farming proclaim the truth about twenty-first-century coffee bars, except through grossly failing to notice all kinds of important differences? The truth is that it's simply not possible to understand anything complicated without focusing on certain elements to reduce that complexity. Economists have certain things they like to focus on, and scarcity is one of them. This focus means that we do not notice the mechanics of the espresso machine, nor the color schemes of the coffee bars, nor other interesting, important facts. But we gain from that focus, too, and one of the things we gain is an understanding of the "system"— the economic system, which is far more all-encompassing than many people realize.

A word of caution is appropriate, though. The simplifications of economic models have been known to lead economists astray. Ricardo himself was an early casualty. He tried to extend his brilliantly successful model of individual farmers and landlords to

explain the division of income in the whole economy: how much went to workers, how much to landlords, and how much to capitalists. It didn't quite work, because Ricardo treated the whole agricultural sector as if it were one vast farm with a single landlord. A unified agricultural sector had nothing to gain from improving the land's productivity with roads or irrigation, because those improvements would also reduce the scarcity of good land. But an individual landlord in competition with the others would have plenty of incentive to make improvements. Tied up in the technical details, Ricardo failed to realize that thousands of landlords competing with each other would make different decisions than a single one.

So Ricardo's model can't explain everything. But we are about to discover that it goes farther than Ricardo himself could ever have imagined. It doesn't just explain the principles behind coffee bars and farming. If applied correctly, it shows that environmental legislation can dramatically affect income distribution. It explains why some industries naturally have high profits, while in other industries high profits are a sure sign of collusion. It even manages to explain why educated people object to immigration by other educated people, while the working classes complain about immigration by other unskilled workers.

Different reasons for high rent

Do you care if you get ripped off?

I do. A lot of things in this life are expensive. Of course, sometimes that expense is a natural outcome of the power of scarcity. For instance, there are not many apartments overlooking Central Park in New York or Hyde Park in London. Because so many people want them, those apartments are expensive, and a lot of people end up being disappointed. There is nothing sinister about that. But it's not nearly so obvious why popcorn is so expensive at the movies—there was no popcorn shortage last time I checked. So the first thing we might want to do is to distinguish between different reasons for things being expensive.

In Ricardo's terms, we would like to know the different causes of high rents. Knowing this about meadows is only mildly interesting (unless you are a farmer) but takes on a sudden significance when applied to the question of why your apartment rent seems so extortionate, or whether banks are ripping us off. But we can start with meadows and apply what we learn more widely.

We know that rents on the best land are determined by the difference in fertility between the best land and the marginal land. So the obvious reason that rents might be high is that the best land produces very valuable crops relative to the marginal land. As mentioned a couple of pages ago, five bushels of grain is a five-dollar rent at a dollar a bushel, but at two hundred thousand dollars a bushel, five bushels of grain is a million-dollar rent. If grain is expensive, it's only natural that the scarce meadows that produce it will also be expensive.

But there's another way to drive rent on meadows up, and it is not nearly so natural. Let's say landlords get together and manage to persuade the local sheriff that there should be what in England they call a "green belt," a broad area of land around the city on which property development is very strongly discouraged by tough planning regulations. The landlords claim that it would be a shame to cover beautiful wild land with farms, and so farming on the land should be made illegal.

The landlords stand to benefit hugely from such a ban, because it would drive up the rents on all legal land. Remember that rents on meadowland are set by the difference between the productivity of meadowland and the productivity of the marginal land. Ban farming on that marginal land, and the rent on meadows will jump; where once the alternative to paying rent and farming on meadows was to farm on grassland rent-free, now there is no alternative. Farmers are much more eager to farm on meadows now that farming on the grassland is illegal, and the rent they're willing to pay is much higher too.

So we've found two reasons why rents might be high. The first is that it's worth paying a lot for good land, because the grain

that good land produces is so valuable. The second is that it's worth paying a lot for good land because the alternatives that should be available are not.

Those readers currently renting property in London may have furrowed brows at this point. London is surrounded by the original "Green Belt," created in the 1930s. Is that why property in London is so expensive to rent or buy—not because it's so much better than the alternative, but because the alternative has been made illegal?

It is a combination of both: it is certainly true that London is unique, and a better place to put plush apartments or office buildings than Siberia, Kansas City, or even Paris. Rents are high, in part, for that reason. But another reason why property in London is expensive is because of the Green Belt. One effect is to keep London from sprawling out across the surrounding region—which many people think is a good idea. The other effect is to transfer a massive amount of money from London tenants to London landlords: the Green Belt keeps rents and house prices in London much higher than they would be, in exactly the same way as a ban on grassland farming keeps rents on meadow and scrub much higher than they would otherwise be.

This is not an argument against the Green Belt. There are lots of benefits in having London's population capped at around six million people, instead of sixteen million or twenty-six million. But it is important that when we are weighing the pros and cons of legislation like the Green Belt, we understand that its effects are more than simply to preserve the environment. Office rents in London's West End are higher than in Manhattan or central Tokyo—in fact, the West End is the most expensive place in the world to rent an office, and it also holds the world record for the most expensive home, at £70m (about 130 million dollars). The Green Belt has made property in London scarce relative to the people who want to use it, and of course, strength comes from scarcity.

Now it's time for your first economics test. Why would improvements in the quality and price of the commuter train services that bring people into New York's Penn Station from the surrounding suburbs please anyone who rents a property in Manhattan? And why might New York landlords be less enthusiastic about such improvements?

The answer is that improved public transportation increases the alternatives to renting a place in the city. When a two-hour commute becomes a one-hour commute, and people are able to get a seat on the train instead of standing, some decide they'd rather save money and move out of Manhattan. Vacant apartments then appear on the market. Scarcity lessens, and rents fall. Improving commuter services wouldn't just affect commuters; it would affect everyone involved in New York's property market.

Are we being ripped off?

One of the problems with being an undercover economist is that you start to see "green belts" of one kind or another all over the place. How can we tell the difference between things that are expensive because they are naturally scarce, and things that are expensive because of artificial means—legislation, regulation, or foul play?

Ricardo's model can help here, too. We need to appreciate a hidden parallel between natural resources, like fields or busy locations, and companies. Fields are ways of turning stuff into different stuff: manure and seed into grain. Companies are the same. A car manufacturer turns steel, electricity, and other ingredients into cars. A gas station turns pumps, big tanks of fuel, and land into gasoline in your tank. A bank turns computers, advanced accounting systems, and cash into banking services. Without perpetrating too much intellectual violence, we can replace "rent" with "profit" throughout Ricardo's model. Rent is the return landlords receive from their property; profit is the return company owners earn from *their* property.

Let's use banking as an example. Imagine that one bank is very good at producing banking services—it has a fantastic corporate culture, strong brand, and has developed the best specialized banking software. Good people work there and other good people join just to learn from them. All this adds up to what economist John Kay (who explicitly invokes Ricardo's model) calls a "sustainable competitive advantage," meaning the sort of edge over the competition that will produce profits year in and year out.

Let's call this uberbank Axel Banking Corporation. A second bank, Bob's Credit and Debt, is not quite so competent: the brand is less trusted, the corporate culture is so-so. It's not bad, but it's not great either. A third bank, Cornelius's Deposit Enterprises, is extremely inefficient: it has a terrible reputation, the tellers are rude to the customers, and control of expenses is nonexistent. Cornelius's bank is less efficient than Bob's outfit and grossly incompetent compared with Axel's Banking Corporation. All this should remind us of the three types of land: meadowland, which is very efficient at producing grain; scrub, which is less efficient; and grassland, which is even less efficient.

Axel's bank, Bob's bank, and Cornelius's bank compete to sell banking services by persuading people to open accounts or take out loans. But Axel's bank is so effective that it can either produce banking services more cheaply or produce better quality services for the same cost. At the end of each year, Axel's bank will earn large profits, and Bob's bank, which serves its customers with less ease, will make something rather more modest, and Cornelius's bank will just break even. If the banking market was tougher, Cornelius's bank would go out of business. If the banking market started to get more attractive, Cornelius's bank would start to make a profit, and a new bank, even less efficient than Cornelius's, would enter the business. The new bank would be the marginal bank, just breaking even.

Without repeating every step of the analysis, we can remind ourselves that the rent on meadowland was set by comparison with the productivity of meadows to that of the marginal grassland. In the same way, Axel's profits are set in comparison with

Cornelius's bank, the marginal bank, which we know should expect to make little or no profits: company profits, like rents, are determined by the alternatives. A company with stiff competition will be less profitable than a company with incompetent rivals.

You are probably thinking of a flaw in the analogy: the acreage of meadows is fixed, but companies can grow. But that's only partly true; companies cannot grow overnight without diluting their reputation and the other capabilities that made them successful. On the other hand, while acreage cannot change, the distinctions between different types of land will shift over time as irrigation, pest control, or fertilizer technology develops. Ricardo's model, which ignores these changes over time, will explain trends in agricultural prices over decades but not over centuries, while it will explain corporate profitability over years, but not decades. As with many economic models, the analysis will work well for a certain time scale—in this case, the short and medium term. For other time scales, different models are needed.

This is all very well . . . but what does it have to do with corporate profiteering?

The newspapers often point to high corporate profits as a sign that the consumer is being screwed. Are they right? Only sometimes. Ricardo's analysis suggests that there are two reasons why average profits of an industry like banking might be high. If customers really value great service and reputation, both Axel and Bob will make a lot of money (Cornelius's bank is the marginal bank and can expect very little). Newspaper hacks will be able to complain about excessive profits. If customers place only a small value on great service, Axel and Bob will be only moderately more profitable than Cornelius (still the marginal bank, still making very little), and average profits should be low. The commentators will be silent. But the motives and strategies used by the industry haven't changed—the only thing that changed was that customers put a premium on great service. Nobody is ripping anybody off; instead, Axel and Bob are being rewarded because they are offering something both scarce and highly valued.

But high profits are not always earned so fairly; sometimes the newspaper outrage is justified. There's a second explanation for high corporate profits. What if a kind of banking "green belt" completely excluded Cornelius's bank from the market? In the real world there are lots of reasons why potential new companies cannot enter a market and compete. At times the consumers have only themselves to blame: new firms struggle to enter the market because customers will deal only with established companies. John Kay shows that certain "embarrassing" products, including condoms and tampons, are highly profitable because new entrants find it hard to create a buzz about their products. More frequently, the firms themselves lobby their governments asking to be protected from competition, and many governments around the world grant monopoly licenses, or are highly restrictive of entry into "sensitive" industries like banking, farming, or telecommunications. Whatever the reason, the effect is the same: established companies, free of competition, enjoy high profits. In fact, because of the similarity between the rents that can be charged on land with few substitutes and the profits enjoyed by a firm with few competitors, economists often call those profits "monopoly rents." It may be a confusing term, but you can blame David Ricardo's model and the lack of imagination shown by economists ever since.

If I want to know whether I am being ripped off by supermarkets, banks, or drug companies, I can find out how profitable those industries are. If they are making high profits, then initially I am suspicious. But if it seems that it is fairly easy to set up a new company and compete, I become less suspicious. It means that the high profits are caused by a natural scarcity: there are not many really good banking organizations in the world, and good banking organizations are much more efficient than bad ones.

Resource "rents"

Landlords and executives are not the only people who like to avoid competition and who like to enjoy monopoly rents. Trade

unions, lobby groups, people studying for a professional qualifi-
cation, and even national governments like them too. Every day
people all around us are trying to avoid competition or reap the
rewards of others who have succeeded in doing so. Economists
call this type of behavior "creating rents" and "rent-seeking."

It's not easy to do this. It turns out that the world is a naturally
competitive place, and it is no simple matter to steer clear of
competition. This is fortunate, because although competition is
uncomfortable if you are on the wrong end of it, it is pleasant to
be on the right end, as the customer. We all benefit when we are
interacting with people who are competing to offer us jobs, news-
papers, or vacations in the sun, just as our mythical landlords
benefited from competition between Bob and Axel.

One way of preventing competition is by controlling a natural
resource such as farmland. There is only so much good farmland
in the world, and only revolutions in agricultural techniques can
change that. But farmland is not the only finite natural resource
in the world. Another example is oil. Some parts of the world can
produce oil cheaply, most notably Saudi Arabia, Kuwait, Iraq,
and other Gulf states. Other parts of the world can produce oil
more expensively—Alaska, Nigeria, Siberia, and Alberta. And
there are many parts of the world that have oil that is so expen-
sive to extract that nobody is even thinking of doing so. At the
moment, places like Alberta produce the marginal oil.

The history of the oil industry is a case study in Ricardo's theory
of rents. Until 1973, the world's oil supply was produced by "oil
meadows," largely in the Middle East. Despite the incredible value
of oil to the industrialized economies, the price of oil was very
low—less than ten dollars a barrel in today's money, because there
was plenty of it available at very low costs. The Organization of
the Petroleum Exporting Countries, OPEC, which was sitting
on most of the oil meadows, decided in 1973 to take some of its
own meadows out of commission, by ordering each member coun-
try to restrict oil production. Oil prices leapt to forty dollars a
barrel, and then to eighty dollars, in today's money. They stayed
high for years, because in the short run there were few alterna-

tive sources of oil. (The equivalent in Ricardo's world would have been to abruptly halt the cultivation of meadowland, leaving a delay before grassland could be cleared and plowed, thereby causing a temporary grain shortage, raising rents.)

At eighty dollars a barrel, plenty of alternatives looked cheap and were adopted over the years: producing electricity using coal instead of oil; building cars that got better gas mileage; and exploring for oil in places like Alberta and Alaska. More and more "energy scrubland" and "energy grassland" was being cultivated. To keep prices high, OPEC was forced to accept a smaller and smaller share of the world oil market. Eventually Saudi Arabia broke ranks in 1985 and expanded production. Prices collapsed in 1986, and until just a couple of years ago the price of oil has roughly tracked the cost of production from marginal fields in places like Alberta—around fifteen to twenty dollars a barrel. In the last couple of years we have been tripped up by a combination of unexpectedly high demand in China with disruptions in Saudi Arabia, Iraq, Nigeria, and Venezuela, all of which have caused oil prices to rise to more than fifty dollars a barrel. Yet even at the lower prices prevailing in the 1990s, the oil produced from the cheapest fields in Saudi Arabia and Kuwait, at a cost of a couple of dollars a barrel, was almost pure profit.

When does crime pay?

A lot of the world's economy isn't closely linked to limited natural resources. That means that people have to find other ways to prevent competition.

One popular method is through violence, which is particularly popular in the drug trade and other organized crime. Drug dealers prefer not to have competitors driving down the price of drugs. Conceivably, by shooting or beating up enough people, a criminal gang could discourage rival gangs from entering the market and thus enjoy large profits. This is illegal, of course, but so is dealing in drugs; if you're risking prison anyway, there is little point in using half measures. If drug dealers want to enjoy strength

from scarcity, they have to go to some lengths to make the competition scarce. Meanwhile, their customers are hardly likely to complain to the police about being ripped off.

Unfortunately for your average drug gang, even violence may not be enough to earn profits. The difficulty is that guns and aggressive young men are both in plentiful supply. Any gang making good money is tempting other gangs to muscle in on its territory—and there will be plenty of contenders. Economist Steven Levitt and sociologist Sudhir Venkatesh managed to get hold of the accounts of one American street gang. It turns out that the "foot-soldiers" sometimes take home as little as $1.70 an hour. Promotion prospects are good, considering the rapid turnover of gang membership (people leave, or get killed, quite often); but even considering these prospects, the average wage is less than ten dollars an hour. This is not much given that over a four-year period, the typical gang member can expect to be shot twice, arrested six times, and has a one-in-four chance of being killed.

Some criminal enterprises are more successful. Mafia groups often get involved in legitimate businesses, such as wholesale laundry, which can make big profits only if entry is deterred. One way to deter entry is to threaten rivals. This is fairly easy, since laundry trucks and laundries themselves are much easier to find and damage than a bag of cocaine. It's even easier to threaten customers. Fans of *The Sopranos* know that the Mafia provides overpriced laundry services to restaurants as a way of extorting money. The reasons are clear enough: restaurants are particularly vulnerable to extortion because it doesn't take much disruption to put off customers, while collecting the extorted cash by providing an expensive service makes the protection money tax deductible. Profitable businesses usually attract competition, but in this case the competition reckon that there must be a safer way to make a living.

This suggests that it isn't violence as such that creates barriers to entry and sustainable profits—it's the effectiveness of an organ-

ization. Axel's bank had it and Cornelius's didn't; the typical street gang lacks it, the Mafia seems to have it in spades.

"Conspiracies against the laity"

Luckily, in genteel corners of the developed world we are usually sheltered from people who use violence to keep out competition. But it does not mean that people have not worked out other ways to keep competitors at bay.

Trade unions are an obvious example. The purpose of a union is to prevent workers from competing with each other for jobs, driving down wages and conditions. If there is a lot of demand for electricians and few people who can do the job, then the electricians have strength from scarcity and should have excellent pay and conditions, with or without a union. If more and more electricians set up shop, this strength is sapped. The new electricians play the role of Bob the farmer. The trade union is designed partly to bargain collectively, but partly to block too much entry into the profession.

As mass-mechanization spread in the nineteenth century, the incentive to unionize was considerable. Workers were a plentiful commodity: all gathered together in urban concentrations, easily substitutable for each other. Without unionization, wages could be kept very low. With it, competition could be excluded and wages would rise—for the lucky ones inside the union. In the United States, trade unions were kept at bay by the law: antitrust laws designed to prevent collusion between large companies were also directed against unions. But as the political climate changed, these laws were ruled inapplicable and trade unions grew in strength.

If trade unions were especially successful, then we might expect unionized industries to enjoy enormous salaries, and there have been times and places—such as the American auto industry in the 1960s and 1970s—when this has been true. But trade unions face several obstacles to this kind of success. When unions are perceived as making unreasonable demands, causing prices to rise

to a level that's deemed unacceptable by a large portion of the public, the public in turn puts pressure on politicians to regulate the unions. Sometimes the unions have their scarcity challenged by international competition, as in the case of American auto workers, who enjoyed excellent wages and job security until the Japanese car industry used more efficient methods and started putting American manufacturers under pressure.

In the case of shrinking industries like the British shipwrights or the car industry in the United States, available jobs are disappearing at such a rate that trade unions have great trouble maintaining their scarcity value; the union can never threaten to cut off the supply of workers fast enough to keep pace with a vanishing demand.

In other industries it is not shrinking demand but powerful employers that curtail the power of the unions. In the United States, Wal-Mart has tremendous bargaining power: there were only two unionized Wal-Marts in North America in the spring of 2004, when Wal-Mart announced that one of them, a branch in Quebec, would be closed because the union was damaging its business model. In the United Kingdom, teachers' wages are low in spite of the fact that there is a shortage of qualified teachers. This is because the government, the single employer, has massive bargaining power. Ordinarily, when there is a shortage of workers, competition between employers would bid up wages. Only a monopoly employer could possibly maintain a situation where there is a serious shortfall of teachers but salaries do not rise to respond. The teachers have some strength from scarcity, but in this case the government has more.

Other professionals, like doctors, actuaries, accountants, and lawyers manage to maintain high wages through other means than unionization, erecting virtual "green belts" to make it hard for potential competitors to set up shop. Typical virtual green belts will include very long qualification periods and professional bodies that give their approval only to a certain number of candidates per year. Many of the organizations that are put forth to

protect us from "unqualified" professionals in fact serve to maintain the high rates of the "qualified" to whom we are directed. In fact, many of us, informally, are happy to seek legal advice from experienced professionals who lack the formal qualification—even medical advice from medical students, foreign doctors, or alternative therapists. But the legal and medical professions do their best to limit the supply of fully qualified professionals and outlaw any low-cost substitutes: if you can't afford the rent on meadow, the scrub and the grassland are forbidden. Small wonder that George Bernard Shaw said that the professions were "all conspiracies against the laity."

And now for something controversial

Immigration has always been an emotive issue for America, and although national security has recently become a concern, the debate continues to revolve around an old question: do immigrants steal our jobs? They may steal your job, but they certainly haven't stolen mine.

Well-educated workers with jobs requiring skill and training, along with businessmen in need of cheap labor, tend to welcome immigration as part of an enriching process, which adds to each nation's economic and cultural life, while poorly educated workers tend to reject any further immigration by unskilled immigrants on the grounds that "they steal our jobs." Perhaps that's too much of a caricature, but it makes sense from a self-interested viewpoint.

As one of those skilled workers I dislike resistance to immigrants and would like to see more immigration. But then, I would, wouldn't I? If you need skilled and unskilled labor together to get useful work done, then it is in my direct interests to see more unskilled workers come to the country, and directly against the interests of the unskilled workers who are already here.

Imagine me and my fellow well-educated citizens as landowners, but instead of "meadow" read "degree." My skills and qualifications are a resource, just as a meadow is a resource. But are

my skills a *scarce* resource? Imagine that I go to work for Wal-Mart's management team. When my skills (let's not be too specific about what they are supposed to be) are combined with the hard work of store assistants and shelf-stackers, we're a productive team. Who gets to enjoy the proceeds depends on whose abilities are scarce. If the country is short of unskilled shelf-stackers, their wages will have to rise to attract people into the job. But if the country is short of skilled managers and full of unskilled shelf-stackers, I'll be paid well for my scarcity value, just as landlords were paid well for scarce land once enough farmers showed up.

Some blame working-class resistance to immigration on racism. An alternative, and more convincing, theory suggests that everybody is acting in his own self interest. New workers are good for people who have assets that become relatively scarcer, whether those assets are meadows or degrees; but it is understandable if new workers are loathed by established ones. In fact, the people who are most harmed by new immigration are the previous group of immigrants, who find their wages nailed to the floor.

The facts support the application of Ricardo's theory to immigration. Skilled immigrants lower the wages of skilled natives, and unskilled immigrants lower the wages of unskilled natives. In the UK, the salaries of nurses in the National Health Service have been kept low by the influx of thirty thousand foreign nurses; immigrants in the UK are nearly 50 percent more likely than natives to have a university degree. In contrast, in the United States, which takes in a far higher percentage of low-skilled immigrants than the UK does, it is unskilled wages that have stayed low: the income of unskilled workers has not improved in thirty years.

What should economists do?

We've been thinking like economists throughout this chapter. But what does that mean? We've used one major economic model

to deepen our understanding of a variety of situations. The chapter has moved from some objective-sounding analysis of who makes money from the cappuccino business to the dangerous political territory of planning restrictions and immigration.

Some economists would claim that there is no difference between their analysis of coffee rents and their analysis of immigration. In an important sense, that's true. Economics is in many ways just like engineering; it will tell you how things work and what is likely to happen if you change them. The economist can show that allowing lots of skilled immigrants will help control the gap between skilled and unskilled wages, while allowing unskilled immigrants will do the reverse. What societies and their leaders do with the information is another matter.

Yet the fact that economics itself is a tool for objective analysis doesn't mean that economists are always objective. Economists study power, poverty, growth, and development. It is hard to wield the models that underlie such subjects and remain unmoved by the real world behind them.

So economists often step beyond their role as engineers of economic policy and become advocates. David Ricardo, for example, was an early campaigner for free trade. He was encouraged by his friend, James Mill, to run for parliament; he won a seat in 1819 when he campaigned for repeal of the Corn Laws, which severely restricted the import of grain. Ricardo's theories had demonstrated clearly that the Corn Laws were shoveling money into the pockets of landlords at the expense of everyone else in the country. Ricardo was not content simply to observe the effects of the Corn Laws, he wanted to abolish them.

Economists come to similar conclusions today about protectionist laws, which, as we will see in chapter 9, protect privileged pressure groups at the expense of the rest of us in the developed world and the developing world alike. Billions of people could benefit from better economic policies. Millions are dying because of bad ones. Sometimes the logic of economics is so compelling that it's impossible for economists not to take a stand.

TWO

What Supermarkets Don't
Want You to Know

Those of you who have visited London recently have probably been to the London Eye, the capital's landmark Ferris wheel. On a sunny day you can purchase a cappuccino from Costa Coffee and sit and sip as the capsules on the wheel rotate high above, occasionally passing between you and the sun . . . one of life's simple pleasures.

Everywhere you look around the Eye you can see vendors with scarce resources, trying to exploit that scarcity. Costa Coffee is the only coffee bar in the immediate area, for instance. There is also a lone souvenir shop doing brisk business. But the most obvious example is the London Eye itself. It towers over most of London's most famous buildings and is the world's largest observation wheel. The scarcity power is clearly considerable, but it is not unlimited: the London Eye may be unique, but it is also optional. People can always choose not to go. Farther along the river, the Millennium Dome (a colossal government-funded white elephant designed for millennial celebrations) is similarly unique: "the largest fabric structure in the world," boasts the local authority. Yet the Dome has proved a commercial disaster because uniqueness alone wasn't enough to persuade people to pay enough to cover the vast costs of its construction. Businesses with scarcity power cannot force us to pay unlimited prices for their products, but they can choose from a variety of strategies to make us pay

more. It's time for the Undercover Economist to get to work and find out more.

As the only coffee provider beside the London Eye, the Costa coffee bar wields plenty of scarcity power over the customer. It's not innate to Costa but is reflected glory from the amazing setting. As we know, because customers will pay high prices for coffee in attractive locations, Costa's rent will be high. Costa's landlords have rented out some of this scarcity value to a coffee bar, just like the owners of Manhattan's skyscrapers, or train stations from Waterloo to Shinjuku. Scarcity is for rent—at the right price.

But how should Costa exploit the scarcity they are renting from the London Eye? They could simply raise the price of a cappuccino from £1.75 (about $3) to £3 (nearly $6). Some people would pay it, but many would not. Remember the Millennium Dome: scarcity gives you power, but not limitless power. Alternatively, they could cut prices and sell much more coffee. They could cover wages and ingredients by charging as little as 60 pence ($1) a cup. But unless they were able to increase their sales dozens of times over, they'd not make enough to cover their rent. That's the dilemma: higher margins per cup, but fewer cups; or lower margins on more cups.

It would be nice for Costa to sidestep that dilemma, by charging 60p to people who are not willing to pay more and £3 to people who are willing to pay a lot to enjoy the coffee and the view. That way they would have the high margins whenever they could get them and still sell coffee at a small profit to the skinflints. How to do it, though? Have a price list saying, "Cappuccino, £3, unless you're only willing to pay 60p"?

Cappuccino for the lavish	£3.00
Cappuccino for the thrifty	60p

It does have a certain something, but I doubt it would catch on with the coffee-buying public of London's South Bank. So Costa has to be more subtle.

For a while, Costa hit upon an elegant strategy: Costa, like most other coffee bars these days, offers "Fair Trade" coffee; theirs comes from a leading fair trade brand called Cafédirect. Cafédirect promises to offer good prices to coffee farmers in poor countries. For several years, customers who wished to support third-world farmers—and such customers are apparently not uncommon in London—were charged an extra ten pence (about eighteen cents). They may have believed that the ten pence went to the struggling coffee farmer. The evidence suggested that almost none of that money went anywhere but Costa's bottom line.

Cafédirect paid farmers a premium of between 40 and 55 pence (up to a dollar) per pound of coffee. That relatively small premium can nearly double the income of a farmer in Guatemala, where the average income is less than $2,000 a year. But since the typical cappuccino is made with a quarter-ounce of coffee beans, the premium paid to the farmer should translate into a cost increase of less than a penny a cup.

Of the extra money that Costa charged, more than 90 percent was going missing between the customer and the farmer. So either Costa and Cafédirect were wasting the money (through higher costs) or it was being added to profits. Fair trade coffee associations make a promise to the producer, not the consumer. If you buy fair trade coffee, you are guaranteed that the producer will receive a good price. But there is no guarantee that *you* will receive a good price. The truth is that fair trade coffee wholesalers could pay two, three, or sometimes four times the market price for coffee in the developing world without adding anything noticeable to the production cost of a cappuccino, because coffee beans make up such a small proportion of that cost. Charging an extra ten pence gave a misleading impression of how much it really cost to get hold of that fair trade coffee. After some inquiries by a certain Undercover Economist, Costa worked out that the whole business gave the wrong impression, and at the end of 2004 began to offer fair trade coffee on request, *without* a price premium. Costa abandoned the premium of fair trade coffee because it was bad public relations, not because it was unprofitable.

But *why* was it profitable to charge a higher markup on the cost of production on fair trade coffee than on normal coffee? Certainly not because Costa objected to the whole idea of fair trade and tried to discourage such idealistic behavior with their pricing. The reason has nothing to do with fair trade at all: it's because fair trade coffee allowed Costa to find customers who are willing to pay a bit more if given a reason to do so. By ordering a fair trade cappuccino, you sent two messages to Costa. One message interested them very little:

"I think that fair trade coffee is a product that should be supported."

The second message is the one that they were straining to hear: "I don't really mind paying a bit extra."

This immediately gave Costa the information they were looking for. They know that socially concerned citizens tend to be less careful with their cash in coffee bars, while unconcerned citizens tend to keep their eyes on the price.

Cappuccino for the concerned	£1.85
Cappuccino for the unconcerned	£1.75

Costa's strategy was designed to get maximum value out of the scarcity power they've rented from the London Eye. They are torn between raising prices and losing customers, or lowering prices and losing margins. If they have to charge the same price to every customer, they will simply have to guess the best trade-off between the two options. But if they can charge a high price to the lavish (or concerned) and a low price to the thrifty (or unconcerned), then they can enjoy the best of both worlds. And there is no need to worry on Costa's behalf that this strategy has now been denied to them. Costa has plenty of alternative ways to identify customers for a price increase. Nor is there anything unusually Machiavellian about Costa Coffee. Any well-run business would seek to charge each customer the maximum price he'd be willing to pay—and they do.

Take a Starbucks, any Starbucks. For the sake of argument, take the Starbucks on P Street and 14th in Washington DC. The price list looks like this:

Hot Chocolate	$2.20
Cappuccino	$2.55
Caffé Mocha	$2.75
White Chocolate Mocha	$3.20
20 oz Cappuccino	$3.40

Or, to translate:

Hot Chocolate—no frills	$2.20
Cappuccino—no frills	$2.55
Mix them together—I feel special	$2.75
Use different powder—	
I feel very special	$3.20
Make it huge—I feel greedy	$3.40

Starbucks isn't merely seeking to offer a variety of alternatives to customers. It's also trying to give the customer every opportunity to signal that they've not been looking at the price. It doesn't cost much more to make a larger cup, to use a flavored syrup, or to add chocolate powder or a squirt of whipped cream. Every single product on the menu above costs Starbucks almost the same to produce, down to the odd nickel or two.

Does this mean that Starbucks is overcharging all of its customers? No. If so, a regular cappuccino or hot chocolate would cost $3.30, and you could have all the frills you wanted for a dime. Perhaps Starbucks would like to do that, but they can't force price-sensitive customers to pay those prices. By charging wildly different prices for products that have largely the same cost, Starbucks is able to smoke out customers who are less sensitive about the price. Starbucks doesn't have a way to identify lavish customers perfectly, so it invites them to hang themselves with a choice of luxurious ropes.

There's one born every minute:
Two ways to find him

There are three common strategies for finding customers who are cavalier about price. Let's cover two for now, and leave the best for last.

The first is what economists call "first degree price discrimination," but we could call it the "unique target" strategy: to evaluate each customer as an individual and charge according to how much he or she is willing to pay. This is the strategy of the used-car salesman or the real estate agent. It usually takes skill and a lot of effort; hardly surprising, then, that it is most often seen for items that have a high value relative to the retailer's time—cars and houses, of course, but also souvenirs in African street stalls, where the impoverished merchant will find it worth bargaining for some time to gain an extra dollar.

Now, however, companies are trying to automate the process of evaluating individual customers to reduce the time it takes. For instance, supermarkets accumulate evidence of what you're willing to pay by giving you "discount cards," which are needed to take advantage of sale prices. In return for getting a lower price on certain items, you allow the stores to keep records of what you buy, and then in turn offer you coupons for discounts on products. It doesn't work perfectly, because supermarkets can only send "money off" coupons, not "money on" coupons. "Money on" coupons have never been a success.

When technology allows, firms with scarcity power may use highly sophisticated methods to target customers. It's no secret anymore that Internet retailers such as Amazon can identify each customer by putting a tracing device called a "cookie" on her computer. Amazon used to tailor their prices based on their records of individual customers. The company really was able to offer "money on" vouchers: two readers buying exactly the same book would be offered a different price based on tendencies shown in previous purchases. Even though it would be more difficult

than for on-line sales, supermarkets could, with the right technology do the same thing—each customer could have an identity tag, and price labels would change according to who was looking at them.

Of course, the "unique target" approach is unpopular. In Amazon's case, customers started to realize that if they deleted the cookies on their computers, they were offered different, often lower prices. And when they found out what the company was doing, there was an outcry. Like Costa, Amazon has promised not to do it any more.

Interestingly, people tend not to object nearly so much to the second approach, the "group target" strategy, which is to offer different prices to members of distinct groups. Who could complain about reduced bus fares for children and the elderly? Surely it must be reasonable for coffee shops to offer a discount to people who work nearby, and for tourist attractions to let locals in for a lower rate? It often *seems* reasonable because people in groups who pay more are usually people who can afford more, and that's because people who can afford more are usually people who care less about price. But we shouldn't forget that this is a convenient coincidence. Companies trying to increase their profits and get the maximum value out of their scarcity are interested in who is *willing* to pay more, rather than who can *afford* to pay more.

For instance, when Disney World in Florida offers admission discounts of over 50 percent to locals, they're not making a statement about the grinding poverty of the Sunshine State. They simply know that for a reduced price, locals are more likely to come regularly. But tourists will probably come once, and once only, whether it is cheap or expensive.

This example gets to the heart of things and tells us what we really mean by "price sensitivity" or "being lavish" or "being cavalier about prices." The important concept is this: when I raise the price, how much do my sales fall? And when I cut the price,

how much do my sales rise? Economists tend to call this "own-price elasticity." Personally I think "price sensitivity" is a bit more descriptive.

Tourists visiting Florida are less price-sensitive than locals, which means that if Disney World raises its prices, locals are more likely to skip a day at the park. By the same token, if the admission price falls, locals may make repeat visits in a way that tourists probably won't. Being rich is sometimes connected with being insensitive to prices, but not always. Business-class air travel is expensive, because companies are willing to pay, and airlines have the scarcity power to take advantage of that fact. Business telephone calls are inexpensive, because although companies would be willing to pay, there is too much competition around for any phone company to force them to.

The same is true of discounts at coffee bars for local workers. The AMT coffee bar in Waterloo station in London will knock 10 percent off the cost of your coffee if you work locally. This isn't because the local workers are poor; they include top government officials and the extravagantly remunerated employees of the gigantic oil company Shell. The discount reflects the fact that local workers are price-sensitive despite being rich. Commuters who pass through Waterloo in a hurry see only one or two coffee bars and are willing to pay high prices for convenience. Local workers pop out of the office at 11 am for coffee and could walk in any direction. They can buy from several cafes, all equally convenient, all of which they will have had a chance to sample. They are bound to be more price-sensitive, even if they are rich.

The "individual target" strategy is difficult, partly because it requires a lot of information and partly because it tends to be very unpopular. Despite the difficulties, however, it's so profitable that companies always explore new ways to do it. The "group target" strategy of discounts for students or locals is less effective but easier to put into action, and it's usually socially acceptable, even welcomed. Either will deliver more profits than simply treating all customers as a homogenous mass.

The third way:
Turkeys voting for Thanksgiving

The cleverest and most common way to persuade turkeys to vote for Thanksgiving is the "self-incrimination" strategy—the one Costa Coffee and Starbucks both use when they persuade some of their customers into confessing that they are not sensitive to price. To get customers to give themselves away, the company has to sell products that are at least slightly different from each other. So they offer products in different quantities (a large cappuccino instead of a small one, or an offer of three for the price of two), or with different features (with whipped cream, or white chocolate, or fair trade ingredients), or even in different locations, because a sandwich in a station kiosk is not the same product as a physically identical sandwich in an out-of-town superstore.

It's reasonable to ask how common this tactic really is. Because the products are different, you never quite know whether the firm is using a price-targeting trick or merely passing on added costs. It could be that it really does cost 10p (about 20¢) more to put fair trade coffee in a cappuccino; maybe cans of whipped cream are expensive to refrigerate and troublesome to clean and the staff hates using them; perhaps large cups of coffee take longer to drink, and so the charge is for table space not coffee—in which case, charging a higher price is not a strategy to get me to incriminate myself but simply Costa passing its costs through to me. But I think it's safe to say that companies are always alert for ways to squeeze the maximum advantage out of whatever scarcity power they have, and price-targeting is the most common way to do that. If it looks like price-targeting, it probably is.

Although use of this strategy is hard to prove, there's plenty of circumstantial evidence around if you know where to look. For instance, the premium you pay for a large cappuccino instead of a small one is the same whether you drink it in the café or take it away. (Except for my favorite coffee shop, the Monmouth in Covent Garden, in London. They are short of space, and will charge a markup for a large cappuccino if you drink it in the

shop. However, they charge less for take-out coffee, and it comes in only one size. I have decided they are far too nice to try to make profits.) That doesn't make sense if it's a charge for taking up space. So we have good reasons to believe that coffee bars try for a "self-targeting" strategy, charging high prices to customers who demonstrate a willingness to pay them.

Coffee bars are not alone

Supermarkets have turned price-targeting into an art, developing a vast array of strategies toward that end. Above the main concourse of London's Liverpool Street station, there's a Marks and Spencer "Simply Food" store, catering to busy commuters on the way in and out of London. We know all about the scarcity value of train stations by now, so perhaps it shouldn't surprise us to find that this store isn't cheap, even compared with another branch of

How far would you walk to save 30p?

About 1,500 feet (500 m) is all that separates two Marks and Spencer stores with somewhat different pricing policies. But for most city dwellers it's just not worth the walk.

Marks and Spencer merely fifteen hundred feet or so away, on Moorgate.

I picked up five products at random in the Liverpool Street store and managed to locate four of them in the Moorgate store. Every single one was about 15 percent cheaper there. Big salads were down from £3.50 to £3.00 ($6.60 to $5.65), sandwiches from £2.20 to £1.90 ($4.15 to $3.55). But even when such discrepancies come to light, few city workers would be willing to stray those several blocks to save thirty pence, about half a dollar. A bold and effective piece of price-targeting.

Other supermarkets are more circumspect about their pricing policy. Going undercover once again, I made a comparison between the smallish Sainsbury's supermarket on Tottenham Court Road in the heart of London's West End, and the large store in Dalston, one of East London's less prosperous neighborhoods. It was harder to find examples of identical products selling for different prices, although by no means impossible. Does this mean that Sainsbury's doesn't price-target as much as M&S? Not at all. They simply go about the whole process with more finesse.

When researching Sainsbury's, my approach was the same as with M&S: walk into the shop and see what caught my eye. As you probably know, what catches our eyes as we walk into the supermarket is no coincidence; it's the result of careful planning designed to throw attractive but profitable products in the path of customers. What constitutes an attractive product depends on who those customers are. On Tottenham Court Road the obvious goods were all quite expensive: Tropicana orange juice at £1.95 ($3.66) a liter, Tropicana "Smoothies" at £1.99 ($3.50) for 100ml, 750ml of Vittel mineral water at 80p ($1.50), and so on. It wasn't that these products were more expensive in Tottenham Court Road than in Dalston (only the Vittel was), it was just that in Dalston, cheaper substitutes sprang into view far more readily.

For instance, I couldn't find inexpensive orange juice in the Tottenham Court Road store, but in Dalston, Sainsbury's own brand of fresh chilled juice was sitting next to the Tropicana at

about half the price, and the concentrated juice was almost six times cheaper than the Tropicana. Brand-name pasta was the same price in both shops, but only in Dalston was it sitting next to Sainsbury's pasta, which again was almost six times cheaper. The effect was to target the whole Tottenham Court Road store at shoppers who are indifferent to prices, but to aim the Dalston stores at shoppers with a sharper eye for a bargain—while of course giving any price-blind Dalston shoppers plenty of opportunity to show their true colors.

Price-gouging the natural way

The best price-targeters pair their efforts to improve profits with apparently virtuous behavior. We've seen how Costa Coffee trumpeted its commitment to fair trade while using it to identify customers with money to burn. It's also good business to offer discounts to the elderly and to students (translation: charge higher prices to people likely to have jobs). Who but a cynic—or an economist—could object to such commendable behavior?

The favored game at the moment has to be price-gouging the natural way, riding the bandwagon of organic food. Organic food is catching on for a variety of reasons, including the fact that in the wake of repeated food health scares, many people think organic food is better for them, or at least won't kill them. The supermarkets have come to the rescue with a plentiful supply of organic products that happen to be marked up far above their additional costs to the supermarket. In British supermarkets, these are often stacked together, apparently for the convenience of the organic shopper but also to the advantage of the supermarkets who thereby reduce the risk that organic shoppers will notice the price of the typical alternative. In Washington DC's Wholefoods store, just across the street from Starbucks, the vast and luxurious fruit and vegetable section contains both organic and conventionally grown produce side by side . . . but always side by side with a completely different product. The organic bananas

are next to the "conventional" (that is, nonorganic) apples; the organic garlic is next to the conventional onions. You will never find the organic bananas next to the conventional bananas, or the organic garlic next to the conventional garlic. The price-comparison would be too sobering.

But is expensive organic food really part of a price-targeting tactic? Organic food should be more expensive: it costs more to produce and, with a shorter shelf life, it is also more expensive to distribute than the standard product. But as with your cappuccino, raw ingredients are only a small part of the price of most food on the supermarket shelves. For example, in the UK, organic milk commands a premium of around fifty cents per quart, but the farmer sees less than twenty cents of this. We should not be surprised that supermarkets are taking the opportunity afforded by the organic food movement to zap customers with well-aimed price increases. My recommendation, if you are convinced of the merits of organic food, is not to let food retailers exploit your enthusiasm: vote with your wallet by supporting any retailer—or direct supplier—who brings the price of organic and nonorganic food closer together.

Bargain shopping and bargain stores

Whenever I mention to people that I live near the Wholefoods supermarket in central Washington DC, they comment on how wonderful the store is: Wholefoods prides itself on being "The World's Leading Natural and Organic Food Supermarket," touts its community involvement, and offers a jungle of fresh fruit and vegetables alongside hormone-free steaks, European cheeses and beers, and luxury chocolates. It's a fun place to shop and offers great food. But my acquaintances also complain about how expensive Wholefoods is. But . . . is it really expensive?

That depends on what you mean by expensive. Presumably people have some price comparison in mind. A fair one would be to compare prices in Wholefoods with prices in Safeway just five

blocks away, a store known to the locals as "Soviet Safeway" be-
cause of the small range of products and the harsh decor. Com-
pare the price of the typical Wholefoods shopper's basket of
goods, and nine times out of ten it will indeed be more expensive
than the typical Safeway shopper's basket of goods. But that says
more about the shoppers than the stores. As a matter of verifi-
able fact, when you compare the prices on the same goods,
Wholefoods is just as inexpensive as Safeway.

Safeway and Wholefoods charge exactly the same for bananas.
Exactly the same for a carton of cherry or grape tomatoes. Ad-
mittedly, Safeway's prices on yellow onions, Irish butter, and
Cheerios are lower. But Wholefoods charges less for mineral
water, Tropicana Premium orange juice, and sweet onions. The
simple truth is that if you bought a big basket of the *same* goods
from Safeway and from Wholefoods, the price tag would prob-
ably come out within a dollar or two—and it would be just as
likely that Wholefoods was cheaper.

That doesn't quite fit with our commonsense belief that some
places are cheap and some places are expensive. But that belief
never made much sense. After all, if some places really did predict-
ably charge more for the same product with similar service in a
similar location, that would imply that all of their customers were
just idiots. Wholefoods is more fun to shop in, but when push
comes to shove, it's still just a supermarket, and you wander around
filling your own cart just as in Safeway.

Wholefoods is not expensive in the sense that it charges more
for the same goods. It is expensive because of where its price-
targeting policies are focused: prices for the basics may be com-
petitive, but the selection in Wholefoods is aimed at customers
with a different view of what "basics" are.

For example: Safeway charges more for Tropicana orange juice
and for Poland Spring sparkling mineral water than Wholefoods
does. For Wholefoods customers Tropicana juice and sparkling
water *are* the basics, and so they need to be priced competitively,
while Safeway customers might well consider that tap water and

concentrated orange juice were perfectly acceptable alternatives. A Safeway customer who buys sparkling water and fresh Tropicana juice is signaling a taste for luxury. A Wholefoods customer may pass by the cheaper option of Tropicana in favor of a more expensive Smoothie made of fresh-squeezed juice at the in-house juice bar.

The basic yellow and sweet onions are priced similarly at both stores. But at Wholefoods, customers have the option to pick fancy varieties: pearl onions, red onions, and even organic onions, at a hefty markup. The Wholefoods shopper who is looking for decently priced products will find them. The Wholefoods shopper who grabs a bag of the first onions he sees will pay dearly for his lack of price-curiosity.

That is why a basket of goods from Wholefoods can cost so much more than a basket of goods from Safeway. It's not because Wholefoods is "expensive" and Wholefoods customers are stupid. It's because Wholefoods offers additional, expensive choices, which Wholefoods shoppers are willing to take because they perceive the quality premium is worth it.

So here's my advice: if you want a bargain, don't try to find a cheap store. Try to *shop* cheaply. Similar products are, very often, priced similarly. An expensive shopping trip is the result of carelessly choosing products with a high markup, rather than wandering into a store with "bad value," because price-targeting accounts for much more of the difference between prices than any difference in value between one store and another.

Mix it up!

Another very common pricing strategy is sale pricing. We're all so used to seeing a storewide sale with hundreds of items reduced in price that we don't pause and ask ourselves why on earth stores do this. When you think hard about it, it becomes quite a puzzling way of setting prices. The effect of a sale is to lower the average price a store charges. But why knock 30 percent off many

of your prices twice a year, when you could knock 5 percent off year-round? Varying prices is a lot of hassle for stores because they need to change their labels and their advertising, so why does it make sense for them to go to the trouble of mixing things up?

One explanation is that sales are an effective form of self-targeting. If some customers shop around for a good deal and some customers do not, it's best for stores to have either high prices to pry cash from the loyal (or lazy) customers, or low prices to win business from the bargain hunters. Middle-of-the-road prices are no good: not high enough to exploit loyal customers, not low enough to attract the bargain-hunters. But that's not the end of the story, because if prices were stable, then surely even the most price-insensitive customers would learn where to get particular goods cheaply. So rather than stick to either high or low prices, shops jump between the two extremes.

One common situation is for two supermarkets to be competing for the same customers. As we've discussed, it's hard for one to be systematically more expensive than the other without losing a lot of business, so they will charge similar prices on average, but both will also mix up their prices. That way, both can distinguish the bargain hunters from those in need of specific products, like people shopping to pick up ingredients for a cookbook recipe they are making for a dinner party. Bargain-hunters will pick up whatever is on sale and make something of it. The dinner-party shoppers come to the supermarket to buy specific products and will be less sensitive to prices. The price-targeting strategy only works because the supermarkets always vary the patterns of their special offers, and because it is too much trouble to go to both stores. If shoppers could reliably predict what was to be discounted, they could choose recipes ahead of time, and even choose the appropriate supermarket to pick up the ingredients wherever they're least expensive.

In fact, it is just as accurate, and more illuminating, to turn the "sale" on its head and view prices as premiums on the sale price rather than discounts on the regular price. The random pattern of sales is also a random pattern of price increases—companies

find it more profitable to increase prices (above the sale price) by a larger amount on an unpredictable basis than by a small amount in a predictable way. Customers find it troublesome to avoid unpredictable price increases—and may not even notice them for lower-value goods—but easy to avoid predictable ones.

Try to spot other odd mix-ups next time you're in the supermarket. Have you noticed that supermarkets often charge ten times as much for fresh chili peppers in a package as for loose fresh chilies? That's because the typical customer buys such small quantities that he doesn't think to check whether they cost four cents or forty. Randomly tripling the price of a vegetable is a favorite trick: customers who notice the markup just buy a different vegetable that week; customers who don't have self-targeted a whopping price rise.

I once spotted a particularly inspired trick while on a search for potato chips. My favorite brand was available on the top shelf in salt and pepper flavor and on the bottom shelf, just a few feet away, in other flavors, all the same size. The top-shelf potato chips cost 25 percent more, and customers who reached for the top shelf demonstrated that they hadn't made a price-comparison between two near-identical products in near-identical locations. They were more interested in snacking.

Admittedly, for some people the difference in flavors is important. Some will notice the higher price for salt and pepper flavor and, irritated, pay anyway. Others will prefer the different flavors and count themselves lucky that they have inexpensive tastes.

But this is an example of a universal truth about supermarkets: they are full of close (or not so close) substitutes, some cheap, some expensive, and with a strong random element to the pricing. The random element is there so that only shoppers who are careful to notice, remember, and compare prices will get the best bargains. If you want to outwit the supermarkets, simple observation is your best weapon. And if you can't be bothered to do that, you really don't need to save money.

Reality check number one:
Does the company really have scarcity power?

It's time for a reality check. When we talk about big companies it is easy to get carried away with notions of how they are infinitely powerful and we are infinitely gullible. Not true.

Remember that no company has power unless it has scarcity, and often that scarcity is something we give them through our own laziness. Nothing is stopping us from walking down the street or driving from one store to another; certainly nothing is stopping us from a bit of mental arithmetic when buying chilies, or from glancing around for two seconds when buying potato chips.

Every store has a tiny amount of scarcity power, if only because it's an effort to walk out and go next door. But some have more scarcity power than others, which is worth thinking about when estimating the risk of being waylaid by price-targeting strategies.

For instance, what is the answer to the question we posed in the previous chapter: why does popcorn cost so much at movie theaters? Is it for the same reason that wine is expensive in restaurants? We know that the first-glance answer in both cases is, "Because once they get you in the door they can charge whatever they want." We also know that this first answer is probably not true. Customers may be dumb, but they're not that dumb. People expect to be charged a lot for wine in restaurants and for popcorn and candy in movie theaters *before* they walk in the door.

Now we have a better answer: it's likely to be a price-targeting strategy. Moviegoers who are sensitive to price will bring their own snacks from home, or go without. People who are not sensitive to price—perhaps because they're on a date and don't want to look stingy—will simply pay for the overpriced popcorn. Very clever.

This is a much better explanation, since in many towns there is only one movie theater, and even in towns with more than one, there is often only one showing the film you want to see.

This gives a theater a lot of scarcity power, and if the manager is smart he'll want to exploit that power to the full.

Yet the same story doesn't ring true for pricey wine at restaurants. The typical restaurant has less scarcity power than a movie theater because in most towns there will be a variety of alternatives. Whenever there is little scarcity power, prices need to reflect costs. Yet even the most ordinary restaurants seem to charge a lot for wine. A better explanation is that one of the big costs in a restaurant business is table space. Restaurateurs would therefore like to charge customers for dawdling, but because they cannot do that, they charge higher prices for products that tend to be consumed in longer meals: not just wine but also appetizers and desserts.

We go to a movie theater to see a movie and to a restaurant to eat, so is the truth also that we always get gouged on "options"? Not at all. One option available in both movie theaters and in restaurants is the option to use the restrooms; this is always an option provided free of charge. Tap water is also free in restaurants. It is not the option that invites the gouging, it's the lack of price sensitivity that allows a business with scarcity power to practice price-targeting.

Reality check number two:
Can the company plug leaks?

Perhaps you are a company director rubbing your hands with glee as you read this, planning to deploy a range of clever price-targeting strategies in your own business. Before you get too excited, you'll need to deal with the leaks in your price-targeting system. There are two potentially catastrophic leaks or great holes in an otherwise brilliant marketing scheme. If you don't deal with them, your plans will be in ruins.

The first problem is that supposedly price-insensitive customers may not play the self-targeting game. It's not hard to persuade price-sensitive customers to steer clear of an expensive product, but sometimes it is more difficult to prevent the price-insensitive

customers from buying the cheaper one. This is not a problem in the case of small price differences; we have already seen that you can get some customers to pay a modest markup in absolute terms, but the markup can be huge in relative terms, just by wrapping some chilies in a plastic bag, or moving a bag of potato chips up onto the top shelf. When it comes to more substantial buying decisions it is not always so easy.

Some of the most extreme examples come from the travel industry: traveling first class by train or air is much more expensive than buying the coach-class seats, but since the fundamental effect is to get people from A to B, it may be hard to wring much money out of the wealthier passengers. In order to price-target effectively, firms may have to exaggerate the differences between the best service and the worst. There is really no reason at all why coach-class train cars shouldn't have tables, as they typically don't in the UK, for instance, except that potential customers for first class might decide to buy a cheaper ticket when they see how comfortable coach has become. So the coach-class passengers have to suffer.

There is a famous example from the early days of the trains in France:

> It is not because of the few thousand francs which would have to be spent to put a roof over the third-class carriage or to upholster the third-class seats that some company or other has open carriages with wooden benches. . . . What the company is trying to do is prevent the passengers who can pay the second-class fare from traveling third class; it hits the poor, not because it wants to hurt them, but to frighten the rich. . . . And it is again for the same reason that the companies, having proved almost cruel to the third-class passengers and mean to the second class ones, become lavish in dealing with first-class customers. Having refused the poor what is necessary, they give the rich what is superfluous.

The shoddy quality of most airport departure areas across the world is surely part of the same phenomenon. If the free depar-

ture areas became comfortable, then airlines would no longer be able to sell business-class tickets on the strength of their "executive" lounges. And it would also explain why flight attendants sometimes physically restrain coach passengers from stepping off the plane before the passengers from first and business class. This is a "service" aimed not at economy-class passengers but at those looking on in pity and disgust from the front of the plane. The message is clear: keep paying for your expensive seats, or next time you might be the wrong side of the flight attendant.

In the supermarkets, we see the same trick: products that seem to be packaged for the express purpose of conveying awful quality. Supermarkets will often produce a store-brand "value" range, displaying crude designs that don't vary whether the product is lemonade, bread, or baked beans. It wouldn't cost much to hire a good designer and print more attractive logos. But that would defeat the object: the packaging is carefully designed to put off customers who are willing to pay more. Even customers who would be willing to pay five times as much for a bottle of lemonade will buy the bargain product unless the supermarket makes some effort to discourage them. So, like the lack of tables in coach-class trains and the uncomfortable seats in airport lounges, the ugly packaging of "value" products is designed to make sure that snooty customers self-target price increases on themselves.

The most surprising examples of all come from the world of computers. For instance, IBM's "LaserWriter E," a low-end laser printer, turned out to be exactly the same piece of equipment as their high-end "LaserWriter"—except that there was an additional chip in the cheaper version to slow it down. The most effective way for IBM to price-target their printers was to design and mass-produce a single printer, then sell it at two prices. But of course to get anyone to buy the expensive printer they had to slow down the cheap one. It seems wasteful, but presumably it was cheaper for IBM to do this than design and manufacture two completely different printers. Intel, the chip manufacturer, played a similar game by selling two very similar processing chips at

different prices. In this case, the inferior chip was actually more expensive to produce: it was made by taking the superior chip and doing extra work to disable one of its features.

Software packages often have two or more versions: one has full functionality (the "professional" package), and the other sells to the mass market at a considerably reduced price. What some people don't realize is that the professional version is typically designed first, and certain features are disabled for the mass-market version. Despite the high price of the professional version, it's the cheaper version that actually has an extra up-front cost for the developer, and of course both versions are sold on CDs, which cost the same to manufacture. Computer hardware, and in particular software, has a strange cost structure because of intensive research and development costs, and relatively low manufacturing costs. At the height of the Internet bubble, giddy gurus were claiming that the different cost structure changes everything—but, as we've seen, the basic rules of making money in the hi-tech business are not so different from the rules for train operators or coffee bars.

The first "leak" in a price-targeting strategy, then, is that rich customers may buy cheap products, unless the products are deliberately sabotaged. The second "leak" is a particularly difficult one for companies using a group-target strategy to plug: their products may leak from one group to another. The risk is that the customers who are being offered a discount buy the product and then resell it at a profit to the customers who are being charged a higher price. Up until now, we've mostly been discussing services that can't be resold (like a bus trip or a visit to Disney World) or products that are probably too much hassle to resell (such as a sandwich or a cup of coffee). That's not coincidence. Services and convenience products are the most fertile grounds for price-targeting strategies, because they don't leak. The really great pricing tricks take place on airlines, in restaurants and cocktail bars (not many bookstores have a "happy hour"), in supermarkets, and at tourist attractions.

In contrast, some products are inherently leaky: they're expensive, easy to transport, and nonperishable. The obvious examples are digital media (CDs, DVDs, and software) and pharmaceuticals. Companies go to tremendous lengths to plug leaks, which in an age where Internet shopping allows us to order products from anywhere in the world are becoming increasingly difficult to prevent. For instance, the DVD industry agreed on a system of regional coding so that DVDs bought in the United States would not work in Europe. But that system is being circumvented by an alliance of customers and DVD-machine suppliers who willingly equip machines to read a DVD from anywhere in the world.

If your instincts are anything like mine, it all seems like a pretty shabby trick. But the same popular opinion that despises the DVD industry for trying to sell their products at different prices in different markets also believes that the big pharmaceutical companies should supply drugs to poor countries at discounted prices. Confusingly, our moral intuitions seem to be sending us contradictory messages.

Maybe the story is as simple as this: when it's an important product like a treatment for HIV/AIDS, the most important thing is to get it to the poor; when it's as trivial as a DVD, our irritation at being ripped off is the dominant emotion. But that doesn't quite add up: DVDs make it to very poor areas, and surely we should be at least somewhat pleased that the poor get to watch movies in bars and village halls across the developing world? Or, conversely, shouldn't we be even more outraged that the pharmaceutical companies are overcharging for crucial treatments in the developed world? An economist cannot solve these ethical conundrums, but economics can unwrap them so that at least the ethical question becomes clearer.

When price-targeting is a good thing

Here is a thought experiment.

Imagine a hypothetical pharmaceutical company called PillCorp, which has developed a uniquely powerful new treatment for HIV/

AIDS. Assume that it doesn't engage in any price-targeting and charges the same price across the globe. PillCorp will set the global price so that the gain in sales from cutting the price exactly balances the loss of margin from a price cut. For example, say that PillCorp cut prices and reduced their margins by half. Unless they doubled sales this would reduce profits. They could raise prices and double their margins, but if sales dropped by more than half that would also reduce profits. PillCorp will maximize profits by pricing at the point where either a price cut or a price increase would slightly damage the bottom line.

The price will be high, because people in rich countries will pay a lot for an effective treatment, and there is no point in losing customers who are paying thousands of dollars in an effort to pick up customers who are paying pennies.

That looks like bad news. PillCorp is using its scarcity power to charge a high price for a life-saving drug. As a result, people in poor countries don't get the drug. People are dying because of PillCorp's greed.

Actually, it's only half bad news. People are also *living* because of PillCorp's greed. PillCorp developed the life-saving treatment because it was encouraged to do so by the hope of a lucrative patent. Pharmaceuticals are very expensive to research and develop, and somebody has to pay the bill. The current system is that public and private insurers pay, and since the United States is easily the largest market, innovation is driven by and largely paid for there.

Although PillCorp is making money by selling its drug at a high uniform global price, they could be doing better and so could everybody else. Economists don't just have in mind a shrug-your-shoulders-life's-like-that-sometimes "could be better." We mean something more precise: PillCorp could be making more money and serving the world better.

Say that a year's supply of drugs for one customer costs $10 for PillCorp to produce, and retails at $1,000. For rich customers willing to pay—or who have insurance that will pay—that's not

really a problem. Each year of treatment transfers $990 from those living with AIDS to those who produced the treatment. But a taxi driver in Cameroon might be willing to pay only $50 a year for treatment; beyond that, he'd rather buy food, or gas for his taxi. Because of PillCorp's global price policy, the taxi driver loses out on the treatment, and PillCorp loses out on the chance to make some profit. But if PillCorp were able to make a one-time discount to the taxi driver and sell him the treatment for any price between $10 and $50—say $30—everybody would be better off. The taxi driver gets treatment for $30 when he was willing to pay $50. PillCorp receives $30 in revenues for a $10 pill—a profit of $20.

That is what economists mean when we say a situation "could be better." If we can point to a change that could make at least one person better off, and nobody worse off, we say that the current situation is **inefficient,** or, in everyday language, that it could be better. (We also say that the current situation is **efficient** if every change that could make at least one person better off will also make somebody else worse off. It doesn't mean that an efficient situation can't be improved; it's just that there is no costless way to improve it.)

Now imagine that PillCorp practices price-targeting, continuing to charge $1,000 in rich Western countries but supplying people in developing countries, like the Cameroon taxi driver, for $30. Suddenly, a whole new market opens up for PillCorp: the new discount allows the company to acquire millions of new customers at a profit of $20 a year, but at the same time, it still makes all the sales it used to make in rich countries.

This assumes the cheap pills don't "leak" back, which in practice is a massive concern for pharmaceutical companies. The current leakage of cheap drugs from Canada is a problem for drug companies who want to take advantage of the high willingness to pay in the United States, but who also sell to Canadian health care providers who refuse to pay high prices for drugs. The risk, if the

leakage continues, is that American providers simply refuse to offer discounts to Canada any more.

The example should also make us realize that the greater price transparency brought about by the Internet and other improvements in communications occasionally has a downside: a company with scarcity power may be discouraged from offering discounted products because they are more likely to leak.

PillCorp's dual-pricing policy creates a much better situation. Customers in rich countries are no worse off. Shareholders in PillCorp are better off. And people living with HIV/AIDS in poor countries are also better off. To use the business-school jargon, this is a win-win situation, or as an economist would say, a clear improvement in efficiency.

This doesn't mean the new situation is perfect; it just means that it is unambiguous progress from the previous situation, where PillCorp's scarcity power was causing a huge inefficiency . . . and huge loss of life in poor countries. Perhaps we are outraged to see the poor denied drugs that cost pennies to produce, not because that is unfair (many things are unfair) but because it is also so wasteful of life.

When price-targeting is a bad thing

PillCorp's new price-targeting program was a win-win affair. But sometimes price-targeting is a losing proposition all around.

Consider another hypothetical organization, TrainCorp, a passenger train company. TrainCorp owns a train that always travels full. Some of the seats go at a discount of $50 to leisure travelers who booked in advance, to senior citizens, to students, or to families. The other tickets cost the full price of $100 and are bought by commuters and other business travelers. This is a fairly standard group-targeting strategy: by giving away a few low-price tickets, TrainCorp restricts supply and acquires the ability to demand high prices by offering tickets to only the buyers with the highest willingness to pay. (It might be profitable for TrainCorp just to fence off some of the seats and restrict sup-

ply that way, but it's even better for them to fill the spare seats if they can.)

We know at once—if we are economists—that this is inefficient. In other words, we can think of something that would make at least one person better off without making anyone else worse off.

That something is to find a commuter who was willing to pay a little less than $100, say $95, and who decided to travel by car instead, and offer him a seat for $90. Where does the seat come from, since the train is full? Well, you take a student who is in no great hurry and was willing to pay a little more than $50, say $55, for the seat and politely throw him off the train. But you refund the price of his ticket, plus an extra $10 for his trouble.

Where do we stand now? The commuter was willing to pay $95 but only paid $90. He's better off by $5. The student was willing to pay $55 for a $50 ticket, so if he'd been allowed to ride, he'd have been only $5 better off. But he has just been given $10, so the student is also happy. And what about TrainCorp? Well, TrainCorp just transformed a $50 ticket into a $90 ticket and made a more profitable sale. Even after paying $10 compensation to the student, the company is $30 ahead. Now everyone's a winner; or they would be if TrainCorp adopted this system instead of its group price-targeting strategy.

But of course, that's not what happens, because if TrainCorp tried it, commuters who were willing to pay $100 would hang around for the $90 tickets, and students who weren't willing to pay $50 would buy tickets anyway and wait to be paid to get off. The whole affair would turn out badly for TrainCorp, who is the one who gets to set the prices.

In case your head is spinning a little, here's the quick-and-dirty summary: the group price-targeting strategy is inefficient because it takes seats away from customers who are willing to pay more, and gives them to customers who are willing to pay less. Yet airlines and railroads still use it, because the alternative of individual price-targeting isn't feasible.

OK, so sometimes price-targeting is less efficient than a uniform price, as in the case of the train; sometimes it's more efficient

than a uniform price, as in the case of the HIV/AIDS drugs. But we can say more than that. Whenever price-targeting fails to expand the number of sales and merely moves products from people who value them more, like commuters, to people who value them less, like students, as in the case of TrainCorp, it will definitely be less efficient than a uniform price. Whenever price-targeting opens up a new market without affecting the old market, as with PillCorp, it will definitely be more efficient than a uniform price.

And there's a middle position. A lot of group price-targeting does a bit of both: it opens up some new markets but also wastefully moves products away from high-value users to low-value users. For example, this book is published in hardcover at a high price, and then the paperback edition emerges later, at a lower price. The aim is to target a higher price at people impatient to hear what I have to say and at libraries. One good result is that the publisher will be able to sell paperbacks more cheaply, because some costs will be offset by the hardcover sales, and so the book will reach more people. One bad result is that the early version is much more expensive than it would be if there was only a single paperback edition, and some buyers will be put off. That's what life is like in a world of scarcity: when companies with scarcity power try to exploit it, the situation will almost always be inefficient, and—equivalently—we economists will almost always be able to think of something better.

I say "almost" because a company, which is able to practice perfectly individualized price-targeting strategy, would never miss a sale: rich or desperate customers would pay a lot, poor or indifferent customers would pay very little, but no customer willing to pay the cost of production would be turned away. The situation would be efficient.

Being realistic, though, it's most unlikely that any company would have so much information about its customers as to be able to make such perfectly efficient sales. The company would need to peer into the heart of every possible customer and find out how badly he or she wanted the product; it would need a supercomputer to operate the cash registers. That just isn't plau-

sible. But perhaps it makes you think. What if you could plug every customer's preferences into a supercomputer? What if you had all the information you needed to never miss a sale? Would the world be a better place?

Something else may have caught your attention. When PillCorp changed its global pricing policy, it did something that was not only profitable but also both efficient and fair. Can we say anything more generally about when private greed will serve the public interest? For the answers to all these questions, and more . . . read on.

Perfect Markets and the "World of Truth"

You might not expect Jim Carrey films and economics to have much in common, but in fact there is much we can learn from the rubber-faced comedian. Consider the film, *Liar, Liar*, which tells the story of Fletcher Reede. As a result of his son's birthday wish, Fletcher Reede finds that he is compelled to tell the truth for twenty-four hours. This is problematic for Fletcher because he is a lawyer—or a *liar*, as his son understands it—and hilarity predictably ensues as a horrified Fletcher incriminates himself by helplessly blurting out truthful answers to every question he is asked. They don't make as much of a feel-good movie, but free markets are just like Fletcher Reede's son—they force you to tell the truth. Yet while the results were humiliating for Jim Carrey's character, we will discover that a world of truth leads to a perfectly efficient economy, one in which it is impossible to make someone better off without making someone else worse off.

In this chapter we'll see what truth means in economic terms, how it leads to efficiency, and why efficiency is good. We'll also explore efficiency's shortcomings: how efficiency isn't always fair, and why we have taxes. As we'll see, taxes are like lies: they interfere with the world of truth. But I'll reveal one way in which taxes can be implemented, which is both fair *and* efficient. This could be good news for seniors struggling to pay their winter heating bills, but bad news for Tiger Woods.

Imagine if you will that Fletcher's son gets his birthday wish, not just for his smooth-talking dad but for the whole world. So, let's buy a cappuccino in the world of truth. Before frothing up the half-and-half for you, the barista looks you up and down and asks:

"What's the most you're willing to pay for this coffee?"

You'd like to lie and pretend that you don't really want it, but the truth just slips out:

"I'm in caffeine withdrawal. Fifteen bucks."

With a smirk, the barista prepares to ring up the extortionate sum, but you have a few questions of your own:

"How much did those coffee beans cost?"

"How much did you pay for the plastic lid and the cup?"

"How much does it cost to raise a cow, and how much milk can you get from one?"

"How much did the electricity cost for the refrigeration, heating, and light in here?"

Now it is the barista's turn to have a Fletcher Reede moment. No matter how she tries to evade the questions or froth up the cost of the cappuccino, she cannot tell a lie. It turns out that the cappuccino costs not fifteen dollars, but less than one. The barista tries to haggle, but you have one more killer question:

"Are any other places within thirty yards selling coffee like this?"

"Yes . . . " she moans, her head thudding to the counter in a gesture of abject defeat.

You walk out of the shop with the coffee safely in your possession for the bargain price of ninety-two cents.

Prices are optional, which means they reveal information

There's a basic truth incorporated into any system of prices. That truth comes from the fact that stores and consumers do not have to buy or sell at a given price—they can always opt out. If you'd been willing to pay only fifty cents for the coffee, nobody could have forced you to raise your offer or forced the barista to drop the price. The sale simply would not have occurred.

Of course, you sometimes hear people complaining that if they want something—say, an apartment on Central Park West—then they have to pay the exorbitant asking price. That's true, but although prices sometimes seem unfairly high, you hardly ever *have* to pay them. You could always use your money to buy an apartment in Harlem or a house in Newark or a million cups of coffee instead.

In a free market, people don't buy things that are worth less to them than the asking price. And people don't sell things that are worth more to them than the asking price (or if they do, it's never for long; firms that routinely sell cups of coffee for half of what they cost to produce will go out of business pretty quickly). The reason is simple: nobody is forcing them to, which means that most transactions that happen in a free market improve efficiency, because they make both parties better off—or at least not worse off—and don't harm anyone else.

Now you can begin to see why I say that prices "tell the truth" and reveal information. In a free market, all the buyers of coffee would prefer to have coffee than the money the coffee cost, which is shorthand for saying they prefer coffee to whatever else they might have spent ninety-two cents on. That is, the value of the product to the customer is equal to or higher than the price; and the cost to the producer equal to or lower than the price. Painfully obvious, perhaps, but the implications turn out to be dramatic.

It may seem trivial to say that in a free market we know customers value coffee more than the money they pay for it. Yet it's

not quite as trivial as it looks. For a start, this "trivial" piece of information is already more than we can say about anything that is paid for outside the market—for example, Washington DC's hugely controversial new baseball stadium. The Montreal Expos baseball team agreed to move to DC on the condition that the DC government subsidize the cost of a new stadium. Some say the subsidy will be $70 million, others that it will be far higher. Maybe this is a good idea, and maybe not. It's not clear how we decide whether this is a good way of spending taxpayers' money.

When decisions are made inside a market system there's no such controversy. If I decide to pay $70 for a ticket to see a baseball game, nobody questions whether it's worth it; I made my choice, so obviously I thought so. This free choice produces information about my priorities and preferences, and when millions of us make choices, market prices aggregate the priorities and preferences of us all.

Perfect markets: *The* truth, the whole truth, and nothing but the truth

So the trivial piece of information that in a free market customers value cappuccinos more than the money they pay for them is not so trivial after all. But we needn't stop there.

Imagine now that the coffee market is not only free but extremely competitive, that entrepreneurs are always starting new firms with fresh ideas and entering the market in an attempt to undercut the incumbent companies. (Profits in a competitive industry are high enough only to pay workers and persuade entrepreneurs that their money isn't better off in a savings account—no higher.) The competition will force the price of coffee down to the "marginal cost"—the cost the coffee bar incurs when making one more cappuccino, which we may remember is just under a dollar. In a perfectly competitive market, the price of coffee would equal the marginal cost of coffee. If the price were lower, firms would go out of business until it rose. If the price were higher, new firms would enter or old firms would expand their output

until it fell. Suddenly, the price is not conveying a vague fact ("this coffee is worth ninety-two cents, or more, to the buyer, and it cost the coffee bar ninety-two cents, or less") but a precise truth ("this coffee cost the coffee bar exactly ninety-two cents").

What if other industries were also perfectly competitive? That would mean that for every product, the price equaled the marginal cost. Every product would be linked to every other product through an ultracomplex network of prices, so when something changes somewhere in the economy (there's a frost in Brazil, or a craze for iPods in the US) everything else would change—maybe imperceptibly, maybe a lot—to adjust. A frost in Brazil, for example, would damage the coffee crop and reduce the worldwide supply of coffee; this would increase the price coffee roasters have to pay to a level that discourages enough coffee drinking to offset the shortfall. Demand for alternative products, like tea, would rise a little, encouraging higher tea prices and extra supply of tea. Demand for complementary products like coffee creamer would fall a little. In Kenya, coffee farmers would enjoy bumper profits and would invest the money in improvements like aluminum roofing for their houses; the price of aluminum would rise and so some farmers would decide to wait before buying. That means demand for bank accounts and safety deposit boxes would rise, although for unfortunate farmers in Brazil with their failed crops, the opposite may be happening. The free-market supercomputer processes the truth about demands and about costs, and gives people the incentive to respond in astonishingly intricate ways.

That may seem like a ridiculous hypothetical scenario. But economists can measure and have measured some of these effects: when frosts hit Brazil, world coffee prices do indeed rise, Kenyan farmers do buy aluminum roofing, the price of roofing does rise, and the farmers do, in fact, time their investment so that they don't pay too much. Even if markets are not perfect, they can convey tremendously complex information.

Governments—or any organizations—find it hard to respond to such complex information. In Tanzania, coffee is not produced in a free market, and the government, rather than the farmers,

receives any windfalls from high coffee prices. Historically, the government has failed to spend the money sensibly, blowing too much on unsustainable salary rises for civil servants, and failing to realize that the price spike was temporary.

To appreciate why markets do such a good job of processing complex information, first think about the customer. We know that he won't buy a cappuccino unless he values it more than anything else he could buy with the same money. But what else could he buy with the same money? In our world of truth, he could buy *anything* that costs the same as, or less than, a cappuccino. If he chooses the coffee he's saying that of all the things in the world that cost the same as coffee, he would like coffee to be made.

Elsewhere, of course, there are other people spending their money not on coffee but on movie tickets, bus fares, or underwear; and there are others choosing not to spend their money at all and to put it in the bank instead. All of these competing demands pull producers to respond. If people want computers, then manufacturers will build factories, hire workers, and buy plastics and metals, which will be diverted from other uses to go into computers. If people want coffee instead of underwear, then more land will be devoted to coffee and less to other uses, like parks or housing or tobacco farming. Lingerie shops will be replaced by coffee shops. Of course, start-up companies will borrow money from banks, and interest rates will rise or fall, depending on the balance between the number of people wanting to save and the number of people wanting to borrow. Interest rates are just another price: the price of spending today instead of next year. (You might have thought that interest rates were set by central bankers like Alan Greenspan at the Federal Reserve or Mervyn King at the Bank of England. Actually, Greenspan and King chair committees that set "nominal" interest rates. True interest rates are interest rates after inflation—set by the market in response to the central bankers.)

The changes don't stop there. The ripples in the price system continue outward. They whip through some parts of the economy

at tremendous speed and cause slow but powerful seismic shifts in others, like education or technology. For example, if there aren't enough trained workers to produce computers, manufacturers like Dell and Compaq will have to train them, or raise wages to poach them from other manufacturers like Apple and Gateway. As the wages for skilled workers rise, people will see that it's worth taking time off and paying to go to college. Manufacturers' interest in producing cheaper or better computers will give a boost to research labs and engineering schools. Higher demand for plastics will raise the price of the raw material—crude oil—which will in turn encourage those who use oil for energy to switch to cheaper substitute fuels or to invest in energy-saving technology. And so it continues. Some of these effects will be tiny. Others will be enormous. Some will have an instant effect. Others will not be realized for decades. But in the world of truth—the world of perfect markets—all of them will have an impact.

What is the result of a set of perfectly competitive markets interconnected like this?

Companies are making things the right way. Any company that wastes resources, over-produces, or uses the wrong technology, will go out of business. Every product is produced in the most efficient way.

Companies are making the right things. The price of a product equals the cost to make it. The price also reflects the terms at which customers can trade off one priority against another. (Two cups of coffee cost the same as one Danish; which would you prefer?) The price is a direct line of communication from what products cost to what customers prefer, and back again.

Things are being made in the right proportions. If too much coffee were being produced, manufacturers would cut prices; and if too little, prices would rise. Either way, the situation would correct itself. In the competitive market, price equals cost; there is no incentive for anyone to produce less (giving up profitable

sales) or to produce more (creating products that cost more than anyone is willing to pay). The competitive rule—price equals cost equals value to the consumer—keeps things efficient.

Things are going to the "right" people. The only people who buy products are the people who are willing to pay the appropriate price. Let's say I confiscate a cappuccino from Axel and give it to Bob. In the world of truth, this is wasteful. Axel was willing to pay for coffee, and Bob was not, which means Axel values coffee more than Bob, and my confiscation is inefficient. Notice that here I am equating "right" with "efficient," an assumption we'll examine and challenge shortly.

So: if the right things are being made right in the right quantities and going to the people who value them most, there is no room for any gains in efficiency. To put it another way, *you can't get more efficient than a perfectly competitive market.* And it all follows perfectly naturally from the truth contained in the price system: prices are true representations of cost to firms, and also true representations of value to customers.

Life without markets

Because Western society relies heavily on free markets, we find it difficult to imagine what it would be like if we didn't, or to take a step back and see quite how profound the effect of the market is. Yet any modern democracy provides goods outside the market system, and looking at the way such goods are provided gives us a hint of the strengths and weaknesses of markets. Think of your friendly local police force, which is paid for by a nonmarket system of taxation. The nonmarket system has some advantages— for one thing, when you dial 911 nobody asks for your credit card details. The government is supposed to afford the same level of protection to the rich and poor, although it does not always seem that way.

But the nonmarket system also has some disadvantages. For instance, if a police officer is rude or incompetent, you don't have

the option to shop for a different police force. If you think that the level of police protection you receive is excessive, it's not up to you to cut back a bit. Neither can you spend more if you decide that you'd like extra service. No, you have to lobby your local politicians and hope they consider your demands.

Government-provided schooling is another example of a nonmarket service that many of us use. In both Britain and the United States, most people send their children to government-funded schools. But those schools are different from each other—different atmospheres, different academic emphases. Most importantly, some are good schools, and some are not. The market solution for schools is similar to the market solution for food: the best food goes to the people who are willing—which also implies able—to pay most for it. But within the government sector there are no prices. What happens instead? Parents line up, haggle, and protest. They move to districts with better schools. In Britain, government-run religious schools often have the best academic records, so atheists take their children to church every Sunday in order to get good references from priests and get their children into these schools.

As with the police, the nonmarket system has the cozy advantage of concealing the fact that the poor don't get the same quality of education that the rich do. But again, the nonmarket system suffers from a serious problem: the truth about values, costs, and benefits has disappeared. It is impossible to tell which parents enroll their children in church schools for religious reasons and which parents are just looking for better results. It is also impossible to know how much parents would be willing to pay for more teachers and better materials. In a market system the truth would emerge about how much it costs to provide good schools, and who would be willing to pay for them. The nonmarket system struggles with these basic questions.

It seems that there is a willingness to pay for good schools, and we see it emerge because house prices are higher in the areas of schools with the best reputation. The nonmarket system, which gives preference to local children, channels the

money that parents are willing to pay for a good school into the hands of property owners near existing good schools. This hardly seems sensible. A market system would simply direct the money to pay for more good schools.

The signaling function of prices

Prices perform two functions, not just one. In a market system, prices provide a way of deciding who gets to enjoy a limited supply of schools: whoever pays most gets to send their children to the best schools, an uncomfortable state of affairs, which the government-school system is designed to prevent. But prices also give the signal to build more schools, hire more teachers or raise their wages if they're in short supply, and buy better materials. In the longer term, a price system will transform a high willingness to pay for good schools into a lot of good schools, just as surely as it will transform a high demand for coffee into a lot of cappuccino.

Don't politicians know that we value good schools already? Should they be making government money available? The difficulty is that politicians hear that we want good schools, but they also hear that we want more police on the streets, a better health service, lots of big roads, excellent welfare benefits, low taxes, and a double-shot caramel Venti latte. It's easy for us to demand all of these things, but prices, by forcing us to put money where our mouths are, uncover the truth. Taxes have their advantages, but many don't contribute to truth because we cannot choose whether or not to pay them, depending on whether each penny is spent according to our wishes. Because prices are optional, they reveal information.

None of this amounts to a knockdown argument against providing a police service or a school system with a nonmarket process. Nonmarket systems have their advantages, but they also lose something important: information, information about wants, needs, and desires, and about inconveniences and costs. Sometimes the loss of information is worthwhile because it is offset by gains in equality or stability. But sometimes the loss of informa-

tion can leave an economy, and a society, floundering in waste and confusion. We think that the value we get from schools and police are more than what they cost us in taxes, but we don't know for sure. Not so with the cappuccino.

Efficiency versus fairness:
Can we handle the truth?

A perfectly competitive market is like a giant supercomputer network. With amazing processing power and sensors in every part of the economy—reaching even inside our brains to read our desires—the market is constantly reoptimizing production and allocating the results perfectly. Remember that when economists say the economy is inefficient, they mean that there's a way to make somebody better off without harming anybody else. While the perfectly competitive market is perfectly efficient, efficiency is not enough to ensure a fair society, or even a society in which we would want to live. After all, it is efficient if Bill Gates has all the money and everybody else starves to death . . . because there is no way to make anybody better off without making Bill Gates worse off. We need something more than efficiency.

So it's hardly surprising we sometimes prefer the cozy white lies: it is expensive, for example, to heat the house of an elderly lady in Minnesota, but we may prefer to subsidize the fuel, not wanting her to face the truth of that expense.

Even more than subsidies, taxes are a common cause of inefficiency: the government taxes market transactions and spends the money on, we hope, good things like police forces and schools. Why are taxes inefficient? Because they destroy the information carried by prices in perfectly competitive, efficient markets: price no longer equals cost, so cost no longer equals value. For example, a sales tax of 10 percent creates a "lie" in the following circumstances:

Cost of cappuccino: ninety cents
- Price of cappuccino in perfectly competitive market: ninety cents

- Price of cappuccino after tax: ninety-nine cents
- Willingness to pay for cappuccino: ninety-five cents
- Cappuccino sold: **none**
- Tax raised: **zero**

There was a sale that could have created five cents of efficiency gains (cappuccino cost ninety cents but was valued at ninety-five cents) but which never happened because of the tax. What's worse, the tax wasn't even paid. If the government were able to waive the tax in such circumstances, they would be no worse off, but the coffee buyer would be better off: a clear efficiency gain.

It's hard for tax officials to know when to charge the tax (situations where taxes will not change buyers' behavior) and when to waive the tax (because potential buyers would have avoided it anyway, by not buying coffee). But they try to do so using the kind of price-targeting strategies outlined in chapter 2. Taxes are often higher when price-sensitivity is low. For example, the government charges high taxes on gasoline and cigarettes, not for environmental and health reasons but because people who buy these products need to drive and are addicted to smoking; they won't change their behavior much even in the face of large taxes.

We are faced with a dilemma. We want to avoid inefficiency, because that would leave us passing up an opportunity to make somebody better off at no cost to anyone else. But taxes cause inefficiency, and most of us think we need taxes to redistribute income (to a greater or lesser extent) from the rich to the poor. We seem to be facing two contradictory imperatives: avoid the needless waste that is "inefficiency," but make sure that wealth is at least somewhat evenly spread. What we need is a way to make our economies both efficient and fair.

Can we enlist markets to help with fairness?

Is it true that we have to choose between the efficiency of perfect markets and the fairness of benevolent government intervention? This seemed to be the conclusion of governments throughout

the free world after the experience of the Great Depression and World War II. President Roosevelt's "New Deal" programs of the 1930s expanded the role of the United States government, in response to the Great Depression. In Britain, Clement Atlee's postwar government took control of much of the health, steel, air travel, petroleum, rail travel, and telephone industries. Government-owned businesses took over partly because in the deprived, exhausted yet hopeful years after the war, economists had some confidence in the experts who had masterminded the war effort and thought they might not do a bad job of organizing the economy efficiently. Few people foresaw the later collapse of government-run economies, whether vast like the Soviet Union and China, or small like Tanzania or North Korea. But even if they had believed that private markets were more efficient, this was neither here nor there in the 1940s: the postwar Labour government in Britain would have been content to live with some inefficiency if it meant a fairer society.

But the old dilemma between efficiency and fairness was about to be shattered by a young New Yorker called Kenneth Arrow, who knew all about unfairness after watching helplessly as a teenager while his father lost his successful business and all his savings in the Great Depression. The desire for social justice stayed with Arrow, but intellectually he couldn't just ignore the question of efficiency. The young economist set his logical mind to wrestling with the tension between the unerring efficiency of the free market and the imperative that some kind of fairness should prevail. His solution was brilliant, twisting the traditional thinking about competitive markets and efficiency on its head. He proved that not only are all perfect markets efficient, *all efficient outcomes can be achieved using a competitive market, by adjusting the starting position.* Arrow went on to win every plaudit available to an economist, and he remains the youngest man ever to win the Nobel Prize for Economics. But why was his insight so important?

I call it the "head start theorem." Instead of focusing on the enormous complexity of a real economy, think of a very simple one-dimensional human challenge: the 100-meter sprint. The fastest

sprinter will win the race. If you wanted all the sprinters to cross the line together, you could just change the rules of the race, ordering the fast runners to slow down and everyone to hold hands as they crossed the line. A waste of talent. Or you could move some starting blocks forward and some starting blocks back, so that although each sprinter was running as fast as he could, obeying the usual rules and objectives of sprinting, the fastest had to cover enough extra ground that he would end up breaking the tape neck-and-neck with the slowest.

Arrow demonstrated that the same approach could work when trying to balance the excesses of competitive markets: instead of interfering with the markets themselves, the trick is to adjust the starting blocks by making lump-sum payments and levying one-time taxes.

An example of a lump-sum tax would be the government taxing everybody eight hundred dollars; or alternatively, taxing everyone over the age of sixty-five eight hundred dollars; or alternatively, taxing everybody whose surname on the birth certificate starts with *H* eight hundred dollars. The point is that unlike an income tax or a sales tax on coffee, a lump-sum tax doesn't affect anybody's behavior, because there is nothing you can do to avoid it. So unlike sales tax, it doesn't lead to an efficiency loss. Similarly, an example of lump-sum redistribution would be to *give* eight hundred dollars to everybody whose name starts with *H*, a policy for which I would be happy to vote.

In the 100-meter sprint, lump-sum taxation is like moving the starting blocks back a few paces. Income tax and sales tax are like asking the best runners to run backwards. Both would have the effect of ensuring a more equal finish, but moving the starting blocks around doesn't slow anybody down.

In the context of a sprint, it's fairly obvious that one of the ways to get a close result is to give the slower runners a head start. In the context of an economy, with literally billions of different goods, desires, raw materials, and talents, the head start theorem is a much bolder claim. But it's true: you can allow the competitive economy to use every skill and every raw material,

take advantage of every opportunity to trade, cooperate, educate, or invest . . . but still get a fair outcome by moving around the starting blocks and letting perfect markets do the rest.

The implication is that in a world of perfect markets, the only thing needed to ensure both fairness and efficiency is a "head start" strategy: a program of appropriate lump-sum taxes and subsidies that puts everyone on equal footing. The perfect markets then find every possible opportunity to make everybody better off from their revised starting points. The question is, can this be done in practice?

Impractical examples

Let's take an example. American political philosopher Robert Nozick deployed a famous argument against taking a view of "justice as fairness." In other words, he disputed the notion that one particular allocation of wealth could be deemed the "best" or "fair" allocation. Nozick's argument invokes Wilt Chamberlain, a basketball star famous in the 1960s and '70s, when Nozick was writing. Chamberlain's talents made him wealthy; Nozick felt this was "just" because Chamberlain's wealth was the outcome of legitimate decisions by fans happy to pay to see him play. The situation may have been "just" in Nozick's sense of the word, but can any situation that leads to a highly unequal distribution of cash be considered "fair"?

Perhaps taxing Chamberlain's income heavily would make the situation fairer, but Nozick warns that if Chamberlain did not really enjoy playing basketball *and* he was loaded down with heavy taxes, he might stop playing altogether. So although this situation might seem more "fair," there would be neither the tax revenue, nor the basketball game: the problem of the cappuccino sales tax all over again. So how is it reasonable to call a distribution of income "fair" when everybody concerned, both fans and player, would prefer the "unfair" outcome?

Thanks to Kenneth Arrow, we now know that, when faced with a modern-day sports star like Tiger Woods, the solution is

to levy a one-time lump-sum tax of several million dollars on him. He would still have the incentive to earn money by playing golf, since he could not avoid the tax by playing less, as he would have to do in order to avoid a heavy income tax. He would no doubt earn enough to pay off the tax bill and still retain enough to buy a family car and a nice house somewhere unassuming. In this scenario, there is no waste or inefficiency, but the result is "fair" in that it produces a much more even allocation of wealth.

The only trouble with this plan is that it's wildly impractical. The problem is not that it's impossible to have taxes that only apply to one individual: President Franklin Roosevelt introduced an income tax rate of 79 percent, but the threshold was so high that the tax was paid by only John D. Rockefeller. Rather, the problem is more that a true lump-sum tax isn't supposed to change behavior at all. Ideally it would have been decided before Tiger Woods was born, because if he could have predicted that he would be liable for a tax as a result of his success he might have chosen a different profession.

This is, of course, quite impossible. But we shouldn't abandon the head start theorem quite yet. While we can't always use lump-sum taxation and redistribution, we can sometimes: and when we can, it's worth considering because it preserves the efficiency and the truth of the competitive market while adding a welcome dose of fairness.

A practical example

A more practical application of the head start theorem could be used to prevent elderly people from getting cold in winter, without damaging the environment. In a typical winter in Britain twenty-five thousand seniors die as a result of inadequate heating. To address this concern, domestic fuel is subject to lower taxes than many other things. But that's a slightly odd way to deal with the problem—an equivalent to the "running backwards" solution. If governments need to raise tax revenue—and all of

them do, it seems—then a first approximation of an efficient strategy would be to have the same sales tax on everything, because that wouldn't distort people's buying decisions too much. A more refined view would recall the "price-targeting" of chapter 2. Because customers cannot easily cut down on fuel consumption, they are not very sensitive to the price of domestic fuel, hence the government should levy a bit more tax on fuel and a bit less on other goods: customers would not change their behavior much and so the inefficiency would be small. An even more sophisticated view (perhaps acquired from a peek ahead at chapter 4) would note that domestic fuel is a nonrenewable resource and using it causes pollution, so the case for higher tax on domestic fuel becomes even stronger.

The case for lower taxes on domestic fuel and higher taxes on other goods is hard to understand, until we start to worry about the elderly shivering in front of a lifeless gas or oil furnace that they cannot afford to switch on. Is this just one of those hard choices that governments sometimes have to make? Not necessarily. Instead of levying the wrong rate of tax on everyone else, better to choose a more sensible rate but give the elderly a head start—because of their poverty and because, being frail, they have an additional need for heating. The simple policy remedy is to raise fuel tax but give extra money to the elderly, money that they could use to switch that furnace on and stay warm.

We know from the head start theorem that given the money, pensioners will find their way to the efficient outcome—which, incidentally, may not involve more fuel being burned. Not every pensioner feels cold, and those who do may find better solutions to the problem. Some may use the money to move to Florida. Some may insulate their homes. Those who did not feel the cold in the first place can spend the money on other things. Nobody will burn extra fuel unless they need to, and if they need to they'll have the money to meet that need.

The lesson of the head start theorem is that when a problem arises, it's worth asking whether the problem can be addressed

by rearranging the starting blocks rather than interfering with the race. This strategy isn't always practical, but because free markets are efficient, it's worth trying to harness that efficiency to meet other goals.

Throughout this chapter, we've been on a flight of fantasy no more plausible than the story of Fletcher Reede. The "world of truth" is a world where markets are complete, free, and competitive. In reality we're about as likely to achieve a world with complete, free, and competitive markets as hotshot lawyers are to start telling the truth to everyone.

You might therefore be asking yourself why you've read a chapter, even a brief one, about some bizarre economists' fantasy. The answer is that the fantasy helps us understand why economic problems arise and also helps us to move in the right direction. We know that a world of perfect markets combined with the head start approach is as good as we're going to get. When real world economies malfunction, we know to look for the market failures—and to do our best to patch them up.

We've already explored one of those failures: some companies have scarcity power and can set prices that are far above their true cost, which is where they would be in a competitive market. This is why economists believe there's an important difference between being in favor of markets and being in favor of business, especially particular businesses. A politician who is in favor of markets believes in the importance of competition and wants to prevent businesses from getting too much scarcity power. A politician who's too influenced by corporate lobbyists will do exactly the reverse.

Whether abetted by politicians or otherwise, companies with scarcity power are one market failure. There are two others. In the next two chapters, we'll encounter them, leaving the curious world of truth behind us and facing up to the real world once again.

FOUR

Crosstown Traffic

We've just learned that in the world of perfect markets, everything is for the best. We know that perfect markets are completely efficient, delivering outcomes that are flawless in every respect except distribution. We also know from the head start theorem that we can fix any complaints about distribution in advance. Presto, every problem solved, or at least every problem concerning the allocation of goods and services.

That's nice to hear, but then why did I spend two hours stuck in traffic on the way to work this morning? The bumper-to-bumper traffic was a stupid waste. All of us could have been riding buses, or carpooling, and we would have reached our destinations in downtown DC in fifteen minutes. Where is the perfect market there? The obvious answer is that, of course, there is no market perfect or otherwise for driving around on the streets. What may be less obvious is that there could be.

Economies that work smoothly because they are full of perfect markets are neither interesting nor realistic. But because perfect markets provide such a clear benchmark, economists find it much easier to start from them and work out what is going wrong, rather than start from scratch and work out what is going right. And this method of thinking about the world will lead us to the cure for crosstown traffic.

What's wrong with my world

I am a happy man, but there are things in my life that infuriate me and that I wish could be different. I wish I didn't have to upgrade my computer software every couple of years at great expense. I wish that I could rely on my doctors to give me appropriate medical treatment when I am ill. I wish Washington's streets were not clogged with traffic and filled with pollution.

These three personal, if common, grumbles correspond to the three key ways in which markets fail to live up to chapter 3's lofty ideals of perfection. Markets fail to work well in the face of scarcity power, as we saw in chapter 2. That is one of the problems with buying computer software—the market is dominated by a single company, Microsoft, which has tremendous power to set high prices. Markets also fail to work well if some decision makers lack information. When I go to my doctor I have no idea if he is giving me good treatment, while he has no need to take into account the cost of the treatment, and my insurance company has every incentive to refuse to pay, without knowing the true situation. (We'll deal with health care in chapter 5.) Finally, markets fail to work well if some people make decisions that affect bystanders: when a driver buys gasoline from a gas station, that is all very well for the driver and the gas station but not for the bystanders, including other drivers, who have to breathe the resulting carbon monoxide.

These three big problems are called "market failures": scarcity power, which we discussed in chapters 1 and 2; missing information, which we will discuss in chapter 5; and the subject of this chapter, decisions that have side effects on bystanders. Economists call the side effect an "externality" because it lies outside the original decision, for instance, the decision to buy gasoline. Whether because of scarcity power, incomplete information, or an externality, when the economy fails to live up to the idealized "world of truth," trouble is in store.

How drivers affect bystanders

Washington DC, London, Tokyo, Atlanta, Los Angeles, and Bangkok, and indeed any of the world's great cities, are full of cars, buses, and trucks. Those vehicles seriously damage the happiness of innocent bystanders. They cause severe air pollution. Admittedly, London's current air pollution is not as severe as the "Great Stink" of the 1850s, in which tens of thousands died of cholera. But still, air pollution from traffic is not trivial: many thousands of people die because other people want to drive. Around seven thousand people a year die prematurely because of traffic pollution in Britain, a little more than one in ten thousand. In the United States, the Environmental Protection Agency estimates that fifteen thousand people die prematurely because of the particulate matter produced from sources such as diesel engines. Within urban areas like London, the cost of delays from congestion are even worse, if you consider the number of hours spent sitting in traffic as being in any way a significant loss of productive or enjoyable life. Then there is the noise, the accidents and the "barrier effect," which discourages people, and particularly children, from walking to school, the local stores, or even to meet their neighbors across the street.

People are not fools: it's almost certainly true that anyone taking a trip in a car is benefiting from driving. But they are doing so at the expense of everyone else around them—the other drivers stuck in traffic, the parents who dare not let their children walk to school, the pedestrians who risk their lives dashing across the street because they are tired of waiting for the light to change, the office workers who even in the sweltering summer cannot open their windows because of the roar of the traffic.

Because each driver who gets into his car is creating misery for other people, the free market cannot deliver a solution to the problem of traffic. The external effects of congestion and pollution are important departures from the "world of truth." In the "world of truth" every act of selfish behavior is turned to the common good. I selfishly buy underwear because I want it, but in

doing so channel resources into the hands of underwear manu-facturers, and do nobody any harm. Textile workers in China, where the underwear is made, selfishly look for the best job, while manufacturers selfishly look for the most capable employees. All of this works to everyone's benefit: goods are manufactured only if people want them, and they are manufactured only by the most appropriate people to do the job. Self-centered motives are put to work for everybody.

Drivers are in a different situation. They do not offer com-pensation for the cost they inflict on other people. When I buy underwear, the money I spend is compensation for all of the costs incurred in making it and selling it to me. When I take the car for a drive then I do not even need to think about the costs in-curred by the rest of society as I avail myself of the free roads.

Different kinds of prices: Marginal and average

It is not quite fair to say that drivers can use the roads for noth-ing. In the United Kingdom, it's not legal to drive a car, or even to park it on public streets, unless you have paid a sizable annual tax called "Vehicle Excise Duty." Many states in the United States have a similar tax. Gas and diesel fuel are also taxed heavily enough to cause great resentment. In the autumn of 2000, for example, a series of protests against high fuel prices prevented fuel reaching the country's gas stations, and brought Britain to a standstill. In Britain, drivers pay £20 billion in taxes on cars and fuel every year; in America, the figure is around $100 billion. To ask "have they paid enough?" is to ask the wrong question. The right ques-tion is, "are they paying for the right things?" The answer is no.

There are two different concepts of price at play here, and the distinction matters. The average price that a driver pays for a journey across a city is quite high if the driver is paying an annual license fee. But the price that the driver pays for one extra trip across the city is low: the trip doesn't burn much fuel and drivers are not charged for extra trips. Once you've paid for the right to

take the car on the street in the first place, you don't get a discount for low mileage: you might as well drive and drive, because it won't put a penny on your tax bill. That is the difference between the average price and the marginal price, which is the price for one extra trip.

To understand why the difference matters, let's turn to alcohol. When I was in college, clubs and societies used to have big parties where some people didn't drink at all and, less surprisingly, most people drank far too much. This was because there were two types of ticket. "Alcoholic" tickets allowed unlimited boozing after payment of an up-front fee of, say, ten pounds (at that time, about fifteen dollars). The other type of ticket was a lot cheaper, and you had to drink rancid orange juice instead and stand in a corner while the drinkers got more and more obnoxious. Turning up and having a couple of beers was a pretty expensive proposition, so most people preferred either to maximize the value of the unlimited drinking opportunity, or opt out of drinking alcohol completely. Of course, the result was chaos, although some people felt it made for pretty good parties.

Since the university felt that the drunkenness represented a problem, they considered dealing with it at the next party by raising the up-front fee to, say, twenty pounds (about thirty dollars). But the likelihood would be that while a few people would switch to being disgruntled orange-juice drinkers or give up on the society altogether, most of the drinkers would decide there wasn't much point in a party without drinking. Grumbling, they would empty the contents of their wallets. Later in the evening, many of them would empty the contents of their stomachs.

The university misunderstood the problem. They understood that people were drinking too much and correctly thought that the solution probably involved raising the price of drinking. The problem is that there are different ways of describing the price of drinking. There's the price of being a drinker: ten pounds. There's the average price of a drink: for the typical student who has twenty

drinks, this is fifty pence. Then there's the *marginal* price of a drink, which is zero. Once you've paid the up-front fee, you might as well keep drinking.

Question: if you were running the university, would you deal with the problem by: (a) raising the up-front fee for drinking?, (b) buying better orange juice?, or (c) scrapping the up-front fee and charging people for what they drank?

Better orange juice might be nice, but the Undercover Economist would humbly suggest that the solution to the underlying problem is *c*.

Now, back to traffic congestion. If you were advising the secretary of transportation you might suggest an analogy with student parties. Currently, potential drivers have two options: they can cough up a large up-front fee and drive as much as they like; or they can not drive at all. This second option, the "orange-juice" option, requires them to bike, use public transportation, or walk—although as with the student party, the more people who choose the first option, the less attractive the second option becomes.

You might even propose some policy options: (a) raise the up-front fee for driving; (b) supply better "orange juice" (more buses, better trains, cycle routes, pedestrian crossings); or (c) scrap the up-front fee and charge people for the trips they drive.

All of these options could be expected to reduce traffic congestion to some extent, perhaps to an important extent. But it is option (c) that attempts to deal with the cause of the problem. Drivers do not live in the "world of truth"; that is they do not pay the true cost of their actions, including the "externalities" or side effects that affect bystanders. Option (c) tries to make them pay that cost; we might call it an "externality charge."

Currently, every potential driver is being offered the same kind of deal as partygoing students: put up a wad of cash in exchange for an unlimited binge, or pay nothing and receive nothing in return. There are no half measures.

Student parties were not livened up excessively by the fact that drinks worked out at fifty pence (less than one dollar) on average: they were livened up excessively by the fact that the next drink was always free. Similarly, congestion is not caused by the fact that the tax on a car trip is fifty cents on average: it is caused by the fact that the next trip is always free.

We must not get obsessed with the question of how much drivers pay on average. Certainly, how much tax any type of person pays on average is an important question of distribution. While distribution is important, however, it doesn't have a big impact on whether our streets are clogged up and our cities are polluted.

What matters much more for congestion is the price drivers pay at the margin; or, to put it another way, the price drivers pay to make one extra trip. Cars don't cause much pollution or congestion, after all: car *trips* are the problem. Universities would encourage appropriate levels of drinking by charging students per drink. Similarly, the Department of Transportation would encourage appropriate levels of driving by making drivers pay for each trip.

Pricing should reflect the damage

I've been oversimplifying, as usual. In most European countries, drivers do pay a tax per mile in the form of a high tax on fuel. But the tax on fuel doesn't closely match the costs that drivers inflict on each other and on nondrivers. People in rural areas pay the taxes (typically they spend between a quarter and a third as much again on gasoline as those in urban areas), but it is the commuters in the London, New York, or Paris rush hours who are causing the most serious congestion, severe air pollution, and noise. The same trips made in the small hours of the morning do not cause congestion, although pollution and noise are still a problem. Make a similar trip between two houses in Alaska and you do not cause congestion. The noise is likely to be heard only by the occasional stray caribou. The damage caused by pollutants is much reduced, because many of them will disperse harmlessly. If

the idea of a charge on driving is that each driver faces the costs of his actions, the rush-hour New York driver should pay more because he is causing more harm to others. Whatever level of externality charge turns out to be appropriate, if it is to reflect the truth, it should vary according to time and place.

The idea of an externality charge is not to discourage everyone from doing anything that might inconvenience anyone else; it is to get them to take into account the inconvenience they cause to others. To take an extreme example: if I go walking in Virginia's Blue Ridge mountains, it is nice to be able to take in the natural beauty of the place in relative solitude, and so it's mildly annoying to find the trails cluttered with other people. They may be inconveniencing me, but it would not be efficient to forbid their trip because it gives them so much pleasure and me so little trouble.

Externality charging needs to strike the right balance between pleasure and trouble; it must reflect the cost of the externality . . . but no more. We should aim to make ours a world where people feel free to do things they enjoy, even if others are mildly inconvenienced, but also one where we all refrain from harming other people if the effort involved to avoid harming them is small. We discovered in chapter 3 that perfect markets deliver this world, at least within the sphere that markets operate. Perfect markets cannot make us smile at passersby or love our families, but they can make sure that we get a cappuccino if and only if we are willing to pay more than the true cost—which includes the cost in time and trouble of the baristas, the bean pickers, the entrepreneurs, the machine manufacturers, and the rest. In other words, perfect markets allow us to feel free to do things that we enjoy only if our enjoyment outweighs the trouble caused to make it all possible.

This is why economists are fairly relaxed when markets seem to be working well. But we are also vigilant for the many market failures. So how do we make sure that when deciding whether to drive across town, I can be sure that the benefit to me outweighs the cost to everybody else? There's no need to worry about costs and benefits that are part of an efficient market transaction. So, if

oil refining and gasoline retailing are perfect markets (contrary to popular belief, they are not far off), then the trouble it took to refine and distribute the gasoline is fully represented in the price. I will not buy gasoline unless the benefit I get from it is greater than the trouble it took to refine and distribute.

Instead, we should worry about costs and benefits missing from the market transaction. The pollution from the gasoline causes local poisoning and global warming, and the majority of the pollution damage when I burn a tank of gasoline is not caused to me or to the oil company. The trick is to mimic perfect markets by getting drivers to pay all of the costs of their actions: since they have already paid the market costs to the oil company, they also need to pay, on top of that, the externality costs. These externality costs are the costs inflicted on others but not borne by the driver or the oil company.

We now have all the elements in place to design an externality charge. We know that there may be costs and benefits that spill over from an individual choice or a market exchange, and if so, this will be inefficient (translation: we could do better, making at least one person better off and nobody worse off). We also know that if we want to change behavior to correct the inefficiency, we need to address prices at the margin, not average prices. Third, we do not need to worry about costs, which have been incorporated into a well-functioning market transaction, only externality costs, which have been left out. Fourth, our marginal pricing should reflect those externality costs accurately. It's not enough simply to ban any behavior we don't like. Instead, we should be focusing on cases where the active person gains small benefits but causes large costs for others.

Two objections to externality charges

A charge for externalities is effectively a government tax, and all government taxes are controversial. Externality charges are often attacked from two opposing ranges of moral high ground.

How much do people spend on fuel?

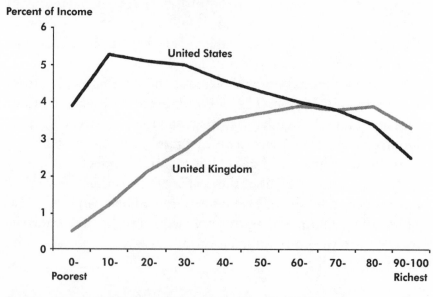

Percent of Income

Source: Smith 1992. Chermick and Reschovsky 1997.

On one flank comes the objection that the externality charge is an unfair tax aimed at a disadvantaged group. Consider the idea of charging drivers to drive at congested times. To such proposals (and they have been widespread) the pro-car lobby argues that drivers pay enough, and it is not fair to price poor drivers off the road. On the other flank come those who strongly object to the activity that is to be taxed on the grounds that after the externality charge has been imposed, the rich will still be able to do whatever it was that was objectionable. In the case of traffic, the anticar lobby claims that it is outrageous that rich drivers can afford to drive around as much as they like, given the environmental damage caused by cars.

Are externality charges unfairly redistributive? They are not aimed at poor people but at voluntary activities: if you decide to stop causing trouble for others, you don't have to pay an externality charge. It is true that the rich can afford to drive more than the poor, but it is just as true that the rich can afford to eat more than the poor. This is unfair too, but if you accept the work-

ings of the price system for typical goods like food, why not road space or clean air? We recognize that food, clothes, and houses cannot be free or we would quickly run out of them. It is because roads are free that we have run out of spare road space.

Furthermore, since the rich do more of most things, externality charges often redistribute money in a desirable way. In the case of congestion charging, the truth is striking: in the United Kingdom, poor people do not drive—they bicycle, walk, or take the bus. The poorest tenth of the population spends almost seven times less on fuel than the richest tenth, as a percentage of their much smaller income. The total spending on fuel by the richest 10 percent is at least thirty times more than by the poorest 10 percent. The conclusion is that congestion charging not only improves efficiency, it also redistributes money by raising more tax from the rich.

That's nice for the defenders of congestion charging in Britain, but useless in the United States, where the poor still drive a lot and so pay larger amounts of tax as a percentage of their incomes. But this needn't be an impossible objection, because externality charges can be designed not to redistribute very much. In the case of roads, the government could scrap the vehicle excise duty, which is a large up-front tax, while starting to levy congestion charges on each trip. This would capture the efficiency benefits of a congestion charge without having major effects on distribution. It is possible to neutralize much of the redistribution caused by the externality charge, while keeping its efficiency-boosting effects. This is a variant of the lump-sum tax on Tiger Woods proposed in chapter 3: we can use lump-sum taxes to redistribute without destroying efficiency.

Having met the attack from the redistributive flank, the economist must face the other way and deal with the enthusiastic charge from the moral high ground of environmentalism. Not every environmentalist opposes pollution and congestion charges, but some do. The reason is that they feel that pollution should simply be illegal, rather than illegal for the poor and affordable for

the rich. Why should the rich be allowed to pollute? More generally, some pressure groups protest against externality charges on the grounds that they allow people to pay and thus continue doing whatever objectionable thing it was that they were doing.

A partial response is to say that even the rich do not pollute for fun. It is true that the rich are more likely to be able to pay a congestion charge, but they will not ignore it. Perhaps they will be careful to make one trip to the store rather than two, or even walk to the local shop rather than drive to somewhere farther away. Externality charges make other alternatives look more attractive, both to rich and to poor.

More fundamentally, we must not confuse the strictness of the externality regulation with the method of the regulation. A congestion charge can be set at one dollar a day, or ten dollars a day, or a thousand dollars a day. What we know is that whatever society decides about the seriousness of the externality, externality charges are the most efficient way to deal with it. Well-designed congestion charges, for instance, are the most efficient way to achieve any given reduction of road use. How much of a reduction is desirable is an open question, but congestion charging can deliver no matter what the answer is.

There are alternatives to congestion charging which stop short of the extreme of an outright ban on driving. The trouble is, they don't work as well. For instance, the government could give everybody vouchers, which allow them to drive up to twenty miles per week. The immediate result of such a plan is that some people, mostly poor, would want to sell their vouchers to others, mostly rich: the poor would rather have the money, the rich would rather have the right to drive. If the government allows vouchers to be traded, they have simply imposed a congestion charge by another means and probably a slightly less efficient one, given the hassle of trading. (The charge is whatever the market value of the vouchers turns out to be.) And if the government bans voucher trading, the plan is clearly inefficient, because people who wish to trade are being prevented from doing so.

Other alternatives such as high parking charges are probably less efficient still, although it is harder to prove this in a paragraph. For instance, high parking charges do discourage some drivers; but the relationship between driving and parking is rather indirect. Some drivers spend extra time on the streets, looking for free spaces. If the government wishes to discourage driving by causing drivers some expense, better to charge them directly and spend the revenue on something useful.

Some interest groups will always complain that externality charges are not tough enough, while others squeal that they are draconian. The economists' defense is that however tough we agree to be, an externality charge is the most efficient way to be tough. For any other policy, the economist can propose an alternative, using an externality charge, which would make some people better off and nobody worse off.

How much is your life worth?

The previous section makes it very clear that the level of any externality charge is bound to be a matter for controversy. For the Undercover Economist, seeking to re-create the "world of truth," the ideal externality charge addresses all the real external costs and *only* the real external costs.

It's worth thinking about what the ideal system would look like for the externalities surrounding driving. Any driver making a trip, which emitted pollutants that damaged the local area, would be charged for the pollution if he drove in a densely populated area. There would be a different charge, which would be imposed for every trip, for emitting carbon dioxide, because it contributes to climate change no matter where on the surface of the planet it is emitted. In each case, the price of the trip would also depend on how clean the vehicle emissions were. Drivers would face additional charges for trips in congested areas at congested times. Older buses, which emit the worst pollutants, would be heavily taxed, and this is likely to lead to an upgrading of their engines. Heavy vehicles would incur a charge for trips on fragile

roads and bridges. SUVs would be taxed because they are more likely to kill other road users in an accident.

Does this mean we should bring back the "luxury tax" on expensive vehicles? Not at all. Such a tax was almost certainly environmentally counterproductive, because it encouraged people to hang on to old, more polluting vehicles: a cheap old car will generally be much dirtier than a fancy modern car. SUVs may be more heavily taxed because they are fuel-inefficient and because their weight and height poses a danger to other vehicles—but not because they are expensive. The aim is to encourage people to drive smaller, lighter, more efficient vehicles, not to encourage people to drive cheaper vehicles.

That sounds complicated. Could it possibly work? It's easy to imagine each car having a little computer linked to a global positioning system to track congestion; the computer would also monitor the vehicle's exhaust. A display on the dashboard would flash up the rate at which the charge was being incurred, perhaps with helpful tips. "Tim, your trip is currently costing you nine cents per minute. Did you know that you could halve this if you got your engine tuned?"

The technology will come; much of it is already available. But there is another difficulty: working out what the costs of the externalities really are. The computer can measure congestion and pollution, but what is the cost of wasting other people's time in a traffic jam? What is the cost of poisoning people with particulates or benzene? Many other externalities involve real external costs and benefits that are very hard to measure: time, health, peace, even death.

For the sake of clarity, it may help to focus on the specific example of pricing the externalities caused by driving. It is hard enough to measure physical facts: how much road damage does one more vehicle do? How much noise does one more vehicle cause? How many accidents? How much delay to other vehicles? How much pollution? What ill-health does that pollution cause? But it is harder still to measure psychological consequences. How

much do people care about various annoyances: foul air, noise, delay, and stress—even illness and death? Not to mention that every individual values these things differently.

It is very tempting to give up in the face of these problems. Surely it is not possible to set a value on noise or delay, and certainly it seems impossible to set a value on human life. But we're kidding ourselves if we think we can opt out of these decisions. Every policy the government adopts, and every individual choice you make, implies that a valuation has been made, even if nobody has been honest enough to own up to it or even admit it to themselves.

Individually, we constantly make decisions that put a value on our own environment, our own time, and even our own lives. If you pay more to avoid a noisy area when you rent an apartment or a hotel room, then you have implicitly put a value on peace and quiet. If you decide to wait for the bus rather than flagging down a cab, you are implicitly putting a value on your time. If you decide you can't be bothered buying a smoke alarm, you have traded off saved time and expense against an increased chance that you will die. However, when you make any of these decisions, you probably don't come clean to anyone, even yourself, about the price you've put on quiet, time, or life.

Governments, too, make decisions that imply that they have worked out how much our lives are worth. Should the government install extra street signs and markings, or spend more money on speed cameras, or improve health care, or fund cancer research—or indeed not do any of these things but cut taxes, improve the quality of universities, or spruce up national parks? Such decisions have to be made; when they are made, embedded within them are assumptions about subjective values, including the value of human life. Estimating externality charges is simply more awkward because, if done properly, it requires that those assumptions be justified and made explicit. Leaving them implicit and unjustified leaves us at best at the mercy of the random drift of political processes, and at worst acquiescing to the self-serving demands of interest groups.

One of the best ways of estimating these subjective values is to look at what people actually do. Economists have a theory of "revealed preference," which is that people's preferences are revealed by the choices that they make as consumers. You bought apples when you could have afforded pears: therefore you preferred apples to pears. For an economist, preference is not just deduced but actually defined by such choices. It is a short step to conclude that people are also rational consumers when it comes to less tangible factors, even when it comes to their health and safety. If you are not willing to pay five dollars to catch a cab and save twenty minutes, then the Undercover Economist concludes that you would rather spend the five dollars on something else. This is not a very dramatic conclusion, but some people find it controversial. He also concludes that peace and quiet is worth an extra fifteen dollars a week to you, on the basis of your rental decision; and observing that you have no smoke alarm, he presumes that you are not willing to spend an hour and pay twenty dollars to reduce your chance of death by one in a million.

Two important sources of information about people's preferences are house prices and wages. House prices contain embedded information about the value people place on all kinds of amenities: shops, greenery, low crime, quiet, the sun through the window in the morning, and so on. Some of these can be quite accurately measured: for instance, the price of two identical houses facing each other across the same street will probably reveal how much people prefer a house that faces the sun. Meanwhile wages can reveal information if there is a salary differential for jobs with very similar skill requirements but different levels of danger.

There are flaws in this method: in particular, what if the peace and quiet comes hand-in-hand with a cul-de-sac, which is safe for your children to play on, and insulation, which will save your heating bills? How much of the fifteen dollars a week is really a payment for quiet surroundings? What if the well-paid but dangerous job on the oil rig also requires you to not drink for six weeks at a time and spend all your spare time indoors? Perhaps

the payment is nothing to do with danger, and everything to do with inconvenience. It will always be hard to disentangle these different factors, and it is impossible to know how well you have succeeded. But with enough information, economists can have what they think is a decent try.

A second problem is that when you bought your smoke alarm, perhaps you thought that it would reduce your chance of death by only one in fifty million, not one in a million. So before we leap to conclusions about how much you value your own life, we really need to find out how likely you thought the smoke alarm was to save it, and recognize that you may quite rationally not bother to invest too much time in finding out.

Controversial and imperfect as these methods are, they reflect an important presumption of mainstream economics: nobody has your best interests at heart quite as much as you do yourself.

Two different gaps in our knowledge

The use of externality pricing does rely on shaky information about how much it is really worth to us to reduce externalities such as noise, accidents, pollution, and congestion. But this is not the only gap in our knowledge; we also do not know the cheapest way of reducing noise, accidents, pollution, and congestion. It is with this second gap that externality pricing comes into its own.

Externality pricing is no worse than any other policy when it comes to facing up to the first kind of shaky information. We now know that any policy—of regulation, pricing, command and control, tax, or "laissez-faire"—contains implicit or explicit assumptions about the scientific evidence on externalities like pollution and congestion, and the subjective preferences of people about their time, convenience, and health. No policy can be more successful than the accuracy of its assumptions.

The real advantage of externality pricing is that it circumvents the second gap in our knowledge. Nobody knows the cheapest way of solving our traffic problems—yet. But externality pricing

brings pollution, congestion, and the rest inside the world of truth, which markets create for us. As long as individuals have to face the truth, or at least our best estimate of the costs of their actions, they will find a way to reduce those costs. The longer they have to respond, the more surprising and innovative the responses can be, as we are about to see.

The New Orleans effect

A visit to New Orleans tells us how profoundly people can react to price signals. New Orleans displays a unique architectural style—the "Camelback" house—based on avoiding tax. In the late nineteenth century, houses were taxed based on the number of stories at the front, so the Camelback design had one story at the front and more at the back. They are charming, but if it was a practical design for a house it would have caught on elsewhere. There is a similar story in Britain, which is full of dingy houses in response to the policy, in force from 1696 to 1851, of taxing people based on the number of windows their homes had.

Advocates of congestion charging believe that it must be easier to persuade people to find a way to make fewer trips by car than it is to persuade people to build their houses in an architecturally innovative but wasteful style. Their expectation is that things wouldn't change much for a few weeks, but over the months and years, we would be living in a society where we could all get around safely and quickly.

Congestion charging can change the small decisions we make every week about whether to drive to a supermarket, or catch the bus, or walk to a local store, or buy food on the Internet. But it will also weigh in the balance with the big decisions. Each year, one in three people change jobs and one in seven people move; every time that happens, there is a clear opportunity to reconsider travel choices in the light of congestion charging.

There's also a domino effect here, as changes in behavior reinforce each other. If more people begin riding buses, there will be more room on the streets and buses will move more quickly . . .

and can cost-effectively run more frequently. If more people join car pools, each person will find potential pool members more quickly and with more similar trips. If more people try to save the congestion charge by working at home a couple of days a week or commuting at a different time of day, more companies will find ways of accommodating them. People may try to live closer to their jobs; or companies may move to more rural areas to allow staff to commute without paying a high congestion charge.

We simply do not know. The attractive thing about externality pricing is that it attacks the problem but makes no assumption about the solution. The congestion charge gives drivers a signal: by bringing your car into town in rush hour, you are imposing a cost on everybody else. The drivers then have a choice: pay compensation, or find a way to avoid imposing the cost. There are many, many ways to avoid that cost, and markets can produce the ingenuity needed to uncover them. When no externalities are present, markets automatically take account of costs and provide incentives for producers to reduce them. When externalities are present, those costs are invisible to the market, but systems such as externality charging provide the missing signal that the cost exists.

When London introduced a congestion-charging zone in early 2003 (charging £5 or about $9 per day to drive into the city center) people responded far more quickly than many critics had expected. After a year, car rides fell by nearly a third. Trips that were exempt from the charge became more popular: there were 15 percent more bus rides, 20 percent more motorcycle rides, and 30 percent more trips by bicycle. Drivers who no longer enter the charging zone have chosen a variety of responses: one quarter drive around it, 55 percent have switched to public transportation, and 20 percent use alternatives like bicycles, car pools, or working from home on some days While the number of trips by car fell, the total delays caused by congestion fell by much more, which suggests that the congestion charge allowed the

streets to be much more efficiently used. And as people have more and more time to adjust to the congestion charge, the cost of dealing efficiently with this externality will fall further.

Battling pollution on the cheap

In the 1990s the Environmental Protection Agency (EPA) in the United States discovered how cost-effectively an externality charge could fight pollution when it decided to attack acid rain. The EPA wanted to reduce sulfur pollution from power stations. It seemed likely that some reduction would be efficient, but reducing pollution has costs as well as benefits. So the regulators were unsure by how much they should demand that pollution be reduced.

The trouble is that polluters will lie to regulators about what the cost of abatement really is. After all, even breathing emits a pollutant, carbon dioxide. But regulators could hardly demand that we all stop breathing to prevent pollution. So which pollution should be reduced? And how? By switching to different methods of power generation? Or reducing power consumption? Or something else? Ask the polluters and they will all tell you that reducing their pollution is like stopping breathing—it would be very expensive to stop, and so somebody else should make the changes.

But it's not really hard to find out the truth. Regulators can find out how much it costs to reduce pollution by telling people either to change their ways or pay a charge. Watch which decision they make. Judge them by their actions.

The EPA tried this in the case of sulfur emissions. They set up an auction for the right to emit sulfur dioxide, which causes acid rain. Polluters were given a quota of emission permits and could either buy more permits in the auction or reduce their emissions by shutting down, installing sulfur scrubbers, or buying cleaner coal. When the EPA simply tried to tell them to install sulfur scrubbers, the power generators argued that it would be very expensive to do so, and they lobbied hard to stop the mandatory

regulation. Even the EPA estimated that the cost of reducing sulfur dioxide emissions by one ton would probably be in the range of $250 to $700 and might be as high as $1,500. But when the EPA conducted the auction in 1993, very few polluters made high bids. The companies had been exaggerating their costs. By 1996 permit prices had fallen to $70 a ton, and even at that price many polluters were buying cleaner coal or installing scrubbers rather than buying permits to continue polluting.

The regulators discovered that getting rid of sulfur dioxide was so cheap that few people were willing to pay much for the right to keep producing it. In the end, the only people willing to pay high prices for permits were student environmental groups buying single permits in an attempt to win fifteen minutes of fame. The clever thing about the auction was not that the sulfur emissions were reduced—that could have been required by law—but that legislators all over the world found out how much sulfur scrubbers *really* cost. It created a basis for further legislation: not making rules in the dark but in full knowledge of the (modest) cost. And it has set an example to the world; for instance, Taiyuan in North-East China is putting a similar plan into place.

Now economists are designing the same kind of auction for carbon dioxide emissions in the hope of reducing the effects of climate change. There is massive controversy about how much emission reduction will cost, but an auction of permits to extract oil, coal, and gas would soon start to tell us. An auction could start gently: in 2007, auctioning permits to extract the same number of tons of carbon as were extracted in 2006. This would require that economic growth take place without any growth in carbon emissions. If many environmentalists are to be believed, the auction wouldn't even sell all the permits, because basic energy efficiency measures cost nothing. We'd soon find out.

Then over the next few years, we would auction fewer and fewer permits. Carbon emissions would probably fall faster than the number of permits, because carbon speculators would be buying the permits and hoarding them. This would cause no problems: the same emissions take place in the end but are delayed. If

it turned out that the permits were expensive, then we would have the information for an informed debate. We could ask if the costs of climate change were worse than the cost of emission reduction. But many economists believe that, like sulfur permits in California, the carbon permits would quickly reveal that decarbonization is cheaper than we expected, and we will wonder why we took so long to start.

Is the environment too important to be a moral issue?

"How did you travel here today?"

"I'm sorry?"

I'm puzzled. Here I am, going to a panel discussion organized by an environmental charity, and a very earnest young member of staff is grilling me before I even get past the door of the lecture hall.

"How did you travel here today? We need to know for our carbon offset program."

"What's a carbon offset program?"

"We want all our meetings to be carbon-neutral. We ask everyone who attends to let us know how far they came and on what mode of transportation, and then we work out how much carbon dioxide was emitted and plant trees to offset the emissions."

The Undercover Economist is about to blow his cover.

"I see. In that case, I came here in an anthracite powered steamer from Australia."

"Sorry . . . how do you spell anthracite?"

"It's just a kind of coal—very dirty, lots of sulfur. OW!"

The Undercover Economist's wife gives him a sharp dig in the ribs.

"Ignore him. We both cycled here."

"Oh."

Apart from being a good example of how irritating an Undercover Economist can be, this true story should, I hope, provoke a few questions. Why would an environmental charity organize a carbon neutral meeting? The obvious answer is "so that it can engage in debate without contributing to climate change." And that is true, but misleading.

The Undercover Economist in me was looking at things from the point of view of efficiency. If planting trees is a good way to deal with climate change, why not forget about the meetings and plant as many as possible? (In which case, everybody should say they came by steamship.) If the awareness-raising debate is the important thing, why not forget about the trees and organize extra debates?

In other words, why be "carbon-neutral" when you can be "carbon-optimal," especially since the meeting was not benzene-neutral, lead-neutral, particulate-neutral, ozone-neutral, sulfur-neutral, congestion-neutral, noise-neutral, or accident-neutral? Instead of working out whether to improve the environment directly (by planting trees), or indirectly (by promoting discussion), the charity was spending considerable energy keeping itself precisely "neutral"—and not even precisely neutral on all externalities, nor even a modest range of environmental toxins, but preserving its neutrality on a single, high-profile pollutant: carbon dioxide. And it was doing so in a very public way.

A kind view would be that the charity was setting a "good example," if acting nonsensically can ever be a good example. An unkind view would be that it was indulging in moral posturing.

This line of reasoning may make economists look too smug for their own good, but it is an important illustration of a wider point. The ethical showboating of an environmental charity can be directly connected to the fact that public policies do not make

evident the environmental costs of our actions. If they did, environmentalists could argue their points from an economic standpoint; much of the moral tone would drain out of the environmental debate, but the environment itself would be much more effectively dealt with.

In a world where environmentalism is merely a moral issue, even the environmentalists themselves cannot work out the environmental impact of everyday decisions. Which is worse: disposable diapers (which clog up landfill sites) or washable diapers (where the washing process uses electricity and releases polluting detergents)? Even with the best will in the world, it is hard to know how to make the right choice.

More importantly, the diaper problem, like any other environmental issue large or small, will certainly not be solved by a tiny minority arguing inconclusively over the morally appropriate individual action. While the Green minority lacks the right signals about environmental damage to act appropriately, the majority of people would not inconvenience themselves even if they understood environmental problems. Both information and incentives are necessary, and as we discovered in chapter 3, markets can provide both.

Economists have long been in the forefront of analyzing environmental problems, and this double difficulty is why they advocate externality pricing. Economists care about the environment but dream of a world where it is no longer an issue that invites moral posturing, but is properly integrated into markets and the world of truth, which would provide both the information and the incentives necessary to persuade ordinary people to behave in an environmentally responsible way. In such a world, we would all have clear signals about the costs of our actions within a market price. Plastics might well be taxed, because they do not biodegrade and so fill landfill sites. This would discourage the use of plastic packaging, disposable plastic bags, and plastic diaper liners. People would use only the more expensive plastics if the convenience it provided was worth the extra money—as it probably is in the case of diapers but might well not be in the case of plastic

packaging. Electricity generation that contributed to climate change would be taxed, too, which would raise electricity prices unless we could develop cleaner fuels. Diaper-washers, and everybody else too, would have an incentive to buy more efficient washing machines and cut down on energy use generally.

Instead of fretting about the environmental impact of our decisions, we would be well aware that if we were willing to pay the externality charge on a product such as a diaper, we would be compensating others for the harm done by our actions, and at the same time we would be confident that that harm was less than our own convenience. We might even find that there are easier ways to improve our environment than by messing around with diapers. They're messy enough already.

Being positive

We've spent a lot of space on what economists call "negative externalities"—unpleasant side effects of actions people get away with scot-free.

Once you start to think about the idea of "negative externalities," you quickly realize that there must be "positive externalities," too. These are *pleasant* side effects of things people do, for which they are not rewarded. If Abraham paints the front of his house and sorts out his garden, the whole street looks better as a result, but nobody will offer to pay for his paint or pruning shears. If Belinda opens an attractive sidewalk café, the streets are more pleasant to walk along, but her clients will be willing to pay only for their own pleasure, not for the pleasure of bystanders. And if Craig decides to vaccinate his son for measles, mumps, and rubella, this means other children are less likely to catch the diseases, but the government can only go so far in encouraging Craig to do this.

"Positive externalities" all seem very agreeable, until you realize that Abraham may decide he can't be bothered to paint his house, Belinda, fearing bankruptcy, may not set up her café, and Craig may decide that he is too worried about the possible side

effects of the vaccines to take his son to the doctor. The rest of us would have benefited if they had gone ahead, but they each decided that on balance it wasn't worthwhile. Just as negative externalities will tend to lead to too much pollution or congestion, positive externalities will leave us undervaccinated, with scruffy neighbors, and a dearth of pleasant cafés. And while negative externalities attract all the attention, positive externalities may be even more important: so many of the things that make life worth living are, in fact, subject to positive externalities and are underprovided: freedom from disease, honesty in public life, vibrant neighborhoods, and technological innovation.

Once we realize the importance of positive externalities, the obvious solution is the mirror image of the policies we considered to deal with negative externalities: instead of an externality charge, an externality subsidy. Vaccinations, for example, are often subsidized by governments or by aid agencies; scientific research, too, usually gets a big dose of government funding. But we need to be realistic about how far all this should go, because although externality charges and subsidies seem a great fix for externalities, there may be an unexpected hiccup.

Too much of a good thing?
Solving externalities without the government

When is an externality not an externality? Here's an example. I may complain about my neighbor's tree damaging my wall, but if it really bothers me I can pay him to let me cut it down. If he refuses the offer then I have to conclude that he gets more pleasure out of the tree than I get nuisance, and in fairness it should stay up. Or perhaps I have the right in law to force my neighbor to cut down the tree. But in that case he can pay me not to exercise that right, and I can spend some of the money fixing my wall. If I have the right to decide then I end up richer; if he has the right to decide he ends up richer. But either way the tree stays up if it's worth more to him and it comes down if it's more irritating to me.

Externalities simply aren't externalities if people can easily get together and negotiate. Remember that they were called "externalities" because they stood outside market transactions. But some of the things that we imagine to stand outside the market can easily be brought into it.

Since these pseudoexternalities can in fact be dealt with very well by the private sector, if the government also steps in with an externality charge, we may find ourselves "solving" the externality twice. This would be just as undesirable as not solving it at all: instead of having too much pollution from power generation, we exaggerate the cost and overcompensate by switching off our freezers and streetlights and walking to restaurants every evening, in the dark.

How would you get this kind of "overdose" of a remedy for externalities? When mentioning the case of Abraham painting the front of his house, I glibly said that the neighbors wouldn't compensate him for his paint, but in fact such things have been known to happen. It's particularly common for landlords to buy paint for tenants to deal with a positive externality: if the tenants repaint, they get a more pleasant apartment, but the landlord will also find it easier to rent it out in the future. Taking into account the advantage to both landlord and tenants, the apartment is worth painting, but without cash from the landlord, the tenants may decide it's not worth the bother. By providing paint the landlord shares the cost as he will also enjoy the benefit. It might well be that in this case, what appeared to be an externality has been "internalized" by bargaining over sharing the costs.

But what if the government has been thinking about subsidies for positive externalities? Imagine that the policy wonks wrongly believe that wherever an apartment is being rented, landlords and tenants will renovate too infrequently and let the place fall apart. It isn't worth it either for the tenants or for the landlord to refurbish more often, but if either of them were taking the other's interests into account, they would agree to do the work. Seeing this positive externality, the government starts dishing out externality subsidies of $500 to tenants who renovate their apartments.

(If you find this implausible, remember that governments certainly grant subsidies for improvements to the energy-efficiency of homes, which produce a positive externality.)

Imagine that the redecorating effort is worth $300 of cleaner living to the tenants and $500 of higher future rents to the landlord, but that it costs $1,000. The government has identified the externality perfectly: $500 of benefits (higher rents) to the landlord that the tenants do not take into account. But note that since $300 plus $500 is less than $1000, the subsidy is not enough to persuade the tenants to redecorate: nor should it be, because the redecorating is clearly more trouble than it is worth to both landlord and tenants.

Unfortunately, the tenants have every incentive to pocket the $500 subsidy and ask the landlord to chip in another, say, $350. Then they are doing very nicely, enjoying a $1,000 renovation for only $150—because 85 percent is paid for by the landlord or the government—and which is worth $300 to them. The landlord is willing to play along, because he pays $350 for a renovation, which is worth $500 to him. But the redecoration should never have happened: after all, the government has spent $500 but managed to make tenants and landlord only $150 each better off: not a very effective way to give money away.

Why does the problem arise? Because the positive externality has been dealt with twice over, once by a government subsidy and once by a process of bargaining. Either solution alone represents an efficient way for a society to deal with externalities and to come to the right conclusion, which in this case is that the positive externality is not large enough to justify the decoration work. Both solutions together mean that there is too much subsidy of positive externalities. The same thing could happen for negative externalities too. If the government taxes my neighbor's dirty gas-powered lawnmower and I also offer to pay him to get rid of it because I dislike the noise and smell, the combination of the taxes and my own offer may persuade him to ditch the monster, even though the fun and convenience he gets from

the thing outweigh any damage to anybody else and he really should be keeping it.

Yet, many externalities are very real. Outside the cozy (if cracked) walls of our gardens or our unpainted apartments, we still have clogged, choking streets. Traffic congestion is not easily solved by sitting down over a cup of coffee and making a deal. There are too many people involved, enforcing the agreement would be impossible, and there would always be a temptation for many to avoid the costly negotiations but hope to enjoy the benefits for free.

Government-imposed externality charging is far more likely to be appropriate in situations where a negotiation over the externality will not work, as in the case of the noise from low-flying aircraft. The more likely people are to be able to sit down around the table and work something out, the more likely government intervention is to screw things up: first, because governments can be swayed by interest groups and so they do not always act in the public interest; second, because of the "overdose" problem; and last, because people know the truth about their costs and benefits better than any government ever could. Externality pricing will work very well for problems such as congestion and climate change, for which individual negotiation is nearly impossible. For smaller-scale situations we must ask whether the government-imposed cures are worse than the disease.

Epilogue: what is economics really about?

This chapter has proposed ways of dealing with some of the major blights on our society: pollution, congestion, and fights with neighbors. We've learned that an externality charge on waste or on driving in congested areas, or a subsidy for research or for vaccinations, is the most efficient way of dealing with many of the problems that the market leaves to one side. Externality charges give people both the information to make the right choices, and the incentives to do so. Such charges do not automatically answer the question of how tough regulation should

be, or what should be regulated, but once our political processes have produced a view about what we want, they provide the most cost-effective way of getting there.

Yet you will often hear so-called experts complaining that taxes on driving or on pollution would be bad for the economy. That sounds worrying. But what is "the economy"? If you spend enough time watching Bloomberg television or reading the *Wall Street Journal* you may come to the mistaken impression that "the economy" is a bunch of rather dull statistics with names like GDP (gross domestic product). GDP measures the total cost of producing everything in the economy in one year—for instance, one extra cappuccino would add $2.55 to GDP—or a little less if some of the ingredients were imported.

And if you think this is "the economy," then the experts may be right. A pollution tax might well make a number like GDP smaller. But who cares? Certainly not economists. We know that GDP measures lots of things that are harmful (sales of weapons, shoddy building work with subsequent expensive repairs, expenditures on commuting) and misses lots of things that are important, such as looking after your children or going for a walk in the mountains.

Most economics has very little to do with GDP. Economics is about who gets what and why. Clean air and smooth-flowing traffic are part of the "economy" in this sense. It's possible that congestion charging would increase GDP because people would get to work more quickly and produce more, and prices in stores would be lower because of more efficient distribution. But it's perfectly possible that congestion charging would reduce GDP. This does not, in fact, matter in the slightest. We know for certain that it would make us better off in a much more meaningful sense: that we would have many new choices open to us about where we go and what we do. There is much more to life than what gets measured in accounts. Even economists know that.

FIVE

The Inside Story

Jerome K. Jerome's nineteenth-century comic travelogue *Three Men in a Boat* begins with Mr. Jerome flipping through a medical dictionary in the British Museum:

> I came to typhoid fever—read the symptoms—discovered that I had typhoid fever, must have had it for months without knowing it—wondered what else I had got; turned up St Vitus's Dance—found, as I expected, that I had that too—began to get interested in my case, and determined to sift it to the bottom, and so started alphabetically—read up ague, and learnt that I was sickening for it, and that the acute stage would commence in about another fortnight. Bright's disease, I was relieved to find, I had only in a modified form, and, so far as that was concerned, I might live for years. Cholera I had, with severe complications; and diphtheria I seemed to have been born with. I plodded conscientiously though the twenty-six letters, and the only malady I could conclude I had not got was housemaid's knee.

If you were Mr. Jerome, what would you do? He decided to go for a trip up the river, but then he was not an economist. My advice in such a situation would be to pick up the phone and buy yourself some really generous medical insurance. After all, since

you know for sure that you will be making expensive claims, why not pay the premium for the best possible care?

Yet this raises a question. If people like Mr. Jerome could rush to buy health insurance if and only if they knew they were ill, who would want to insure them?

Inside information

This is more than an idle question. Economists have known for a while that if one party to a deal has inside information and the other does not, then markets may not work as well as we would hope. That makes intuitive sense. But it wasn't until an American economist named George Akerlof published a revolutionary paper in 1970 that the profession realized quite how profound and dramatic the problem might be.

Akerlof chose as his example the market for used cars and showed that even if the market is highly competitive, it simply cannot work if sellers know a lot about the quality of their cars and buyers do not. To take a stark example, let's say that half the used cars on sale are "peaches," and half are "lemons." The peaches are worth more to prospective buyers than to sellers—otherwise the buyers wouldn't be buyers—say, $5,000 to prospective buyers and $4,000 to sellers. The lemons are worthless pieces of junk. Sellers know whether the car they're selling is a lemon or a peach. Buyers have to guess.

A buyer who doesn't mind taking a fair gamble might think that anything between $2,000 and $2,500 would be a reasonable price for a car that has a 50-percent chance of being a peach, and a 50-percent chance of being a lemon. The seller would also think this was a fair deal for a 50/50 prospect, but the seller doesn't face a 50/50 prospect: the seller knows for certain whether the car is a peach or a lemon. The problem is that a seller with a lemon would bite your hand off if offered $2,500, but a seller with a peach would find it rather insulting. Wandering around offering $2,500 for a car, you quickly discover that only lemons are for sale at that price. Of course, if you offered $4,001 you

would also see the peaches on the market—but the lemons won't go away, and $4,001 is not an attractive price for a car that only has a 50-percent chance of running properly.

This isn't just a trivial problem around the fringes of the market. In this scenario, there *is no market*. No seller is willing to sell a peach for less than $4,000, but no buyer is willing to offer that much on a car that has a 50-percent chance of being a lemon. Sellers don't offer peaches for sale, buyers know that they won't, and in the end the only cars that are traded are worthless lemons, which get passed around for next to nothing. Less extreme assumptions about the problem lead to less extreme breakdowns of the market, but the conclusions are similar: if some people know more than others about the quality of a product, then some high-quality products may not be traded at all, or not be traded very much.

Anyone who has ever tried to buy a secondhand car will appreciate that Akerlof was on to something. The market doesn't work nearly as well as it should; secondhand cars tend to be cheap and of poor quality. Sellers with good cars want to hold out for a good price, but because they cannot *prove* that a good car really is a peach, they cannot get that price and prefer to keep the car for themselves. You might expect that the sellers would benefit from their inside information, but in fact there are no winners: smart buyers simply don't show up to play a rigged game.

Let's be clear about how dramatic and how worrying this problem is. What Akerlof described is not a market where some people get ripped off; it's much more serious than that. He described a market that should exist and simply doesn't because of the corrosive force of inside information. Sellers with good cars should be trading with buyers—each trade produces $1,000 of value, because that's the difference between the value to the seller and the value to the buyer. If the price is close to $4,000, the buyer gets more of that value, and if it is close to $5,000, the seller gets more. But Akerlof showed that none of those value-creating trades happen because the buyers will not buy without proof, and the sellers cannot offer proof.

The market for used cars is not the only one affected by inside information. Think about furniture in a rented apartment—why is it never built to last? Akerlof's model provides an answer. Apartments have many noticeable, even obvious, attributes that can influence our decision whether or not to rent—size, location, interior design, and so on. But there are also qualities that are difficult to observe—for instance, whether the furniture is durable. The landlord has little incentive to provide expensive, hardwearing furniture, since this is not one of the features that potential tenants can recognize before they move in, and so not one for which they are willing to pay. (Of course, the landlord might also go for cheap, fragile furniture because he expects the tenants to trash whatever he puts in the flat. But that fear is equally an argument to get in more durable stuff.) As a result, there is a market for rental apartments with flimsy furniture but not a market for rental apartments with durable furniture.

Inside information also means that you can't get a decent meal in a tourist trap like London's Leicester Square, Times Square in Manhattan, or the Plaka in Athens. With few exceptions, the hungry visitor will pay a lot for mediocre cuisine. Tourists are willing to pay high prices because they have no sense of where better alternatives, even just a few streets away, might be found. But the tourist-trap phenomenon is not just about high prices. If it was, we would see a wide range of restaurants, charming little bistros, and downscale pasta or burger joints, all kinds of food from superb to disastrous, all charging a premium. Instead, we see a truncated market—high-quality places, whether the good food is fried chicken or fine dining, are simply not to be found. The reason is simple enough; tourists will only be making a single visit and will find it hard to pick out the great food from the bad. Good restaurants all locate where they are more likely to be appreciated by more informed locals. The bad ones remain . . . the "lemons" of the restaurant trade.

It's worth emphasizing that Akerlof is not describing universal ignorance but a situation where one side knows more than the

other. If buyers and sellers were both ignorant about whether a car was a lemon or a peach there would be no problem: buyers would be willing to pay up to $2,500 for a car that had a 50/50 chance of being a peach; sellers, equally ignorant, would be willing to accept any offer over $2,000. Of course they will strike a deal. It's only when one negotiator knows too much and the other too little that agreement becomes impossible. Because the problem is caused by an uneven grasp on the facts, economists tend to call it "asymmetric information." Ripping the "world of truth" apart, this imbalance in information can completely destroy perfect markets.

Inside information and health insurance

Akerlof's "lemons" problem would be troublesome enough if it applied only to secondhand cars, furnished accommodations, and dubious restaurants in the world's beauty spots. Unfortunately, it also damages the market for more important goods—most notably, health insurance.

Health insurance is important because illnesses are extremely unpredictable and sometimes cost a lot to treat. Not only can some medical treatment be very expensive, it is often impossible to postpone it until a more convenient moment. It can also coincide with periods of low income because people are more likely to need medical care after retirement, and because those who need medical care may also be too ill to work.

So health insurance is a valuable product. If the health insurance market doesn't work well, the results will be excessively high premiums and a large number of uninsured people. This will sound very familiar to readers in the United States, where markets do not, in fact, do a good job of providing medical insurance, precisely because of Akerlof's "lemons" problem.

Let's say that people who are likely prone to sickness are "lemons"; people who are likely to stay healthy are "peaches." If, like Jerome K. Jerome, I suspect myself to be a lemon, I'd be well

advised to buy all the medical insurance going. On the other hand, if you feel fine and all your ancestors lived to be a hundred, then perhaps you will buy medical insurance only if it is extremely cheap. After all, you hardly expect to need it.

Thanks to Akerlof's proof that markets whose players have asymmetric information are doomed, we know that the insurance market may disappear just as the market for good-quality used cars did. You, whose body is a succulent peach, will not find the typical insurance package a good deal; while Mr. Jerome and I, whose bodies are bitter little lemons, will embrace the typical insurance package with open arms. The result is that the insurance company only sells insurance to people who are confident they will use it. As a result, the insurer loses clients who are unlikely to make claims and acquires the unwanted clients who are likely to make costly claims, and then the insurer has to cut back on benefits and raise premiums. People of middling health now find the insurance is too expensive and cancel it, forcing the insurance company to raise premiums even higher to stay in business. More and more people cancel their policies, and in the end only the most sickly of the lemons will buy insurance and at a price that will be nearly impossible to afford.

The insurance companies will, of course, try to repair the insurance market by finding out more information about their customers. Do they smoke? How old are they? Did their parents die of hereditary diseases at the age of thirty-five, or in sports car accidents at the age of a hundred? With more genetic information becoming available, insurance companies will be able to gain an increasingly accurate picture of the costs of providing medical insurance to particular individuals. Previously the insurance market was constrained by the presence of inside information: insurers knew less than those they were insuring. But if insurance companies can continue to close that information gap, they will be willing to provide insurance to more people.

This might sound like the price targeting used by Starbucks and Wholefoods in chapter 2, but in fact it's a different game.

When Starbucks tries to price-target, it knows its own costs and is simply trying to find out whether it can get away with a higher price for some customers. The health insurance companies face a more fundamental task: they don't know how much it will cost to cover the claims of each customer, and if they can't work this out with more accuracy than the customer can, they will simply go bust under the burden of claims. The effects are different, too: price-targeting is a way of getting a larger slice of the pie by squeezing more money from customers, while finding out about insurance customers can create a new pie by making trades possible when previously there were none.

Unfortunately, the insurance market would be saved at some cost: what we would find is that lemons, like Mr. Jerome and me, would be able to buy insurance only at enormous rates. Peaches like you could pick it up for a nominal sum. Both premiums would reflect an actuarially fair rate, which means a rate that covers no more and no less than the likely medical expenses. If companies had really accurate information, perhaps obtainable from the genetic tests of the future, then someone who was likely to get ill would pay hundreds of thousands of dollars in premiums; but this would hardly be insurance at all.

By assessing our individual backgrounds and predicting the cost of providing benefits to each of us, the insurance industry manages to stay afloat; if companies did not raise prices for lemons like me and Mr. Jerome, they would soon go out of business. The problem is that people who expect to have expensive medical needs—the elderly and the chronically ill, for example—will find that their insurance company does not really give them much insurance at all. Because their premiums are adjusted to take these expenses into account, they will pay more for insurance than they would for the out-of-pocket medical costs they would face without insurance.

The curious conclusion, which is obvious in retrospect, is that an insurance policy depends on mutual ignorance. An insurance company can only insure me against an event like a burglary, a fire, or a medical bill if neither of us has any idea whether it will

happen. If we could predict the future, insurance would be mean-ingless. If my insurance company could predict fires much better than I could, it would sell me insurance only if I didn't need it. And if I knew that my house would burn down, the insurance company should be calling the police rather than selling me fire insurance. Since insurance depends on mutual ignorance, then any advance in medical science, which pushes back the bound-aries of ignorance—whether for the insurers, the insured, or both, will weaken the basis of insurance. The more we know, the less we can insure. This is a worrying prospect if we want to give people a chance to protect themselves against the high costs of bad luck.

Making lemonade

A slightly vexing aphorism recommends, "If life deals you lem-ons, make lemonade." How can we make lemonade out of Akerlof's lemons? To return to Akerlof's original example of the market for secondhand cars, both buyers and sellers have an incentive to try to fix the problem: sellers want to get a decent price for their peaches, and buyers want to buy peaches. If inside information is wrecking the chance of a mutually beneficial deal, both sides will want to find a way to bridge the information gap.

Akerlof won the Nobel Prize in 2001 for his work on the prob-lem of asymmetric information; he shared it with two econo-mists who proposed partial solutions. Michael Spence argued that the person with the information might be able to communicate it in a way that the person without the information could trust. Joe Stiglitz looked at the problem in reverse and explored ways in which the person without the information might uncover it.

Spence realized that it wasn't enough for a seller of peaches sim-ply to say, "All my cars are peaches," because talk is cheap. A seller of lemons can also say, "All my cars are peaches." The buyer wouldn't know who was telling the truth, so the claim itself doesn't carry any information. Spence realized that a real signal of quality would be one that a lemon-seller could not make, or at least, could not afford to make.

An example would be buying an expensive car showroom, an investment affordable only by a businessman who plans to stick around for the long term. A peach-seller expects satisfied customers to return, and to tell their friends about his reliable, trustworthy cars. Over the years the sales would pay for the showroom. A lemon-seller couldn't operate like that; instead, he would sell a few overhyped lemons and then have to move someplace where his reputation for dishonesty could not follow.

It's for this reason that banks always used to build such impressive buildings. In the days before government oversight, who knew whether they were depositing their money with a fly-by-night operation? Customers realize that crooks planning to run off with the money do not first clad their branches with bronze and marble. This is one reason, too, why you will pay more at an established store than at a market stall if you buy a product about which you lack inside information about quality and durability. The established store will still be there to refund your money in the case of a complaint, and that very possibility gives you an assurance that a complaint is less likely to be necessary.

Other economists have used Spence's theory to explain enormously expensive advertising campaigns with no informational content. What, after all, is the information contained within a soft-drink advertisement? "Coca-Cola. Real." Pardon? The only information that potential customers can glean from such an advertisement is that it was expensive to make, and that therefore the Coca-Cola company plans to stick around with the same commitment to high-quality products that it always had.

Spence himself first used his insight to show why students might choose to pursue a degree in philosophy, which is difficult but does not lead to specific career opportunities, like an economics degree or a marketing degree. Assume that employers would like to hire smart, diligent workers but can't tell from an interview who is smart or diligent. Assume also that everyone has to work hard to obtain a philosophy degree, but lazy, dumb people find it particularly troublesome.

Spence then shows that smart, diligent people can prove they're smart and diligent by going to the trouble of getting a philosophy degree. It's not that lazy, dumb people can't get that degree but that they wouldn't want to: employers will pay philosophy graduates enough to compensate them for the trouble but not enough to persuade lazy, dumb people to bother. The employers are willing to do this despite the fact that the philosophy degree itself does not improve the candidate's productivity at all. It is merely a credible signal, because a philosophy degree is too much trouble for lazy, dumb people to acquire. Since Spence himself majored in philosophy at Princeton, perhaps there is something in his idea.

Spence proved that one way to bridge the information gap in markets previously hindered by inside information is for trustworthy vendors to find ways to signal their reliability. High-quality job applicants, banks, used-car salesmen, and soft-drink manufacturers may find it worthwhile to spend excessive amounts of time and money (by pursuing a degree that does not really add to one's qualifications, paying for lavish decorations, buildings, and advertising) simply to distinguish themselves from low-quality job applicants, banks, used-car salesmen, or soft-drink manufacturers.

Spence's ideas suggest that the lemons problem is not insoluble, but they are not particularly reassuring. In some variations of Spence's model, everyone would be better off if the wasteful signal were impossible. If studying philosophy was banned, employers would be unable to distinguish between lazy workers and smart workers and would pay both the same wages, an average of their expected productivity. The lazy workers would be better off; the smart workers might also be better off if the new, lower, wage is more than the old wage minus the cost of getting a philosophy degree. And the employers don't mind; they employ worse workers on average but also have to pay less for them. Akerlof showed that inside information could reduce people's ability to find trades that made both sides better off. Spence showed a way of making those trades possible but also found that the social cost of doing so can be too high.

While Spence asked what the informed side could do to credibly signal information, Stiglitz studied what the uninformed side could do to uncover it. He explicitly considered markets for insurance and concluded that the uninformed insurer was not completely helpless in the face of customers who could predict the likelihood of needing to file insurance claims. The insurer could offer different deals, for instance, reducing the premium but increasing the deductible. This has the effect of reducing the level of insurance: the low premium makes the insurance cheaper, but the higher deductible, which is the amount by which any claim is reduced, means that any claim would pay out less. Low-risk customers would be attracted by that kind of deal, because the insurance is cheaper and they don't expect to claim very often anyway, but high-risk customers would rather pay the higher premium because they expect to claim frequently, so a high deductible will cost them a lot. So insurers could persuade different types of customer to reveal their inside information. This is a little like the self-targeting strategy used by coffee bars in chapter 2. Starbucks offers frills like whipped cream and flavored syrup to persuade customers to reveal whether or not they are price conscious. Aetna Insurance offers four different packages to individuals, with deductibles ranging from $500 to $5,000, to entice policy buyers to reveal their predictions for how many insurance claims they will file. But again, Stiglitz did not conclude that Akerlof's lemons problem could be costlessly solved. On the contrary, he showed that in response to inside information, banks might deny loans to whole sections of society, firms might prefer to pay high wages to privileged insiders rather than lower wages to more workers, and insurance companies would prefer to exclude high-risk individuals. Spence and Stiglitz both showed that you can make lemonade from Akerlof's lemons—but that you cannot get rid of the bitter aftertaste.

Lemons, health care, and the United States

The difficulty of solving the lemons problem may explain why the American health-care system is malfunctioning so badly. The

United States relies upon private health insurance to provide much of the financing for medical costs. This is unusual: in Britain, Canada, and Spain, for example, health-care costs are largely paid for by the government. In Austria, Belgium, France, Germany, and the Netherlands, medical costs are paid for by a system of "social insurance": it is compulsory for most people to buy insurance, but insurance premiums are tied by law to income rather than to the risk of a claim.

The United States system makes it voluntary to buy insurance, and premiums are linked to risk, not to income. But these market-based principles, beloved of many Americans, do not seem to be delivering health care that makes them happy. A recent survey revealed that only 17 percent of respondents in the United States were content with their health-care system and thought no substantial reforms were necessary. Why the discontent?

The superficial reasons are simple enough to describe: the system is hugely expensive, very bureaucratic, and extremely patchy. The expense first: US health care costs a third more, per person, than that of the closest rival, super-rich Switzerland, and twice what many European countries spend. The United States government alone spends more per person than the combination of public and private expenditure in Britain, despite the fact that the British government provides free health care for all residents, while the American government spending program covers only the elderly (Medicare) and some of the marginalized (Medicaid). Most Americans worry about health-care costs and would be stunned to discover that the British government spends less per person than the American government but still manages to provide free health care for everyone. In fact, if you figure in the costs of providing health insurance to government employees and providing tax breaks to encourage private health care, the US government spending on health care, per person, is the highest in the world.

Bureaucracy next. Researchers at the Harvard Medical School found that the administrative costs of the US system, public and private, exceed $1,000 per person. In other words, when you count

all the taxes, premiums, and out-of-pocket expenses, the typical American spends as much on doctor's receptionists and the like as citizens of Singapore and the Czech Republic spend on their entire medical care. Both places are countries with health outcomes very similar to those in the United States: life expectancy and "healthy life" expectancy (a statistic that distinguishes a long healthy life and a long life plagued by years of severe disability) are a shade lower in the Czech Republic than in the United States; and in Singapore they are a little higher than in the United States. The cost of US bureaucracy is also more than three times the $307 cost per person for the administration of the Canadian health system, which produces noticeably superior health outcomes.

Then there is the patchy coverage of the system. Health insurance is usually packaged together with a job, which reduces the efficiency of the labor market; workers are hesitant to quit their jobs without lining another job up first for fear of being uninsured. Worse, 15 percent of citizens have no insurance coverage of any kind—which should be a stunning statistic for the world's richest economy, but probably isn't because it has been lamented for so many years. Compare it to Germany, where 0.2 percent of the population has no coverage, or to Canada or Britain, where everyone is provided for by the government.

Given what we have learned from George Akerlof and his lemons, the troubles of the US health-care system should be no surprise. We should expect a voluntary private insurance system to be patchy. A few people who have more pressing costs than health insurance (for example, the young poor, who have little money and rightly expect that they are unlikely to become seriously ill) will drop out of the system. As a result, health insurance companies, needing to cover their costs, will raise the premiums for the average client, driving out more and more people. Unlike the very stark lemons model, the market does not completely collapse; this is partly because many people find that the risks of having to pay for medical treatment are so worrying that they're willing to pay substantially more than an actuarially fair premium.

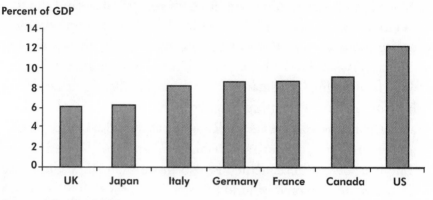

The US spends most on medical care

Source: Cutler 2002.

As a result, the process of unraveling stops, but not before many people have been excluded from the system.

Thanks to Spence and Stiglitz, we should also expect insurance companies to devise ways to get around this lemons problem, but that although the solutions may be effective they will probably also be wasteful. The huge bureaucratic burden of the US system is one of the results, as insurance companies struggle to monitor the risks, behavior, and expenses of their customers. The clunky linkage of health insurance with jobs is another result: at first sight, there is no reason why a job should come with health insurance, any more than it should come with a house or free food. Employees are frequently forced to buy the health insurance that is packaged with their job. This packaging compels the healthiest members of society to buy insurance packages and so helps prevent the unraveling of the market. But this solution doesn't come cheap: health-care plans are not chosen by their beneficiaries, who would aim to get the ideal coverage for the right price, but by human resource managers with other priorities, such as making their own lives easy with a "one-size-fits-all" bulk purchase. The result is likely to be further wasteful spending.

Not every drawback of the US health-care system should be blamed on Akerlof's lemons problem. Even without the diffi-

culty of inside information, the system of insurance is problematic, because patients are not always able to choose their treatment. With the insurance company picking up the bill, choosing the appropriate treatment is always going to be something of a matter of negotiation. When you ask somebody else to pay for your health care, don't be surprised if you don't get exactly what you would have chosen yourself.

Nevertheless, it is striking that partial coverage, inefficiency, and high costs are not only the defining characteristics of private health insurance, they are also exactly what we would have predicted armed only with the theoretical models of Akerlof, Spence, and Stiglitz.

Imperfect information—
the whole story

The lemons problem ("adverse selection" in the economists' jargon), when inside information guts a market because ignorant buyers are unwilling to pay for quality they cannot observe, is one example of the broader problem of inside information ("asymmetric information" in the jargon). Inside information also produces an obstacle called "moral hazard." The concept is simple: if you compensate people when bad things happen to them, they may get careless.

If my car is insured against theft, I will park wherever I find a space, even on a deserted street that doesn't seem entirely safe. If my insurance doesn't cover theft I may choose to pay a little extra to park in a lot with an attendant. If I lose my job and the government pays unemployment benefit, I may not hurry to find a new job quite as quickly as I would if I had no income whatsoever. If the money in my checking account is insured against a bank failure, why bother to check that the bank is financially sound?

Moral hazard is an inevitable problem in the real economy. While it is impossible for insurance companies (or anyone else)

to avoid moral hazard altogether, they can take steps to reduce it. For example, they do not offer insurance against being fired or becoming pregnant, which is a shame, because it would be great to have that kind of insurance. The reason is easy to see: it is easy to arrange to be fired or to get pregnant. There are many people who would like to leave their jobs and many others who would like to have children, and such people would be particularly eager to buy an insurance policy that would pay them handsomely for putting their plans into action. As a result, moral hazard destroys the market for private unemployment insurance.

On the other hand, public unemployment insurance still exists, in spite of moral hazard. It is not polite to say so, but it is obvious that paying people to be unemployed encourages unemployment. Yet if a government scrapped unemployment benefit, there would still be jobless people, and supporting the jobless is something that every civilized society should do. The truth is that we have a trade-off: it is bad to encourage unemployment but good to support those without incomes.

Both governments and private insurers will try to protect themselves against moral hazard. One of the most common ways insurance companies do this is by modifying the insurance policy to provide incomplete insurance, in the form of a deductible. If my car insurance deductible is $200, the fear of losing that money probably won't persuade me to take extravagant safety precautions, but it should be enough to make me check that my car is locked.

Another way insurance companies can fight moral hazard is by gaining access to the inside information. Health insurers will want to know whether I am a smoker before they set my premiums. Of course, I could lie, but it wouldn't be too hard for insurers to expose my lie; a simple medical examination would reveal that I smoke. When most governments pay unemployment benefits, they do so on the condition that recipients are actively looking for work. Because the government cannot monitor people's job searches perfectly, it pays out only meager unemployment benefits. Yet if the government could really tell how hard unem-

ployed people were looking for jobs, then it would be possible to pay more generous benefits to genuinely deserving recipients.

The problems of imperfect information include adverse selection (lemons) and moral hazard, but there are other, broader, and vaguer issues. For example, my boss would like to pay me extra if I try harder to do a good job, but because he has only a vague idea how hard I am trying, my performance bonus is only a small part of my salary. If my boss could observe my skill and effort perfectly, he could make my entire salary performance-related. Another example: let's say I would like to eat at the best-value restaurant in town; I don't know what it is, so I look for a familiar brand name, where I know I can't go wrong. Knowing that customers won't bother trying to find the cheapest place around, established restaurants are able to charge more than they should.

Do these information problems destroy markets completely? They certainly don't help, but it would be wrong to exaggerate the problems. In spite of asymmetric information, markets do often work well, because people produce ingenious solutions to improve the quality of information—or to reduce the damage caused by imperfect information.

When I buy complicated equipment like a camera, I talk to friends and consult websites and consumer magazines, which I hope will give me useful information about the products I am trying to choose between. Expert reviews providing "inside information" can be particularly helpful when we are ignorant about what we're buying. I rely on them all the time in another market, which suffers from severe information problems: the market for vacations. I'm the kind of person who likes to visit new places, but often I have no idea where to go or what will be fun, where is tacky and who offers a good deal, where is beautiful and where is dangerous. If the problem were insoluble we wouldn't bother to take vacations at all. (Or we might demand that governments provided them, which in my mind conjures up images of being on a waiting list for years before enjoying organized team games

and artificial cheer in an overcast concrete resort.) Instead, we simply buy decent guidebooks and try to learn more on our own.

Health-care provision, yet again, provides a particularly acute example of the problem. It's one thing to check a guidebook to find out what to do on vacation. It's quite another to consult a guidebook to find a heart surgeon. Yet the basic information problem is the same as the one faced by vacationers. Heart surgery patients try to learn more about which doctors have good reputations, which procedures have the highest success rate, and which hospitals provide the best recovery care. Still, most patients would admit that they really don't have much idea just how good their doctor really is.

Market failure versus government failure

This is not exactly comforting. A health-care system based on private insurance will be, as we have discovered, patchy, costly, and bureaucratic. What's more, it will offer patients choices, such as the choice of heart surgeon, that they are not very well qualified to make. So could the government do better? After all, every chapter of this book so far—with the exception of chapter 3—has lamented the causes and costs of market failures. It's tempting to look to the government to sort things out.

Unfortunately, while markets can fail, governments can fail too. Politicians and bureaucrats have their own motivations. Scarcity power, externalities, and imperfect information do not magically disappear when the economy is run or regulated by governments. When market failure and government failure are both present, the choice is often between the lesser of two evils.

An intriguing case in point is Britain's National Health Service (NHS), which offers health care to all citizens. It is almost completely free, although people with jobs need to pay a token amount for prescription drugs. It provides universal coverage: if you walk into any doctor's surgery or any hospital in the country, you will be treated free of charge.

As you would expect, the system gets overcrowded, people often have to wait, and patient choice is not a major feature of the system: you accept whatever treatment the doctor says is appropriate, or nothing. Overall, the medical outcomes are not bad, but the waiting lines for treatment have been a major bone of contention for many years. The same survey, which found 17 percent of American citizens approved of the US health-care system, reports that only 25 percent of the British are happy with their own system—better, but hardly a resounding endorsement.

If you were going blind in Britain, you would be well aware of a recent example of the difficulties faced by such a system. The Royal National Institute of the Blind, along with other organizations representing people with vision problems, has been campaigning vigorously against a ruling by the National Institute for Clinical Excellence (NICE), an agency that evaluates treatments and decides whether the National Health Service should pay for them or not. Heart surgery is on the approved list; nose jobs are not.

The controversy stems from NICE's half-hearted endorsement of a new treatment called photodynamic therapy. The therapy uses a drug called "Visudyne" or verteporfin, combined with a low-intensity laser treatment, to destroy lesions under the surface of the eye's retina, usually without damaging the retina itself. If the lesions are not treated they can irreversibly damage the center of the retina, called the macula. The resultant condition, age-related macular degeneration (ARMD), destroys central vision so that the victim cannot recognize faces, read, or drive. It is the leading cause of blindness in the United Kingdom.

In 2002 NICE filed a report recommending photodynamic therapy only in more extreme cases, only when both eyes are affected, and only in the eye that is less seriously damaged. The implication is that even treated patients will lose their sight in one eye, while others whose sight might be improved are denied treatment altogether.

It is easy to condemn NICE without appreciating its methods and the situation it is in. The basic challenge confronting the

National Health Service is that it has a limited amount of money to spend and an unlimited number of ways of spending it. It is no good asking patients, who pay little or nothing for treatment and will as a result demand more of everything. So NICE must resolve the inevitable dilemmas, determining who will get what type of health care, and who will be left to fend for himself.

How can medical spending be decided under such conditions? What would *you* do if you were in charge of NICE? It's a near-impossible task, but you would probably work out the costs and the effects of each treatment, and then you'd compare them to each other. Sometimes this is quite simple: a treatment with a 20-percent chance of preventing another heart attack is better than a treatment with a 10-percent chance of preventing another heart attack. Under pressure to make decisions, you might go farther and say the first treatment is twice as good, and should be used if it is less than twice as expensive. Even to go that far would be a stretch. How, then, would you compare a treatment that increases the chance of walking again after an accident, with a treatment that reduces the likelihood of going blind? Impossible! But if you were running NICE you would have to try.

The way NICE does it is to calculate the impact of each treatment in "Quality-Adjusted Life Years," or QUALYs. A treatment that saves ten years of life is better than a treatment that saves five years of life; a treatment that gives somebody ten years of able-bodied life is better than a treatment that gives somebody ten years alive but in a coma. Evidently, the value-judgments involved are extraordinarily difficult. Yet they must be made in a system that provides health care free of charge.

As an example, think of the problems involved in judging the QUALY impact of photodynamic therapy, which reduces the chance of blindness. The best way for the Royal National Institute of the Blind to get a higher priority for photodynamic therapy is to argue that a year alive but blind is worth much less than a year alive and fully sighted. If NICE accepts this view, treatments curing blindness will become very valuable on the QUALY mea-

sure, which places years alive and fully sighted high above years alive but blind.

But hang on. The strict logic of the view that "it's bad to be blind" would suggest that while that claim places a high priority on vision treatments, it places a low priority on treating people for *other* illnesses if they are already blind. If two people, one blind and one sighted, simultaneously turn up in a hospital in coronary arrest and there is time to treat only one, the QUALY methodology offers a truly unpalatable conclusion; that it is more worthwhile to help the person who can see rather than the blind patient.

We could backtrack and argue that in fact there is no difference in the value of life for the blind compared with the sighted. That is certainly more comfortable. Unfortunately, in conjunction with the QUALY methodology, this produces the conclusion that there is no point in spending anything at all on photodynamic therapy—or indeed on a pair of glasses. If treatments do not improve the value of people's lives then they are not worth spending money on, particularly when there are many causes, such as treatment for cancer, which certainly do improve the value of people's lives.

It is no wonder that the Royal National Institute of the Blind steers well clear of even mentioning QUALYs. It simply argues that photodynamic therapy is proven to improve vision and so should be comprehensively available. I do not blame the RNIB. But given the problem NICE is trying to solve—allocating finite resources among an unlimited range of medical treatments—it is easy to understand the position NICE takes: in particular the apparently heartless ruling that treatment should be applied in only one eye, leaving the other to go blind. The dispassionate perspective of QUALY analysis argues that the difference between having two good eyes and one good eye is less significant than the difference between having one good eye and none at all. Small wonder that the calculations tend to churn out embarrassing recommendations. But a free service will always be in demand, and it is hard to see a better way of rationing it.

Fixing health care with
keyhole economics

Keyhole surgery techniques allow surgeons to operate without making large incisions, minimizing the risk of complications and side effects. Economists often advocate a similar strategy when trying to fix a policy problem: target the problem as closely as possible rather than attempting something a little more drastic.

How, then, can we fix health care? The insurance-based market solution is misfiring badly in the United States, in large part because of the problem identified by Akerlof's lemons model. The result: expensive, bureaucratic care . . . and even that, only for some.

The British approach has been to sweep away the market completely and replace it with a system governed by the decisions of bureaucrats like NICE rather than directed by market prices, as though part of the old Soviet Union had been transplanted into the hospitals and surgeries of the English shires. Fortunately, political and bureaucratic decisions are much more accountable in the United Kingdom than in the USSR, so the system works fairly well. But this is a colossal and wide-reaching response to the serious but rather specific problem of inside information. We owe it to ourselves to ask: is there a "keyhole" solution, which could fix health care without sacrificing the ability of patients to decide how much they value their own eyes?

Keyhole economics would first identify the specific market failures, which fall into three categories: scarcity power, externalities, and imperfect information, plus the issue of fairness. Scarcity power is a potential problem, but for most treatments not a significant one. In the United Kingdom, for example, there are roughly fifteen hundred patients per general practitioner (the doctor who is the first port of call for most patients using the National Health Service). So, a small town of nine thousand people can support six doctors, probably more than enough to encourage real competition, in a country where 90 percent of people live in urban areas. Some special treatments will wield

greater scarcity power—people fly from Australia and New Zealand to Hawaii for treatment with the Leksell Gamma Knife, a device for treating brain tumors. So there are some situations, but few, where scarcity power is a concern.

Externalities, too, are important only in select cases: for instance, for public health projects to restrict communicable diseases. (If everybody else had been using condoms to protect themselves from HIV/AIDS, I would not have needed to bother.) Yet neither externalities nor scarcity power are so severe or widespread that government provision becomes an attractive alternative. The keyhole solution would be some light-touch regulatory oversight to prevent the exploitation of scarcity power, coupled with focused subsidies to boost inoculation programs.

Fairness is not, strictly speaking, a market failure; it is something that even perfect markets do not necessarily provide. But we care deeply about fairness when it comes to medical care, both because we do not want the poor to be deprived, and because the cost of health care can vary dramatically, depending on the luck of each individual. In a civilized society we will want to make sure that everyone can afford some standard of medical care. The best way to do this is to tackle the general problem of poverty (think back to the "head start theorem" discussed in chapter 3) using redistributive taxes. After all, why spend so much to provide free medical care to poor people while ignoring the fact that they cannot afford healthy food or a safe house to live in?

That leaves inside information as the big obstacle to a well-functioning health-care system. The economic analysis we've done suggests that government provision is ineffective because decision making is out of patients' hands, and resources are rationed by political processes. Meanwhile, the overwhelming problem for the market provision of medical care is inside information, and more specifically its tendency to destroy insurance markets.

This diagnosis suggests a two-part keyhole treatment. The first part is to ensure the widespread availability of information: it should be easy to get a second opinion, easy to call a help-line, and easy to get information from libraries, clinics, the Internet,

even supermarkets. In the United Kingdom, people do not pay much attention to this information because doctors make the decisions. If we were asked to take responsibility for our own medical care we would pay much closer attention, and many more resources (public and private) would respond to our demands to know more.

The second part is to give patients an opportunity to use this information. In a privatized, insurance-based system the insurance company tends to make a lot of choices; in a government-provided system the government makes the choices. In a market-based system without insurance, the patient makes the choices. Much better. But the patient also has to pay for unpredictable and potentially catastrophic health-care costs.

How to give patients choice and responsibility without putting an unbearable burden on them? The best system would be one that compels patients to pay for many of the costs, thus providing an incentive to inform themselves and to make choices that are both in their interests and reasonably cost-effective but which leaves the most severe costs to the government or insurance. This might work, because most medical bills are not catastrophic and so do not need insurance.

How might such a system work, in more detail? The aim would be to give maximum responsibility and choice to patients, therefore requiring them to spend their own money rather than that of governments or insurers, but to make sure that nobody faced catastrophic medical bills and to make sure that even the poor had enough money to buy medical care.

These requirements suggest: people should pay for all medical care; but insurance should cover the largest bills; and that everyone should have a savings account dedicated to medical expenses, to which the government would contribute in the case of the poor or the chronically ill.

Catastrophe insurance, which pays out only when a particular course of treatment is very expensive, is fairly cheap. The savings are no problem either: simply reduce each person's tax bill by,

say $1,500 a year—this is very roughly the cost, in taxes, of both the UK and the US public health systems—and make them put the money in a savings account. For people who pay less than $1,500 in tax a year, the government would contribute money to make up the shortfall. Since the system is compulsory, no adverse selection takes place.

If you participated in such a program, how would it work for you? Your health-care savings would automatically go into a high-interest bank account. They would build up gradually throughout your life. For most people, medical bills are low in their younger years. So you could expect to have thirty thousand dollars in your account when you turn forty; more, if you've managed to keep your spending low and watched the money earn interest. Thirty thousand dollars buys a lot of medical care. Of course, it could all be consumed by a single expensive procedure, except that catastrophe insurance restricts your expenses.

If you reach retirement age with money still in your medical savings account beyond some minimum, you can put the excess toward your pension. When you die, you can pass the savings to other people's savings accounts (usually your spouse or children). So at every point in your life, you would have an incentive to spend money only on health care that you feel is absolutely necessary. If you felt that the right treatment for you was a bit of preventive maintenance—a course of shiatsu, say—then that would be your choice. You might well consider giving up smoking, given how much it would cost you in medical bills over the years. The catastrophe insurance would still pay for your lung transplant, of course, but no humane system can avoid moral hazard completely.

If one day your optician told you that you were suffering from age-related macular degeneration, but that a treatment with photodynamic therapy would increase your chances of maintaining your sight for a few more years . . . well, the choice would be yours. The photodynamic therapy drug, Visudyne, costs $1,500 a treatment. It would increase your chance of keeping good sight

from about 40 percent to 60 percent. No need to start talking about QUALYs: it's your money, and your choice.

The exception would be if you had a catastrophic expense, in which case the insurance company would prefer to pay for the cheapest treatment while you would want the best—a difficult problem, but no different from the conflict of interest faced for every single treatment in our medical systems today. The new system simply means that that inherent conflict of interest happens far more rarely.

It is common to provide goods and services on the private market, but one of the main alternatives—certainly, the main ideological alternative—has been to provide them using a political market instead. Medical goods and services are among the most difficult to distribute. We have tried using political markets, but they have let us down badly, and for obvious reasons.

At first sight, the private market failures, exemplified by the US system, are also obvious. But when we closely examine the market failures, it's the lack of information that is most serious, and the insurance market suffers the most serious consequences. American citizens receive much of their medical care through the intermediation of this badly malfunctioning market.

With some imagination, and some economics, we can step back from the troubles of our current systems and think about how to fix them. In Singapore, the system sketched in the last few pages has been successful for almost two decades. The typical Singaporean lives to the age of eighty, and the cost of the system (both public and private) is a thousand dollars per person—less than the cost of the bureaucracy alone in the United States. Each year, the typical Singaporean pays about seven hundred dollars privately (the average American pays twenty-five hundred dollars privately) and the government spends three hundred dollars per person (five times less than the British government and seven times less than the American government). Keyhole economics works.

The reason why Singapore's success is uncommon is probably that policy debates get stuck with one side claiming that we should rely on the market, and the other side asserting that the government would do a better job. So, government or market? We've learned that the question doesn't make any sense in isolation. To answer it we need to understand why markets might work, and how and why they fail.

We learned in chapter 3 exactly why markets work: because our choices as consumers between competing producers gives them both the right incentives and the right information to produce the right amount of exactly what we want. And we've also learned that scarcity power, externalities, and inside information can each ruin the way markets do this.

In the case of health care, the market works poorly because while we want the reassurance of knowing they can afford expensive medical bills, inside information eats away at the insurance by driving away low-risk customers and forcing premiums to rise. Private companies have developed ways to get around the problem, but they are expensive and bureaucratic. Singapore's government had the power to tackle the problem head on, by using forced saving and catastrophe insurance to make sure costs were manageable but keeping the power of patient choice at the heart of the system. Governments can replace markets, but they will often do better to try to fix them. They are unlikely to succeed unless they appreciate exactly what the problem is in the first place.

SIX

Rational Insanity

"My vision is that in a few years there will only be two or three big Internet portals—everybody will go to one of them to be directed to wherever they want to go on the Internet. That will be worth hundreds of billions of dollars. If you want to succeed, you'll have to be one of those portals."

So spoke Graham Bailey (not his real name) in 1998. Bailey was a partner in a management consulting firm and was making this passionate speech to any potential client who would listen. For all I know, he believed it then and believes it now. But when I heard it, I did not. There were not many skeptics at the time. 1998 was the year when the frenzy about the dot-coms was really starting to mount.

One of the most famous dot-coms was the Internet bookshop, Amazon.com. (It was rapidly becoming the vogue to set up companies named after website addresses.) Amazon started selling books over the internet in 1995, and in 2003 it sold over $5 billion worth of merchandise. Amazon's rapid growth and its fight to become profitable is remarkable, but not as remarkable as the price of its shares. In 1997 Amazon shares were first sold to the public, at a starting price of $18.

A lot has happened since then. In 1999, Amazon shares soared to over $100, even after stock-splits reduced the intrinsic value of each share. At the time it was said that Amazon.com was valued

at more than all the regular bookshops in the world. But then Amazon shares plummeted. By the summer of 2001 Amazon shares were trading around $8. In 2002, the company was getting good write-ups in the financial press—but shares were still in the doldrums. Yet, since then they have recovered to $40 a share. Which price was the mistake: $100, or $8? Or both?

The answer would be useful, not least because Amazon's roller-coaster performance is common. So can the Undercover Economist say anything about why share prices acted the way they did, and how they might behave in the future?

A random walk

Economists face a serious problem in trying to say anything sensible about stock prices. Economists work by studying rational behavior, but the more rational the behavior of stock-market investors, the more erratic the behavior of the stock market becomes.

Here's why. Rational people would buy shares today if it was obvious that they would go up tomorrow, and sell them if it was obvious that they would fall. But this means that any forecast that shares will obviously rise tomorrow will be wrong: shares will rise today instead because people will buy them, and keep buying them until they are no longer so cheap that they will obviously rise tomorrow. In fact, rational investors should be able to second-guess any predictable movements in the stock market or in the price of any particular share—if it's predictable then, given the money at stake, they will predict it.

But that means that if investors really are rational, there won't be any predictable share movements at all. All the predictability should be sucked out of the stock market very quickly because all trends will be anticipated. The only thing that is left is unpredictable news. As a result of the fact that only random news moves share prices, those prices, and the indices measuring the stock market as a whole, should fluctuate completely at random. Math-

ematicians call the behavior "a random walk"—equally likely on any day to rise as to fall.

More correctly, the stock market should exhibit a "random walk with a trend," meaning that it should on average edge up as the months go past, so that it is competitive compared with other potential investments such as money in a savings account, or property. If it was expected to edge up by more than that trend, it would already have done so, and similarly if it was expected to edge up by less, or to fall, it would already have underperformed. This is the reason people hold shares at all. The trend doesn't alter the basic analysis, though, and on any given day the trend is dwarfed by random movements.

This theory should hold even if not every investor is rational. The ones who are should be enough to force the market into a random walk, providing they are throwing plenty of money into good shares and out of bad ones. Throwing money around shouldn't be too difficult, since presumably the smarter investors make more money.

Should we believe the "random walk" theory? We certainly shouldn't expect it to be absolutely true. If it was, that would be a paradox: perfectly informed investors produce a random market, but a random market doesn't reward anybody for becoming perfectly informed. It wouldn't be worth anybody's while to invest time and effort to analyze the market or uncover new information, if everybody else was doing the same. On the other hand, a market full of unexploited opportunities would offer big profits to any investor willing to research them, which would then lead to fewer unexploited opportunities. Somewhere in the middle is a balancing point: a nearly random market with enough quirks to reward the informed investors who keep it nearly random.

You can see the same phenomenon at work at the supermarket checkout. Which line is the quickest? The simple answer is that it's just not worth worrying about. If it was obvious which line was the quickest, people would already have joined it, and it wouldn't be the quickest any more. Stand in any line and don't

worry about it. Yet if people really just stood in any line, then there would be predictable patterns that an expert shopper could exploit; for example, if people start at the entrance and work their way across the store, the shortest line should be back near the entrance. But if enough experts knew that, it wouldn't be the shortest any more. The truth is that busy, smart, agile, and experienced shoppers are a bit better at calling the fastest lines and can probably average a quicker time than the rest of us. But not by much.

Value and price—
beyond the random walk

Assuming that what is true of supermarket lines is also true of stock-market prices, economists should be able to throw some light on the market, but not very much. Many economists do work for investment funds. They are as wrong nearly as often as they are right, but not quite. Our modified random walk theory tells us that this is what we should expect.

So, what do these economists do to provide investment funds with such tiny edges over the market? The starting point is to view stock shares for what they are: a claim on the future profits of a company. Here's an example. Let's say there are 100 shares of timharford.com. If I own one share, I have a right to 1 percent of timharford.com's profits for as long as I hold the share. If timharford.com makes $100 per year, forever, then I get $1 per year, forever. If timharford.com makes $1,000 per year for the next ten years, then nothing, then I get $10 per year for ten years, then nothing.

That's all very simple. A slight complication is that companies do not necessarily return their profits directly to shareholders. Amazon.com earned eight cents per share in 2003, so might have been expected to pay a "dividend" to shareholders of eight cents a share; but Amazon.com didn't pay a dividend in 2003, nor in any of the years before. That doesn't mean that Amazon.com shareholders are being defrauded. The management is using the money for other things, such as paying off Amazon.com's debt

or investing to expand the business. If these things are done wisely, profits will rise over time. Instead of being paid a dividend, Amazon.com shareholders would be compensated by a share price higher than it would otherwise have been, in anticipation of these later profits. Even if they sell the share before any dividend is paid, they should get a better price for it because of future dividend payments.

If it was easy to tell the future it would be easy to say how much it was worth to own a share in timharford.com. Let's say that everybody knows timharford.com will make $100 per year, forever. Then holding one share will bring in $1 per year, forever. How much is that worth? If I put $10 in a savings account earning 10-percent interest, that will also get me $1 per year, forever. So one share in timharford.com is like $10 in a savings account at 10 percent. At interest rates of 10 percent I should be willing to pay $10 for one share in timharford.com. Interest rates of 5 percent make shares twice as attractive relative to a savings account; interest rates of 1 percent make them ten times as attractive. I should be willing to pay $100 for one share in timharford.com with interest rates at 1 percent forever, because it would earn me a dollar a year, just the same as $100 in a savings account. (This is one of the reasons that stock markets rise when interest rates are expected to fall, and fall when interest rates are expected to rise.)

Amazon.com shares were valued at $40 in October of 2004. But with long-term interest rates in the United States of about 4 percent, I needed only $2 in a savings account at that point to earn eight cents a year. Since Amazon.com earned eight cents per share in 2003, the share should have been trading at $2, not $40. Something else must have been justifying those prices.

That "something else" is the future. Real companies do not reliably make a certain profit every year. Investors have to judge their future profitability, in whatever way they can. Perhaps timharford.com will not make $100 a year but $1 billion a year because of a dramatic expansion. Perhaps timharford.com will go bust tomorrow. Because of this uncertainty, most reasonable people will want a discount: one risk-free share at 1 percent interest might

have been worth $100, but one risky share, expected to produce the same return of $1 a year (but who can tell?) would be worth less, perhaps $90, $70, or even $30. How much less they are worth depends on how risky the share really is, and on how much the typical investor worries about that risk.

That suggests that investors in Amazon.com don't expect long-term profits of eight cents a share, but something much higher. Instead of buying a share at $40 and making eight cents, they could put $40 in a savings account and make $1.60 (since long-term interest rates are 4 percent). Amazon.com shareholders clearly expect earnings per share to rise to $1.60 and beyond to compensate them for their risk. To do this, Amazon.com profits would have to rise from $35 million to about $1 billion a year.

What I have just described is a view of the stock market based on *fundamentals*—in other words, on the recognition that in the end, shares are called shares for a reason: they give you a right to have a share in the profits of a real company. In the long run the share price has to reflect that. Economists can help to work out what the fundamental value of the share is, which is what I have just done. If the price of the share is lower than the fundamental value, that tells you that the share is cheap and you should make money buying it. In the long run, share prices have to reflect the funda-mental profits of companies. At the extreme, even if a good-value share stays undervalued forever, you should still make money holding it and pocketing the dividends. In the short run, share prices should also reflect the fundamental prospects of the com-pany, too. After all who would buy a share for $10 when every-body knows it is really worth $1 in the long run? And who would sell a share for $1 when everybody knows it is really worth $10 in the long run? As long as the big investors are sensible, share prices should reflect fundamentals in both the long run and the short run. But are investors sensible?

The most famous economist of the twentieth century, John Maynard Keynes, compared the stock market to a silly newspa-

per competition in which readers were invited to pick several pretty faces from a hundred photographs. The winner was a reader who chose girls closest to the general opinion.

> It is not a case of choosing those which, to the best of one's judgment, are really the prettiest, nor even those which average opinion genuinely thinks the prettiest. We have reached the third degree where we devote our intelligences to anticipating what average opinion expects the average opinion to be. And there are some, I believe, who practice the fourth, fifth, and higher degrees.

A modern day example is the "Grolsch" method of picking shares. I met an investor who told me he had bought lots of shares in the brewer, Grolsch, because he'd been to lots of parties around the City of London and Grolsch beer was being served at all of them. Other beers, which had previously been popular, like Stella Artois or Heineken, seemed to have disappeared from the scene. Naively, I told him that parties in the City weren't necessarily a good indicator of Grolsch's worldwide sales; Grolsch could be doing well in the City but badly everywhere else, in which case the company's long-term profits would fall and buying the shares would have been a mistake. The investor told me that he knew that was true, but it didn't matter. He reckoned that if Grolsch was big in the City, lots of City investors would figure it was made by a successful company and buy the share. The share price would go up—for a while—and he could sell at a profit. The fundamentals only mattered if he planned to hold the share for a long time, long enough for the real picture, whatever it was, to become clear. And what was the real picture? Over the next year, Grolsch shares fell by about a third from £24 to £17.5; they then bounced right back in just a couple of months. At the time of writing in March 2005, they are almost exactly where they were when we first had the conversation.

The Grolsch method is not interested in the value of the share. It's simply an attempt to take advantage of what mistakes you

think other investors will make. Yet given what we now know about rational stock markets and the random walk, why would we expect investors to make such easily exploitable mistakes?

Rational fools

Why indeed? Consider the story of Tony Dye, Chief Investment Officer of Philips & Drew, which manages investments such as pension funds on behalf of large clients. Tony Dye concluded in 1996 that at a level of 4000, the FTSE 100 (the index that reflects the performance of the London Stock Exchange's 100 largest companies) was overvalued, and he moved a chunk of his clients' money into cash, effectively, putting it into a savings account. Having withdrawn £7 billion from the stock market, he was then judged day by day on his decision by his clients, his peers, and the newspapers. He was mocked and nicknamed "Dr. Doom." As the FTSE continued to climb throughout the late 1990s, Dye looked increasingly stupid. In 1999, Philips & Drew lost more clients than any other fund manager. Based on returns to clients, it ranked sixty-six out of sixty-seven competitors in the final three months of 1999. Dye continued to insist that the stock market was overvalued, shunned Internet and telecom shares, and kept an unusual proportion of his client's investments in cash. The end was inevitable: his early retirement was announced at the beginning of March 2000, and the broad conclusion was that he had been forced out. The *Times* of London called Philips & Drew "a standing joke," and Dye's successor acknowledged that Dye had suffered: "That's a lonely place. The last few years have not been the easiest in terms of the flak he has had to put up with."

Dye lost his job, but he was right. Before Philips & Drew had time to change its strategy, the stock market turned. Internet, telecom, and technology stocks plummeted. The stock market as a whole slumped. The unfashionable "value" shares, which Dye had been holding, did well, and cash was also better than crash-

ing Internet shares. Philips & Drew soared to the top of the pension fund performance tables, earning its clients 6.4 percent in the three months up to June 2000—the equivalent of more than 28-percent annual return in a sharply falling market. The FTSE fell and fell and fell, from over 6400 at the time of Mr. Dye's departure to under 3300 three years later. Dye had concluded in 1996 that his clients would be better off selling shares with the market at 4000 and putting the money in a savings account. He was eventually proved right seven years later.

Tony Dye was right, but was he sensible? The hundreds of fund managers who were proved disastrously wrong kept their jobs because they were all wrong in a big herd. Tony Dye decided to follow his own path. He was vindicated in the end, but not before he had been ridiculed by the press, abandoned by his clients, and forced out by his employer. Fund managers face lopsided incentives: if they decide to take a different view from the crowd, they will win a few clients if they are successful but lose their jobs if they are not. Much safer to run with the herd.

This isn't to say that share prices are completely out of touch with reality—simply that many major fund managers, who make decisions concerning vast sums of money, are being paid to follow fashion instead of pick the right shares. That's bound to mean that the stock market will make mistakes.

Taking the long view

It can take many years for those mistakes to become apparent. Who is to say for sure that the Internet bubble really was a bubble? The truth might be that we're making a mistake today when stock prices have fallen so far. There are no definitive answers, but I find that taking a long, long look back certainly raises the right questions. At the peak of the market in 2000, it was fashionable to try to get people to buy into the stock market, or a stock-market related product such as a pension, by showing a graph of stock prices, which looked something like this:

Does the stock market do this . . .?

Source: Shiller 2001.

The idea of this graph is to show you that the stock market (in this case, a much-quoted US stock index, the S&P 500) has climbed very quickly, and if you had invested in the early 1980s you would have done very nicely indeed.

The real message is a little bit more alarming. The numbers up the side of the graph are "historical price/earnings ratios." They show how the price of shares is related to the history of company profits over the previous ten years. So in 1980, the price of typical S&P 500 shares was nine times the typical S&P 500 company's average profit during the 1970s (the graph, and all these figures, are adjusted to remove the effect of inflation). Shares that had brought $100 a year of profits in the 1970s cost $900 to buy in 1980. By 1990, shares that had brought $100 a year of profits during the 1980s would cost $1,800 to buy. This means that investors in 1990 were optimistic that the 1990s would be

better than the 1980s, while investors in 1980 were less optimistic that the 1980s would be better than the 1970s.

By 2000, investors were willing to pay $4,500 for shares that had brought $100 of profits throughout the 1990s. If investors in 1990 were optimistic relative to investors in 1980, the investors in 2000 were absolutely delirious. Part of that was a willingness to pay more for shares because people were more familiar with shares and more tolerant of the risks. But mostly it reflected a view—and an unconscious, unquestioned view—that future profitability would be much better than past profitability, in a way that had never happened before.

Let's be clear about what a massive assumption that was. It wasn't a question about whether company profits were increasing. On average, over the medium term, they always have increased in a bumpy uphill ride as the economy expands. But price/earnings ratios like those shown in the graph have always taken into account the fact that because the economy is growing, tomorrow's profits will probably be larger than today's profits. Investors in 2000 were betting on more than that. They were betting that tomorrow's profits would be much, much larger than today's profits—in a way that had never been seen in the history of the stock markets, not when the railroads came, nor when America was electrified, nor in the great expansion of the 1950s and 1960s.

The graph of price/earnings shouldn't rise like the north face of the Eiger. It should be fairly flat, bouncing up and down a bit perhaps, but over the long term never really changing much. A stable ratio of 16 says that I am willing to pay $16 for a share that has in the past given profits of $1 a year, $1,600 for a portfolio that has in the past given profits of $100 a year, or $16 billion for a company that has in the past given profits of $1 billion a year. As the companies on the stock market grow, profits may grow from $10 million to $100 million to $1billion, but the *ratio* shouldn't usually change over time. (It does change with interest rates and attitudes to risk, but these effects aren't nearly enough to explain what happened in the late 1990s.)

. . . or this? The long view.

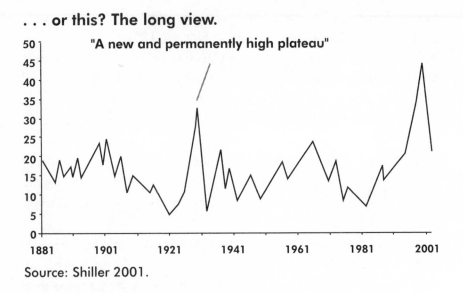

When pension salesmen showed me graphs like this in 2000, what they hoped they were telling me was that the stock market was going to keep soaring. But what I saw was a message that it was bound to crash. Historically, long-term price-earnings ratios have always been around 16. They have often drifted away from 16 but have always returned to that figure. Yale economist Robert Shiller has devoted some effort to establishing this pattern of always drifting back to a P/E ratio of 16, and he has collected price/earnings ratios back to 1881. (Robert Shiller's data is used in the graphs for both figures. In fact, the first figure is just an extract from the second. The impression the two graphs give is rather different.) What comes out very clearly from Shiller's data is that a ratio over 30 is not normal. It only happened once before the 1990s, in 1928. As in 2000, people in 1928 came up with many rationalizations for the high share prices at the time. Irving Fisher, one of Shiller's predecessors as a noted Yale economist, famously declared that shares had reached "a new and permanently high plateau." Fisher was no fool; a very influential thinker in monetary economics, he wrote a book called *The Wall Street Crash—And After*, giving what must at the time have seemed like excellent reasons for expecting share prices to stay high.

After the initial dramatic swing down in the stock market at the end of the 1920s, the start of the Wall Street Crash, Fisher argued that future profits would be excellent, due to efficiencies resulting from recent large mergers, the application of new technology, the improvement of management expertise, and the expertise of the Federal Reserve. The analysis seems reasonable . . . and strangely familiar.

Unfortunately, despite the title, Fisher's book was not published after the Wall Street Crash. It was published just after the first act of what turned out to be a much longer drama. Further dramatic falls in share prices followed. So, too, did the Great Depression.

Thinking sensibly about scarcity

We are probably not on the verge of another depression. Some die-hard optimists would even claim that the stock market will bounce to justify its bubble valuations. James Glassman and Kevin Hassett, the authors of *Dow 36,000*, a book that made the eponymous prediction, were unrepentant in August 2002 after the Dow had slumped to around 8000 and have continued to defend their book. They point out, correctly, that nobody could call the market in the short term; they predict a rebound for the market over time. (They are no longer emphasizing the fact that in *Dow 36,000* they predicted that the market might take "three or five years" to soar . . . that is, until the end of 2004.) Glassman and Hassett argue that the stock market has been undervalued for a hundred years, so the historical data produced by Robert Shiller does not prove that investors in the future will make the same mistake. Perhaps investors have indeed been wrong for the past century. As we've already discovered, once economists abandon the view that people are acting sensibly, it is very hard for us to say very much at all.

A more productive line of inquiry is to ask whether, as bubble valuations suggested, company profits will really be so dramatically much higher in the next few years. It's tempting to think that this is an argument about the power of the internet, cell phones,

computers, and other recent technological advances. Many Internet fans did indeed argue that it was reasonable to pay an enormous amount of money for a company like Amazon because the internet was "transforming everything."

Unfortunately, that is not the point. Maybe the Internet really is a transformational technology like electricity, mass chemical production, or the railroads. The answer will emerge over time, but that answer does not actually matter much for the stock market. The hidden premise is that if we are in an economic revolution, shares should be very valuable. This premise is wrong. Shares should rise in price only if there's good reason to think that future profits will be high. As we know, profits derive from scarcity; for instance, ownership of scarce land (protected by legal title), a scarce brand (protected by trademark), or an organization with unique capabilities (protected by nothing more than the fact that most effective organizations are hard to copy). So share prices should rise only if economic transformation increases the degree to which organizations control scarce resources.

It's easy to see that there might be a link between economic transformation and the control of scarcity. It's far less easy to see what it is, and it seems unlikely that it is as straightforward as "new technologies will increase corporate control of scarce resources." Some companies will gain; others will lose. Historically, there has been no clear link between economic transformation and high profits for the average company. In fact, the reverse is often true: economic transformation destroys the profitability of old firms (by replacing or duplicating their scarce assets), while the new firms that replace them often face a high failure rate and very large costs of building their businesses. The advantages are enjoyed by workers who are paid higher wages on average and by customers who pay lower prices or get new and better goods and services. For example, Amazon's profits of $30 million in 2003 should be weighed against the fall in global music industry profits of around $2.5 billion in the same year, a drop that industry executives blame on Internet music down-

loads and easy piracy. The Internet can destroy profits as well as enable them.

This has always been the case with previous revolutionary technologies such as railroads or electricity. Because I didn't understand the point well enough at the time, I once made the mistake of entering into a sportsman's bet with the economist John Kay. He wondered what would have happened if you had bought shares in the Great Western Railway, the most famous of all the rail companies in Britain, the birthplace of train travel. He speculated that even had you bought them on the first day they were available, and held them for the long term, your returns would have been quite modest, say, less than 10 percent a year. I couldn't conceive that one of the most successful companies of the railroad revolution could have possibly returned such a modest sum to shareholders. Off I went to flick through dusty nineteenth-century editions of *The Economist* and find out the answer. Of course, Kay was right. Not long after the Great Western Railway shares were put on sale for £100 a share in 1835, there was a tremendous burst of speculation in rail shares. Great Western shares peaked at £224 in 1845, ten years after the company was formed. Then they crashed and never reached that level again in the century-long life of the company. The long-term investor would have received dividend payments and would have made a respectable but unremarkable 5-percent annual return on his initial £100 investment. Somebody buying at the peak of the frenzy would have lost money but would have done far better than the backers of countless rail companies, which simply went bankrupt without completing their lines.

So, even the best rail companies weren't great investments, and the worst were financial disasters. But nobody disputes the fact that the railroads completely transformed developed economies. Conservative estimates are that they added 5–15 percent to the total value of the US economy by 1890—a staggering amount, when you think about it. But competition to build and operate rail lines kept profits modest. As long as competition is strong, the railroads had little scarcity power.

Scarcity and technology

In the case of the dot-coms and other high technology companies, the case for scarcity is even harder to make. A few have done well, it's true; for instance, IBM, Microsoft, and Intel. IBM was an enormously successful company: at the end of the 1970s it was the most profitable company ever. But at the beginning of the 1980s, it nearly went bankrupt and has only recovered by radically and painfully transforming itself into a completely different business. Intel has not suffered the same disintegration, although operating profits did fall by over three quarters in 2001. But Intel is famous for its incessant drive to keep innovating to stay ahead of the competition. (The chairman, Andy Grove, wrote a book titled *Only the Paranoid Survive.*)

Only Microsoft, which replaced IBM as the titan of the computer industry, seems to have had a comfortable time. Perhaps it is the great success of Microsoft, which has helped to fuel the frenzy to find the "next Microsoft." Most companies are not Microsoft and never will be. In truth, as far as the share price is concerned, even Microsoft is not Microsoft, because its share price at the end of the 1990s reflected not its current situation but an expectation of what Microsoft could eventually become. The view of investors, perhaps correctly, is that by controlling a number of important industry standards, Microsoft really does have genuine, lasting scarcity power, which will generate massive profits for many years to come.

For the gaggle of dot-com pretenders, the contrast could not have been greater. Many of them had businesses that could have been duplicated at minimal cost in a matter of months, and it was that fact alone that should have made it clear that their shares were really worth next to nothing. It did not matter whether the economy was changing, because the economy will never change so much that companies with no scarcity power become highly profitable.

Which brings us back to Graham Bailey and management consulting in late 1998. The implicit idea behind his story was this: it

doesn't matter whether you have any scarcity power. It doesn't matter if anyone in the world can do what you do. What matters is that you get there first. It's a gold-rush vision—the first claim has priority. If somehow Internet companies could stake out "territory" on the Internet, other companies would find it impossible to move in and dislodge them.

When you make that implicit idea explicit you can see that it appeals to the great American myths, but doesn't really have a lot behind it. Settlers and prospectors had a set of property rights, admittedly rough-and-ready ones, to defend their claim. But Internet companies do not—they have a domain name and maybe some brand recognition. But easy come, easy go: why on earth should the first company to set up an Internet business face no effective competition? It is quite easy for customers to find out about new businesses. It is effortless for them to visit their websites—much easier than it is to visit a new store. In fact, the advantage to businesses who move first looks smaller than it has ever been in the past. As Bailey was speaking, a tiny company was being established in a garage in California. It provided Internet search technology but was performing just a few hundred searches an hour. The company's name was Google.

Google is the living proof that moving first counts for nothing on the Internet. What counts is being best. Google came to the game late, at a time when Yahoo! appeared to have established itself as the king of all search engines, but has become synonymous with Web searching itself. The question for Google is whether a new company, sitting in a garage somewhere, is about to do to them what they did to their rivals. On the Internet, every company is vulnerable to competition. The Web eats into scarcity power.

The lessons for your own stock market investment are clear enough. First, remembering the struggle to find the fastest line at a supermarket, bear in mind that all stock prices incorporate tremendous expert knowledge. If you plan to try to make serious money, better have a clear idea what you think you know, and

what market insiders are ignoring. Second, remember that long-lasting profitability for a company comes from having some capability that others cannot match: a powerful brand in a conservative market—think of Trojan condoms; control of a standard like Microsoft's; or simple superior expertise, like General Electric. Perhaps eBay has such a capability, drawn from its locked-in base of loyal buyers and sellers. Very few other Internet companies do, and if you looked inside Graham Bailey's story thoughtfully you would have found it very unconvincing in 1998. His consulting firm went bankrupt in April 2001.

The Men Who Knew
the Value of Nothing

Someone who knows the price of
everything and the value of nothing.

Oscar Wilde's definition of a cynic,
now commonly applied to economists.

Imagine hiring an economist to sell your house. He designs a
clever-looking kind of auction, which he assures you should raise
the $300,000 you think your house is worth. The bids come in,
and to your horror and the economist's embarrassment you some-
how end up with less than $3,000. You're left homeless and nearly
penniless, your wife divorces you, and you spend the rest of your
days in a dank basement.

Meanwhile, your next-door neighbor also decides to sell his
house and engages a different economist, who also designs a
clever-looking kind of auction. Your neighbor also expects
$300,000, but the bidding just keeps on going up and he ends up
with $2.3 million.

Far-fetched? Not at all. Something very similar actually hap-
pened, not to homeowners but to governments. The real estate
in this situation was constituted not of bricks and mortar but of
thin air, wavelengths of radio spectrum, to be exact, which cell-
phone companies use to operate their networks. Over the past
few years, governments across the world have been selling the
rights to use this spectrum to telecom companies. There is a

limited amount of the spectrum available, and as we have learned, where there is scarcity there is money to be made. Unfortunately, not all of the economists who were hired as consultants knew how to set up the auction so that it was likely to produce a good price. One auction really did raise less than 1 percent of what was hoped for, while another raised ten times as much as expected.

This wasn't down to luck but to cleverness in some cases and blundering in others. Auctioning air, like playing poker, is a game of great skill—and one that was played for very high stakes indeed.

Love, war, and poker

Many of those who knew the mathematician John von Neumann regarded him as the "best brain in the world," and they had a chance to compare him with some stiff competition, given that one of von Neumann's colleagues at Princeton was Albert Einstein. Von Neumann was a genius around whom grew a mythology of almost superhuman intelligence. According to one story, Von Neumann was asked to assist with the design of a new supercomputer, required to solve a new and important mathematical problem, which was beyond the capacities of existing supercomputers. He asked to have the problem explained to him, solved it in moments with pen and paper, and then turned down the request.

Von Neumann made dramatic strides in logic, set theory, geometry, meteorology, and other fields of mathematics, and he took a central role in developing quantum mechanics, nuclear weapons, and the computer. But it's his role as the founder of game theory that interests us here.

A game, to a game theorist, is any activity in which your prediction of what another person will do affects what you decide to do. Such games include poker, nuclear war, love, or bidding for thin air in an auction. Game theory can seem deceptively simple: for instance, the game "driving" is thoroughly straightforward.

In "driving," I receive an acceptable payoff if I drive on the right and so do you. I also receive an acceptable payoff if I drive on the left side, and you do too. If one of us chooses to behave otherwise, I receive a very bad payoff—a ride in an ambulance. (You also receive a bad payoff if we have a head-on collision, but in game theory I don't usually care about your payoff for its own sake. I care about your payoffs only because they help me predict your behavior.)

Games are often described in just that way, using little stories or anecdotes, but these stories conceal the fact that for a game theorist, games are mathematical objects. The great game theorists are brilliant mathematicians, such as Von Neumann himself, or Nobel Prize winner John Nash, the subject of *A Beautiful Mind*. As in the case of all game theory, Nash's revolutionary new way to predict a game's outcome was an inspired application of well-understood mathematics.

Von Neumann was fascinated by poker, and as he turned his mind to the game he developed mathematical tools that are not only handy for economists but for people trying to understand everything from dating to evolutionary biology or the cold war.

The fundamentals of poker are simple: players conceal their cards until the final showdown, when the player with the best cards wins the pot, full of all the accumulated bets. Each player has to keep betting to stay in the game, but some will give up along the way, preferring to forfeit a little money rather than risk losing much more in the showdown. If all the other players give up, you can win the pot without ever showing your cards.

If you were playing poker, your basic challenge would be to work out whether it was worth paying to stay in the game. Probability theory won't get you very far. It is not enough to calculate the odds that the hand you hold is better than the other hands hidden around the table. You need to analyze your opponents' moves. Is a small bet a sign of weakness, or a trick to tempt you to raise the stakes against hidden strength? And do big bets mean a big hand—or a bluff? At the same time you must recognize that

your opponents will be trying to interpret your own bets, and you must be careful not to be predictable.

Poker is full of spirals of second-guessing: "If he thinks that I think that he thinks that I have four kings, then. . . ." Poker is a game both of luck and of skill, and most importantly, it is a game of secrets: each player has access to information hidden to the others. In chess, a game of pure skill, the battle takes place in plain sight of everyone. In poker, no player can see the whole truth.

This is where game theory comes in. Von Neumann believed that if he could analyze poker using mathematics, he could shine a spotlight onto all kinds of human interactions. Poker is a game where a small number of players try to outwit each other in an environment of luck, secrets, and skilled calculation. But poker is not the only situation to fit that description. Think of generals fighting a war, or even—if you're a cynic like me—men and women playing the great game of love itself. Many human interactions can be interpreted as battles of wits, like poker. All these interactions came to be described by theorists as "games" and explored using game theory.

Economic life is no exception. Von Neumann teamed up with the economist Oskar Morgenstern to write the bible of game theory, *Theory of Games and Economic Behavior*, which was published just before the end of World War II. Ever since, game theory and economics have had a close relationship: game theory is taught to most students studying economics, and several game theorists have been awarded the Nobel Prize for Economic Sciences.

If you want examples of real-life "economic games," think of bargaining between landlord and tenant, between government and trade union, between used-car salesman and used-car buyer. Think of oil producing nations deciding whether to adhere to OPEC rules to help drive up oil prices, or produce flat out and take advantage of the high prices that others have created.

Or, to take the example we'll explore in most depth in this chapter, think of a collection of eager telecom corporations try-

ing to acquire radio-spectrum licenses from a government with a limited number to offer. Every bidder has some idea of how profitable it would be to own a license (and so how valuable a license is), but nobody knows precisely how profitable. The government's challenge is to find out some secrets: to determine which of the telecom companies can best use the licenses, and how much the licenses are worth to them. Ideally the government would want to assign the licenses to the firms who will use them best. Since the government is to be divvying up a valuable public asset, they also want to get the best value for the taxpayer.

Poker and the spectrum license problem are both games in Von Neumann's sense. There is an even closer similarity: in both cases, it's important to put large sums of money at the heart of the process. Without stakes, poker makes no sense. To a gambler, any game may be regarded as "more interesting" if there is money riding on it, but in poker, money is central to the play of the game. This is because bets communicate strength and weakness in poker—if players are not betting with real money, the "communication" is meaningless. As we know well by now, talk is cheap. Bluffing only has consequences if real money is at stake.

The same is true of spectrum licenses. Economists specializing in game theory argued that the allocation of public assets, from the right to drill oil to the right to use radio spectrum, ought to be determined by methods similar to those that determine a game of poker. In order to sift out competing companies' cheap talk and empty promises, the government had to impose high stakes and, to use an old phrase, force each negotiator to "put his money where his mouth is."

Games within games:
How to sell a $300,000 house for $3,000

The US government employed game theorists to help sell spectrum rights throughout the second half of the 1990s. This was not an easy task: a company bidding for a Los Angeles license

and a San Diego license might want both of them, or neither, because it is cheaper to run adjacent networks. But how to bid sensibly on Los Angeles before knowing who will get San Diego? This is a complex problem represented by a complex piece of game theory. The theorists duly designed a complex set of parallel auctions.

The first sales were highly successful (and very lucrative for the government), but after a few auctions things went wrong. The theorists had got the complex things right but made some simple mistakes, like publishing the bids without rounding them to the nearest few thousand dollars. Firms took advantage by making bids which contained area codes. This allowed them to signal which licenses they'd prefer, and so carve up the US telecom market without having to bid aggressively against each other. This scheme didn't even require an (illegal) agreement, because the auction allowed such clear signals. It looked like cheating, but nobody could prove it. Three years after the first auctions, an auction in April 1997 raised less than 1 percent of the expected revenue because, claimed many commentators, firms had learned to cheat by avoiding competition with each other.

This is the equivalent of selling your $300,000 house for less than $3,000. It seems hard to understand how this might happen, but it's simple. If there are only a small number of potential buyers for your house, they could agree among themselves not to bid against each other. The one who buys the house cheaply needs to find some way to compensate the others. The most obvious form of compensation would be to agree not to bid against them in future auctions. In the same way, telecom firms seemed to work out a way of agreeing not to bid against each other for spectrum licenses in different regions. It was a humiliation for game theory, only slightly better than having given away the licenses for nothing.

An alternative way of seeing the problems of the American auctions is that the game theorists failed to see that what they had analyzed was only part of a wider game. The government was like the poker player blissfully unaware of hidden cameras in

the room; oblivious to the fact that the other players, by a series of nods and winks, are taking turns winning his money. The game he thinks he's playing isn't the real game at all.

Game theory for dummies

Whether applied to colluding at auctions or cheating at cards, it must be clear by now that game theory is as much art as it is mathematics. All games need some simplifying assumptions before they can be modeled; if the theorists use the wrong assumptions (for example, that bidders won't use area codes to coordinate a carve-up) then they will produce perfect solutions to the wrong problems.

One of the most difficult challenges of all is rooted in the very origins of game theory: it was developed by men of nearly superhuman intellect like Nash and Von Neumann. That is both its great strength and its great weakness, because for game theory to be successful, it has to provide insight into what mere mortals do. Game theory expresses the way people would act as the solution to a mathematical equation. It presumes hyperrational players who are able instantly to solve very tough problems, and this description starts to look unrealistic if game theory is to be a practical tool for explaining how real people actually behave. Nash and Von Neumann really could solve such problems instantly. The rest of us cannot.

For instance, game theory tells us that chess is not worth playing because in theory its outcome is predetermined: one player can force a result. However, we do not know whether it is black or white that can force the result, we do not know whether the forced result is a win or a draw, and we certainly do not know how the game would be played. We only know that in theory, the forced result is possible. In practice even the strongest players (computer or human) do not know this optimal strategy, and in practice the outcome of a game of chess is far from being predetermined. So what use is a theory that tells us that chess would be trivial, if only we were all smart enough to know how to play it?

Not all of us think like a genius. Most of us would try to bluff at poker with a halfway good hand; Von Neumann showed that the correct play is to bluff with the worst possible hand. Chris "Jesus" Ferguson, a disciple of Von Neumann, proved it when he won the World Series of Poker in 2000. But poker with your buddies in the garage is not the World Series; what can game theory say about players who get drunk and bluff badly?

This is not a knockdown objection to game theory. It is possible to model mistakes, forgetfulness, misinformation, and any other kind of failure on the part of the players to live up to the impossibly high standards of John Von Neumann. The trouble is that the more mistakes that need to be taken into account, the more complicated and the less useful game theory becomes. It is always useful for the game theorist to draw on experience as well as pure theory, because if the game becomes too complex for the players to understand, then the theory becomes nearly useless for practical purposes since it tells us nothing about what they will actually do.

Enter the auctioneers

In late 1996, I saw one of the country's leading auction theorists illustrating this point—in passing—in a seminar on applying game theory to auctions. As part of his talk, Paul Klemperer confiscated the wallets of two members of the audience, counted the money they contained, and then offered to sell that (unknown) sum of money back to whichever of the victims would bid highest. The two members of the audience, put on the spot, were quite unable to work out what the optimal strategy was for bidding in the auction.

The difficulty—which is a challenge for bidders in many auctions, including spectrum auctions—is that the two victims just didn't know the value of what they were bidding for. They knew part of the value, of course, because they knew how much money had been in their own wallet. But each knew nothing about the contents of the other's wallet. In a spectrum auction, the prob-

lem is similar: each bidder has his own forecasts and technology plans, but each knows that other bidders will probably have different insights. The optimal strategy would take advantage of any information revealed by other players' bids—but this is not easy. (In the wallet game, one solution is for each player to keep bidding until he reaches twice the sum in his own wallet. The player with the fatter wallet would win but pay less than the combined contents of the wallets. Bidding more aggressively risks paying too much.)

The failure of the two dumbfounded "volunteers" to work out how to bid in the auction was more remarkable because they were Ken Binmore and Tilman Börgers, themselves experts in the game theory of auctions. Klemperer, Binmore, and Börgers were about to become members of the team of academics who designed the mechanism for distributing the licenses in the UK for "third generation" (3G) cell-phone services.

They had two serious difficulties to wrestle with. First, to avoid being outmaneuvered by cheating bidders as the US authorities had been. Second, even if they couldn't find the optimal strategy for each others' auctions on the spot, how could they expect a collection of businessmen to behave as game theory predicts? And if those businessmen behaved unpredictably, who was to say what might happen?

John Maynard Keynes, the most influential economist of the twentieth century, longed for a day when economists were no longer archtheorists but instead, "rather like dentists," consulted to fix everyday problems and give straightforward advice. Economics is not there yet, and any economist who wishes to be even half as helpful as a dentist must temper economic theories with heavy doses of the hard lessons of real life: players cheat; bidders make mistakes; appearances matter. Auctions, like games of poker and chess, do not always unfold in the way the game theorist would predict.

The New Zealand government, which auctioned radio spectrum as early as 1990 with advice from some economists who

seemed to have a slender grasp on reality, learned such lessons the hard way. The auctions were held without making sure that there was any interest from bidders, without minimum prices, and using a theoretical curiosity called a "Vickrey auction," which led to considerable embarrassment. (The auction was named after its inventor, Nobel laureate William Vickrey, who made major early advances in applying game theory to auctions.)

The Vickrey auction is a second-price sealed-bid auction. The "sealed bid" means that each bidder writes down a single bid and seals it in an envelope. When the envelopes are opened, the highest bidder wins. "Second-price" is the curious rule that the winner pays not his bid but that of the second-highest bidder. The elegant reasoning behind this auction is that no bidder ever has an incentive to shave his bid in an effort to make more profit; making a lower bid affects his chance of winning but not the price. To a theorist, this doesn't seem odd at all: after all, in a traditional auction at Sotheby's or Christies, the price is also set by the second-highest bidder, because bidding stops when the second-highest bidder drops out. To the press and many others, this Vickrey auction looked nothing short of crazy. The problem with the Vickrey auction is not substantive but stylistic: in a traditional auction nobody ever finds out the maximum price the highest bidder would have been willing to pay, but in a Vickrey auction that fact is made public. Justifiably, New Zealanders wanted to know why a bidder who had offered NZ$100,000 (about $72,000) for a license only had to pay NZ$6 ($4+) or why one who had offered NZ$7 ($5+) million was only coughing up NZ$5,000 (around $3,600). These figures were embarrassing. The theorists knew that on average, Vickrey auctions make just as much money as other auctions because, by not demanding payment of the highest bid, they encourage all bidders to offer more. But what the theorists knew did not matter to the press and to the public: the harsh reality is that Vickrey auctions were seen as a failure of the New Zealand government.

Game theory can help predict some problems, such as cheating in the US auction. Others, such as the public reaction in New

Zealand, simply don't show up in the theoretical analysis. Economists who aspire to dentistry have to think carefully and learn from mistakes: new ones will continue to be discovered the hard way.

Why use an auction?

When the UK government started to consider using an auction to sell spectrum rights, they were taking a bold step. After initial success, the US auctions had fallen apart because the game theory used to construct them had been far too narrowly conceived. The New Zealand government had made itself a laughing stock. And they weren't the only ones: Australia had also run auctions for TV licenses and left loopholes in the bidding rules, which had been so badly exploited that the minister responsible lost his job. Why did Britain even consider using an auction, given the risks?

Like the US government, the UK government wanted to sell the licenses to the companies that could use them best and to raise money while doing so. Of course, there was an additional unstated aim: to avoid embarrassment for bureaucrats and politicians alike. For the taxpayers of New Zealand and the United States, an auction that raised some money was better than simply giving the licenses away, but for a politician, giving away public assets is a great way to make friends and allies. Auction theorists therefore had to make a strong case for auctions.

That case relies on game theory, which clearly demonstrates the power of simple auctions. One of the trickiest problems is making sure that the licenses end up in the right hands. With a limited number of licenses it would be a criminal waste if one of them went to timharford.com, an Internet-bubble company with no relevant experience and no capability to use the valuable asset. The licenses should go, instead, to companies that will use them to deliver the best quality services at the lowest cost. Competition between license holders will then set prices.

So what is the best way to identify the most capable companies? One possibility is simply to ask them, but companies will

boast and bluster. Some will point to their experience, others to the latest technology. But would any really tell the truth? Talk is cheap.

Another idea that might seem more promising is to appoint experts to decide which companies are most deserving. But in the fast-moving world of cell telephony, most experts would have some financial interest in one company or another—who is expert yet totally detached from the industry? Even if a truly impartial expert could be found, he would still have little success in penetrating trade secrets and judging the true potential of rival technologies.

Game theory shows how a simple auction can cut through all the complexity and solve the problem elegantly. For simplicity, imagine a straightforward auction of a single license, which is like a traditional auction where bidders yell out higher and higher offers, with one difference: anyone who stays in the room is presumed to be willing to pay the current high bid. Anyone who drops out must leave the room and not reenter. This slightly different auction is easier for game theory to analyze, but also closely reflects many of the actual auctions used to sell licenses.

Each bidder must now make a straightforward judgment about what the license is worth. The better their innovative ideas and the cheaper their technology, the more money they will make if they win a license. Of course, none of the companies can perfectly forecast what profits they would make with a license, but each is in a better position than any external expert to make the judgment.

When the auction starts and the price begins to rise, bidders will start to drop out once the asking price for the license exceeds their own estimate of its value to them. Companies without confidence in their business plans and technologies will be the first to go. If the price rises a long way without anyone leaving the room, each bidder learns that the others are confident about the prospects for the market as a whole. (This provides the distinction between this auction and a traditional auction at Sotheby's—

while a Sotheby's auction is in progress you never know who is still a potential bidder and who is just watching.) If some bidders leave surprisingly early, the rest should take note and revise their own assumptions. The auction neatly summarizes the collective wisdom of all the bidders.

Meanwhile, nobody is in a position to lie. Talk is cheap, but bidding is expensive. No company will drop out while the price is still lower than their prediction of the license's value, and no company will keep bidding once the price rises too high. In a sense, the auction is like Von Neumann's game of poker: because money is at stake, the bids have to be taken very seriously. In another sense, it is not like poker at all, because the auction makes it absolutely impossible to bluff.

The auction forces each bidder to tell the truth about his own estimate of the license's value. At the same time, the auction broadcasts the collective view to all the bidders, so that they can update their own opinions accordingly. What's more, it collects cash while it does so.

Game theory also shows that this simple auction is generally a better cash-generating machine than the alternative ways of negotiating a sale. This is not obvious. One alternative would be for the seller to run an auction but to set a reserve price (open or secret) below which he will not sell. Another would be to negotiate in secret with several buyers in parallel and lie about how the negotiations were going. Or the seller could make a one-shot, "take-it-or-leave-it" offer to each seller in turn. Or something else. Given the perplexing array of possibilities, how can a seller choose the most lucrative way of making a sale?

Game theory slices through to the core of the problem. In the mid-1990s, Klemperer and Jeremy Bulow (who became another member of the auction design team) published a paper showing if the simplicity of the auction attracted just one extra serious bidder, that straightforward auction would raise more money than any other kind of negotiating set-up.

In addition to the central claim that auctions really do raise more cash, the paper finally focused the attention of auction theorists on what should have been obvious: if you want a successful auction, you need plenty of serious bidders.

The UK auction in action

The UK auction design team certainly went all-out to make sure those serious bidders turned up. By March 2000, the UK auction was ready to go with thirteen registered bidders who had paid £50-million deposits and were hooked up to the Internet to submit their bids remotely. The team had been advertising the auction for more than a year in advance and had made sure they were the first European nation to hold an auction for third generation phone licenses. The result promised to be a highly competitive auction.

The team had been focusing obsessively on the details. They'd tested the auction design using computer simulations and test-runs with London students playing the role of telecom executives. They crawled over the fine print of the auction, trying to eliminate loopholes. They even gave themselves options to postpone the auction if something suspicious appeared to be going on. But despite all this preparation, nobody really knew if the auction would work, or whether it would be yet another bungle by the economists.

The auction was set to run in short rounds—lasting half an hour or so—during which the bidders had to submit new bids or withdraw. Those who chose not to enter a valid bid had to drop out of the auction; each bidder was allowed to "pass" three times before finally withdrawing. There would be a couple of rounds every day, maybe more once the bidders became comfortable with the bidding process. Each of the rounds would be posted promptly on the Internet; this auction was to take place in full view of the world.

The initial expectations were that the auction might raise a lot of money: two or three billion pounds, enough to knock a penny

off the UK income tax for the year. While the team was obviously nervous, they were thrilled to have nine new companies join the four established players in the bidding, and they expected the auction to be a success.

They attributed the interest from new companies in part to the fact that five licenses were available. Originally, the engineers had believed that the airwaves could accommodate four licenses, operating on adjacent wavelengths of radio spectrum and each covering the entire country. But with four established companies, an auction for four licenses would have had obvious winners and the new entrants would not have bothered turning up simply to get beaten. The economists on the project were therefore very relieved when the engineers worked out that there was enough radio spectrum available for one extra license. This license, called "license A," was reserved for new companies who were not currently operating in the UK cell-phone market.

The idea of the auction was that competition for license A would drive up the prices of the other four licenses. Any firm not currently in the lead for a license had to keep bidding or withdraw; but as long as firms kept making legal bids, they could switch bids from one license to another. The firms would obviously choose to bid on whichever license appeared to offer the best value at the time. This meant that the hot competition for license A kept the auctions for the other licenses simmering nicely—every time the price of A rose above the rest, the other licenses looked like bargains. Entrants would peel away and challenge the established companies for the licenses they had staked out for themselves. When the established firms raised the price, the underdogs flipped back to bidding on license A.

Although the simultaneous auction of five licenses is complex to explain, it is quite simple for a bidder to understand the best strategy. Because bidders never know when the auction is going to end, they need to make sure they are always comfortable in their current position. The best strategy is to look at all the licenses and submit a new high bid on whichever license looks like the best value. If none looks like a good value at that time, then

the right move is to withdraw. The simplicity of the auction may help to explain why so many companies decided to bid, and unlike World Series Poker or the wallet game, it is close to being idiot-proof.

Imagine selling your house in a prolonged auction that goes on for weeks and weeks. You've heard the stories about other auctions, and you're afraid that instead of getting the $300,000 you expect, you'll end up like your unfortunate neighbor, divorced and penniless. The first week is agony. But the price slowly starts to rise, and your blood pressure starts to fall. Eventually the bidding gets to $250,000—you realize that, whatever happens, you're not going to do too badly. A few days later the bidding reaches $300,000 and you're smiling. From here on everything is a bonus; maybe you'll get $310,000, or $320,000, or even $350,000. Who knows? Then the price keeps going up. It hits $320,000. It reaches $350,000. $400,000. $500,000. What's happening? You can scarcely believe it.

This unexpected turn of events is similar to what happened in the UK spectrum auction, except the stakes were ten thousand times higher: not £300,000 but £3 billion. For a week, the bidding went smoothly; the rules about continuous bidding kept the total revenue rising steadily. After about twenty-five rounds of bidding, bidders were committed to around £400 million for each license. After fifty rounds of bidding the total stood at £3 billion: what the government had been hoping to raise. (In comparison, the deposits, even though they had been raised to £100 million, were starting to look a little trivial.) But something extraordinary was happening. Bidders were staying in the auction. All thirteen companies continued submitting bids regularly and the prices of the licenses kept rising without any sign of slowing down.

As the auction rolled on, the press started to take interest. Photographs of the design team began appearing in the newspapers. Journalists struggled to explain exactly what the team had done, but everybody started to realize that something remarkable was happening.

The bidding moved through round sixty (total revenue: £4 billion). Round seventy (£5 billion). Round eighty (£7 billion). The end of March came and went. The price was still rising.

The auction designers were keeping quiet about what they thought of all this, but behind closed doors they were both excited and nervous. The auction was becoming a victim of its own success: it was lasting too long. There were jitters on the US stock market—what if a stock-market crash spread to the UK, destroyed the confidence of the bidders, and brought the whole auction to a sudden stop? The deposit of a £100 million suddenly looked pretty small. Maybe the bidders would just walk away. Perhaps the bidding should be speeded up? It turned out that there was no need to worry.

On the morning of April 3, almost a month after the first bid had been cast, with more than £10 billion (£200 or almost $400 per person in the UK) raised, something finally happened. After round ninety-four had finished, it was announced that one of the bidders, Crescent, had dropped out. The auction then started to change quickly. That afternoon, in round ninety-five, a second bidder, the 3G-UK consortium, dropped out. The next morning, in round ninety-seven, a third bidder, Spectrum, also quit. Some other bidders were stalling for time by playing their "waivers" to stay in without raising a bid. In round ninety-eight Epsilon withdrew. The next day, at lunchtime on April 5, One-Tel quit.

After ninety-three rounds of bidding without any withdrawals, the auction had lost five bidders in eight rounds over the course of three days. Now only eight bidders remained. Why was the bidding stuttering so suddenly? Perhaps it was pride: nobody wanted to be the first to drop out, but once Crescent quit, others who had been waiting for the chance also quit soon after.

Game theorists have an alternative explanation: bidders were learning from each others' bids about what the 3G licenses were likely to be worth. This was one of the advantages of the auction's transparent design. A commonly used alternative would simply have been to run a "sealed bid" auction where everyone handed

in an envelope containing a single bid. But such an auction would have left every bidder guessing in the dark, probably leading to much more conservative bidding and a much less profitable outcome for the government. With an open auction, even when the bidding rose higher than anyone had expected, each bidder could see that its twelve competitors were making equally large offers and shared confidence that the licenses would prove hugely valuable. Each company had its own business plan, its own technology partners, its own sales projections. All of these were speculative, but the transparent auction gathered signals of these plans together and put the information at the disposal of all the bidders. (The auction also put the information at the disposal of the government and collected revenue on that basis at the same time—all very neat.)

Crescent's withdrawal sent a signal to the other bidders that the company felt the licenses were not worth a higher bid. Taking into account Crescent's doubts, other bidders who were also having second thoughts were tipped into withdrawing. Crescent set off a spiral: each new withdrawal reinforced the news that the bidding was getting too high.

Of course, the companies who dropped out were just sticking with the herd, but remember that herds run together for good reasons. The transparent auction was designed to spread information around, so it was hardly surprising that bidders looked at the same facts and came to the same conclusions.

The auction had seen a sudden run of withdrawals but it was far from over. By the middle of April the total revenue of the auction topped £29 billion. The government's profit was almost enough to halve the basic rate of income tax for a year. What actually happened was that the British chancellor, Gordon Brown, launched a generous round of spending in the run-up to the election without a large increase in taxes or borrowing. The British public was given an enormous free lunch, courtesy of the telecom boom and the painstaking determination of the auction designers to take advantage of it.

The last three withdrawals happened gradually over the course of April. Just after breakfast on April 27, NTL Mobile announced

that it would be withdrawing, and suddenly all the excitement was over. A company called TIW was the new name in cell telephony, having paid £4,384,700,000 for license A. Vodafone had won its bloody struggle with British Telecom and was the proud holder of license B, at a price of almost £6 billion. British Telecom settled for a smaller license. The auction raised £22.5 billion and in the process had become the biggest auction in modern history.

If you had been selling your $300,000 house at an auction, which exceeded expectations like this one, you would eventually have closed the deal at $2.25 million—and you'd have had to pinch yourself the next morning to check that you weren't dreaming.

Remember: strength from scarcity

Critics of the auctions assumed that because the telecoms had paid so much for the licenses, they would in turn charge consumers very high prices for 3G services. But did the auctions ruin 3G? Consider the following sentence:

> If 3G licenses are very expensive, then firms will charge customers more.

It seems persuasive, but think like an economist for a moment: if 3G licenses are very cheap, will firms charge customers less? What if the government gave the licenses away for nothing, would firms charge customers nothing? And if the government paid telecom companies to take the licenses off its hands, would firms give each customer a cash bonus along with her free wireless service?

We learned way back in chapters 1 and 2 that firms will charge the maximum they possibly can, under any circumstance. We also know that their ability to do this is limited by their scarcity power.

For the UK, the crucial determinant is that there are five licenses. Five licenses are few enough to give each company enough

scarcity power to be able to charge quite high prices. If only two licenses were available, then the scarcity power would be greater and the prices would be higher. If twenty licenses were available, the scarcity power would be less and the prices would be lower. It is the scarcity power, and not the price of the licenses, which determines the price for customers.

In the UK there was scarcity built into the amount of radio spectrum available: five licenses were the most the technicians could offer. It does not make any difference to the customer how much the licenses cost, but it does matter to the taxpayers, who would like the government to get a lot of money for this valuable public resource, and the telecoms' shareholders, who would like their companies to dish out as little as possible.

The hangover

In the previous chapter we heard all about the stock market crash, which (in retrospect) began to unfold during the series of European 3G auctions. Telecoms were among the worst sufferers, and their distress has been widely reported. In Europe alone, telecom companies lost $700 billion in stock market value in the two and a half years following the first 3G auction.

Many people have blamed the auctions for the woes of the telecoms, and argued that the UK design team, far from being clever by raising so much money, stupidly crippled the industry by charging such outrageous sums. Less widely reported is that the most seriously afflicted firms did not win 3G licenses—they are US firms who did not participate in the European auctions, or troubled cable companies such as NTL and Telewest, who withdrew from the 3G auctions without spending anything. The 3G license winners, such as Vodafone, remain successful firms, sadder and wiser after the telecom bubble, perhaps, but still perfectly viable.

Telecom executives may curse the British auctions since 3G remains commercially unproven and threatened by competitors like Wi-Fi, but the public should celebrate them. All the compa-

nies involved were convinced that the 3G licenses offered tremendous scarcity value, and these auctions successfully secured a fair price for that apparent value. John von Neumann's successors used game theory to achieve one of the most spectacular, if controversial, policy triumphs that economics had ever seen. The men who knew the "value of nothing" had shown that economists, like dentists, could finally earn their keep.

EIGHT

Why Poor Countries
Are Poor

They call Douala "the Armpit of Africa." The description is perfect. Lodged neatly beneath the bulging shoulder of West Africa, the malaria-infested city of Douala is humid, unattractive, and it stinks. But if you live in Cameroon, Douala is where the action is. Cameroon is a very poor country indeed; the average Cameroonian is eight times poorer than the average citizen of the world and almost fifty times poorer than the typical American. In late 2001 I went to Douala to find out why.

I'm not sure who first applied the "armpit" label but I wouldn't be surprised if it was Cameroon's Ministry of Tourism. We all know that in most countries the Ministry of Defense is in charge of attacking other countries and that the Ministry of Employment presides over the unemployment lines. Cameroon's Ministry of Tourism is in that noble tradition. Its job is to discourage tourists from getting into the country.

One colleague had warned me that the Cameroonian embassy in London would be so obstructive that I'd have to go to Paris to get my tourist visa. In the end I had less trouble because I had a man on the inside: a friend in Cameroon paid the equivalent of a half-day's wages to get me an official stamp of invitation. Armed with this official stamp, I paid another five days' Cameroonian wages to get my visa, in a process that required only three trips to the embassy and some mild groveling. Funnily

enough, my companions and I did not meet many tourists in our three weeks in Cameroon.

But I don't want to give too much credit to the Ministry of Tourism. Discouraging tourists is a real team effort. According to Transparency International, Cameroon is one of the most corrupt countries in the world. In 1999, it was the most corrupt country surveyed. When I visited in 2001 it was the fifth most corrupt, an improvement much celebrated by the government. A moment's reflection should tell you that earning the title of "Most Corrupt Country in the World" takes some effort. Because Transparency International ranks countries based on international perceptions of corruption, a winning strategy is to concentrate on screwing bribes out of foreign businessmen—for instance, at the airport. But the Cameroon authorities have spread themselves too thin, because Cameroon is massively corrupt at every level and does not just target foreigners. Perhaps it's this lack of focus that has caused them to slip from the top spot.

That's not to say that Douala international airport is a well-oiled machine. Far from it: it's a humid, chaotic shambles where you have to fight your way through packed crowds despite the fact that the place deals with only three or four flights a day. Thankfully, on a torrid evening, we were guided out by my friend Andrew and his driver, Sam, who would have whisked us immediately to the cooler hillside town of Buea, if Douala were at all conducive to being whisked anywhere. It isn't. Douala, a city of two million people, has no real roads.

A typical Douala street is fifty yards wide, from shack to shack. This is not because the space is required for tree-lined boulevards. It's packed with street vendors, slouched beside a tray of peanuts or an impromptu plantain barbeque; and with little clusters of people, standing around a motorbike, or drinking beer or palm wine, or cooking on a small fire. Piles of rubble and vast holes mark unfinished construction or demolition work. Along the middle is a strip of potholes, which twenty years ago had been a road. Down that strip drive four streams of traffic, mostly taxis. The streams on the outside are usually made up of stationary— or nearly stationary—cabs picking up fares, while the taxis on

the inside weave in and out of the potholes and other cars with all the unpredictability of balls in a lottery machine. There are no hard and fast rules. Sometimes a taxi on the shoulder, over-loaded with passengers, will lurch off and overtake the stuttering traffic on the inside; often the road is more potholed than the shoulder. The noise is incredible, because not only does every man, woman, and child in Douala seem to carry a boom box with the volume stuck on full, but the car horn has become a form of universal communication. I worked out some of the most common phrases:

> BEEEP—"You don't see me, but I have spare seats in my cab."
>
> BEEEP—"I see you, but I do not have spare seats in my cab."
>
> BEEEP—"I cannot take your fare because I'm going in a different direction."
>
> BEEEP—"I can take your fare . . . get in."
>
> BEEEP—"In a moment I will swerve around a pothole, and knock you over. Move!"

Douala used to have buses, but the buses can no longer cope with the decaying roads. So the taxis are all that is left. The cabs are beaten-up old Toyotas, carrying four in the back and three in the front, sprayed New York yellow, each with a unique slogan: for instance, "God is great," "In God We Trust," "Powered by God," or "Toss Man."

Nobody who sees a Douala street scene can conclude that Cameroon is poor because of a lack of entrepreneurial spirit. But poor it is, and it's getting poorer. Is there anything to be done to reverse the decline and help Cameroon grow richer instead? That's no small question. As Nobel laureate Robert Lucas put it:

> The consequences for human welfare involved in questions like these are simply staggering: Once one starts to think about them, it is hard to think about anything else.

The missing jigsaw piece

Economists used to think that economic wealth came from a combination of *man-made resources* (roads, factories, machines, telephone systems), *human resources* (hard work and education) and *technological resources* (technical know-how, or simply hi-tech machinery). Obviously, then, poor countries grew into rich countries by investing money in physical resources and by improving human and technological resources with education and technology transfer programs.

What's wrong with this picture? Nothing, as far as it goes. Education, factories, infrastructure, and technical know-how are indeed in abundance in rich countries and severely lacking in poor ones. But the picture is incomplete: a puzzle with the most important piece missing.

The first clue that something is amiss with the traditional story is its implication that poor countries should have been catching up with rich ones for the past century or so, and the farther behind they are, the faster the catch-up should be. The poorer countries should catch up quickly because in a country, which has very little in the way of infrastructure or education, new investments have the biggest rewards. Rich countries don't gain much from further investment: this is called "diminishing returns." For instance, a few roads in a poor country can open up whole new areas for trade; in a rich country, a few more roads just relieve a little congestion. The first few telephones in a poor country are of huge importance; in a rich country, phones are used by schoolkids to send text messages in class. A little more education in a poor country can make all the difference; in a rich country, people with degrees often can't find jobs. And of course, it should be much easier for a poor country to copy technology than for a rich country to invent it: the citizens of Douala can enjoy taxis without waiting for a Cameroonian Gottlieb Daimler to reinvent the internal combustion engine.

When you look at places like Taiwan, South Korea, or China, which have been doubling their incomes every decade or quicker,

the theory of catch-up seems reasonable. But many poor countries are not growing faster than rich ones; in fact, they are growing more slowly or, like Cameroon, getting poorer. In order to patch up the traditional story, economists combined their "diminishing returns" model with one that also takes into account "increasing returns." The new theory says that sometimes the more you have, the faster you grow: phones are useful if other people have phones; roads are useful if everyone has a car; technology is easier to invent if you've done a lot of inventing before.

That story would explain why rich countries stay rich and poor countries fall farther behind, but it doesn't explain how countries like China, Taiwan, and South Korea—not to mention Botswana, Chile, India, Mauritius, and Singapore—are catching up. These dynamic countries, not Japan, the United States, or Switzerland have become the fastest-growing economies on the planet. Fifty years ago, they were mired in poverty—lacking man-made, human, technical, and sometimes natural resources—and have grown much richer since then. Along the way they have improved education, technology, and infrastructure.

And why not? Since technology is so widely available and increasingly inexpensive, that is really what economists should expect of every developing country. In a world of diminishing returns, the poorest countries gain the most from new technology, infrastructure, and education. South Korea, for example, acquired technology by encouraging foreign companies to invest or by paying licensing fees. It wasn't free: in addition to the fees, the investing companies sent profits back home. But the gains to Korean workers and investors, in the form of economic growth, were fifty times greater than the fees and profits that left the country.

As for education and infrastructure, since the returns seem to be so high, there should be no shortage of investors willing to fund infrastructure projects or lend money to students or indeed to governments who provide free education. Banks, domestic and foreign, should be lining up to lend people the money to get through school or to build a new road or a new power plant. In

turn, poor people, or poor countries, should be very happy to take out such loans, confident that investment returns are so high that the repayments will not be difficult. Even if, for some reason, that didn't happen, the World Bank, established after World War II with the express aim of providing loans to countries for reconstruction and development, lends billions of dollars a year to developing countries. Investment money is clearly not the issue—either the investments are not being made, or they are not delivering the returns the traditional models predict.

Even the "increasing returns" model suggests that it should be possible for poor countries to grow richer as long as they can make a number of complementary investments all at once, such as factories, roads, electricity, and ports, to allow goods to be manufactured and exported. This "big push" theory of investment was advanced by the economist Paul Rosenstein-Rodan, who spent some time at the World Bank in its early years. Whether through a big push or otherwise, many poor countries have managed to grow quickly over the past few decades, so why have so many others been left behind?

A theory of government banditry

As our car slowly bumped and lurched through the crowds, I tried to make sense of it all by asking Sam, the driver, about the country.

"Sam, how long was it since the roads were last fixed?"

"The roads, they have not been fixed for nineteen years." (President Paul Biya came to power in November 1982 and had been in office for nineteen years by the time I visited Cameroon. Four years later, in 2005, he is still in power. He recently described his opponents as "political amateurs"—they are certainly out of practice.)

"Don't people complain about the roads?"

"They complain, but nothing is done. The government tells us there is no money. But there is plenty of money coming

from the World Bank and from France and Britain and America—but they put it in their pockets. They do not spend it on the roads."

"Are there elections in Cameroon?"

"Yes! There are elections. President Biya is always reelected with a 90-percent majority."

"Do 90 percent of people vote for President Biya?"

"No, they do not. He is very unpopular. But still there is a 90-percent majority."

You do not have to spend a long time in Cameroon to realize how much people resent the government. Much of government activity appears to be designed expressly to steal money from the people of Cameroon. I was warned so starkly about government corruption, and the likelihood that officials at the airport would attempt to relieve me of my wad of francs, that I was more nervous about that than any risk of malaria or a gunpoint mugging in the back streets of Douala.

Many people have an optimistic view of politicians and civil servants—that they are all serving the people and doing their best to look after the interests of the country. Other people are more cynical, suggesting that many politicians are incompetent and often trade off the public interest against their own chances of reelection.

An economist called Mancur Olson suggested a working assumption that government motivations are darker still and produced a remarkable and simple theory of why stable dictatorships should be worse for economic growth than democracies, but better than anarchies. Olson supposed that governments are simply bandits, people with the biggest guns who will turn up and take everything. That's the starting point of his analysis—a starting point that you will have no trouble accepting if you spend five minutes looking around you in Cameroon. As Sam said, "There is plenty of money . . . but they put it in their pockets."

So imagine a dictator with a tenure of one week: effectively, a bandit with a roving army who sweeps in, takes whatever he wishes, and leaves again. Assuming he's neither malevolent nor kindhearted, but purely self-interested, what incentive does he have to leave anything? The answer is none . . . unless he plans on coming back next year.

But imagine that the roaming bandit likes the climate of a certain spot and decides to settle down, building a palace and encouraging his army to avail themselves of the locals. Desperately unfair though it is, the locals are probably better off now that the dictator has decided to stay. A purely self-interested dictator will realize that he cannot destroy the economy and starve the people if he plans on sticking around, because then he would exhaust all the resources and have nothing to steal the following year. And so a dictator who lays claim to a land is a preferable leader than one who moves around constantly in search of new victims to plunder.

Although it may seem totally unrelated, biology offers a helpful archetype for the political economist here: viruses and bacteria tend to become much less virulent over time, because the most extreme strains die out rapidly. When syphilis was first recorded in Europe in the late fifteenth century, it was described as being a tremendously aggressive disease, which quickly killed the victim. This is not a terribly successful strategy—it's much better to be a virus that allows its victims to live, at least for a little while, to spread the disease. So mutant strains of syphilis that killed people less quickly turned out to be much more successful and longer-lasting that the more virulent strains.

The evolution of diseases certainly stuck in my mind when I thought of President Biya. I cannot confirm that he fits Olson's description of a self-interested dictator. But if he did, it wouldn't be in his interests to take too much from the Cameroonian people, because otherwise there would be nothing to take next year. As long as he feels secure in his tenure, he will not wish to kill the golden goose. Like the disease whose very existence relies on the bodies it afflicts, Biya would have to keep the Cameroonian

economy functioning in order to keep stealing from it. This suggests that a leader who confidently expects to be in power for twenty years will do more to cultivate his economy than one who expects to flee the country after twenty weeks. Twenty years of an "elected dictator" is probably better than twenty years of one coup after another. Long live President Biya?

This is not to say that Mancur Olson's theory predicts that stable dictatorships should do good things for their countries, simply that they should damage the economy less than unstable ones. But leaders like Biya who are confident of always winning elections, are still very detrimental to the people and economies of their countries. Staying with the simplifying assumption that Biya has absolute power over the distribution of Cameroon's income, he might decide to steal, say, half of it every year in the form of "tax," which goes into his personal bank account. That would be bad news for his victims, of course, but also bad news for Cameroon's long-term growth. Think of a small businessman considering an investment of $1,000 in a new power generator for his workshop. The investment is expected to generate income of $100 a year. That's 10 percent, a pretty good return. But since Biya might take half of it, the return falls to a much less attractive 5 percent. The businessman decides not to make the investment after all, so he misses out and so does Biya. That's an extreme example of the phenomenon we discovered in chapter 3: taxes cause inefficiency. Biya's taxes are more arbitrary and larger, but the fundamental effect on the economy is similar in nature.

Of course, Biya might make his own investments, for instance, providing roads or bridges to encourage commerce. While they would be expensive in the short-term, they would help the economy to prosper leaving Biya with opportunities to steal later. But the flip side of the same problem applies: Biya would be stealing only half of the benefits, not nearly enough to encourage him to provide the infrastructure that Cameroon needs. When Biya came to power in 1982, he inherited colonial-era roads that had

yet to fall apart completely. If he had inherited a country without any infrastructure, it would have been in his interests to build it up to some extent. Because that infrastructure was already in place, Biya needed to calculate whether it was worth maintaining, or whether he could simply live off the legacy of the past. In 1982 he probably thought that the roads would last into the 1990s, which was as long as he could reasonably expect to hold onto the reins of power. And so he decided to live off the capital of the past and never bothered to invest in any type of infrastructure for his people. As long as there was enough to get him through his rule, why bother spending money that could otherwise go right into his personal retirement fund?

Am I being unfair to President Biya? Perhaps a little. In the 2004 elections, which took place after my visit to Cameroon, Biya secured about 75 percent of the vote in an election, which many observers regarded as at least passably fair. According to Olson's theory, a leader who needs to secure broader support for his policies will need to spend more government revenues on wealth-creating goods and services like roads and courts, and less on himself and his cronies. The fact that Biya has failed to do this but remains in office provokes two questions: first, is it possible that the elections were not as democratic as some observers have concluded? Second, could Biya provide wealth-creating goods and services even if he wanted?

Bandits, bandits everywhere

Perhaps Biya is not in control as much as it first appears. If you want to drive from the town of Buea to Bamenda, farther north, the most popular way to make the trip is by bus; minibuses ply all long-distance routes in Cameroon. Designed to seat ten people in comfort, they will depart as soon as thirteen paying passengers have boarded. The relatively capacious seat beside the driver is worth fighting for. The vehicles are old boneshakers, but the system works pretty well.

It would work a lot better if not for the malign influence of government. Sometimes the problem is simply neglect. For example the quickest, though certainly not the most direct, route from Buea to Bamenda is through the French-speaking part of Cameroon, which has better roads. Simply drive east for two hours, north for two hours and then west for two hours. This is much faster than driving directly north on the appalling roads of the English-speaking region of Cameroon. Biya's government tends to ignore the interests of the politically impotent English-speaking regions. The English-speaking minority complains that when donors funded Cameroon's beltway, the government just sent them the receipts but didn't bother to build the English section.

The second obstacle, literally, is the multitude of police road-blocks. Bullying gendarmes, often drunk, stop every minibus and try their best to extract bribes from the passengers. They usually fail but from time to time they become determined. My friend Andrew was once hauled off a bus and harassed for several hours. The eventual pretext for the bribe was his lack of a yellow-fever certificate, which you need when you enter the country but not when riding a bus. The gendarme explained patiently that Cameroon had to be protected from disease. The price of two beers convinced him that an epidemic had been prevented, and Andrew caught the next bus, three hours later.

This is even less efficient than Mancur Olson's model predicts. Olson himself would have admitted that his theory in its starkest form underestimates the damage that bad governments inflict on their people. President Biya needs to keep hundreds of thousands of armed police and army officers happy, as well as many civil servants and other supporters. In a "perfect" dictatorship, he would simply impose the least-damaging taxes possible in whatever quantity was necessary and distribute the proceeds to his supporters. This approach to government turns out to be impracticable because it requires far more information about and control over the economy than a poor government can possibly muster. The substitute is government-tolerated corruption on a massive scale.

The corruption is not only unfair, it is also hugely wasteful. Gendarmes spend their time harassing travelers in return for rather modest returns. The costs are enormous. An entire police force is too busy extracting bribes to catch criminals. A four-hour trip takes five hours. Travelers will have to take costly steps to protect themselves: carrying less money, traveling less often or at busier times of day, bringing extra paperwork to help fend off attempts to extract bribes.

The blockades and crooked police officers comprise a particularly visible form of corruption, but there are metaphorical roadblocks throughout the Cameroonian economy. The World Bank threw light on them when it recently started collecting data about simple business regulations. The bank discovered that in order to set up a small business, an entrepreneur in Cameroon must spend on official fees nearly as much as the average Cameroonian makes in two years. (My expenditure on a tourist visa pales into insignificance in comparison.) To buy or sell property costs nearly a fifth of the property's value. To get the courts to enforce an unpaid invoice takes nearly two years, costs over a third of the invoice's value, and requires fifty-eight separate procedures. These ridiculous regulations are good news for the bureaucrats who enforce them. Every procedure is an opportunity to extract a bribe. The slower the standard processes, the greater is the temptation to pay "speed money." As a result, President Biya enjoys the support of enough officials to keep him firmly in power.

Yet that is not the only result. Inflexible labor regulations help make sure that only experienced professional men are given formal contracts; women and young people have to fend for themselves in the gray market. Red tape discourages new businesses. Slow courts mean that entrepreneurs are forced to turn down attractive opportunities with new customers, because they know they cannot protect themselves if they are cheated. Poor countries have the worst examples of such regulations, and that is one of the major reasons they are poor. Governments

in rich countries usually perform these basic bureaucratic tasks quickly and cheaply, whereas governments in poor countries draw out the processes in hopes of pocketing some extra cash themselves.

Institutions matter

Government banditry, widespread waste, and oppressive regulations designed to make it easier to extract bribes: all are elements of that missing piece of the growth and development puzzle. Over the past ten years or so, economists working on development issues have converged on the mantra that "institutions matter." Of course, it is hard to describe what an "institution" really is; it is even harder to convert a bad institution into a good one.

But progress is being made. Mancur Olson's theory of government banditry helps us understand, in a simplified form, how different kinds of government might affect the incentives of everyone in the country, although it gives us little guidance as to how to make things better.

The World Bank's measurement of red tape gives us an excellent sense of one kind of institution: simple business regulations. The project also shows how simple publicity can improve some of those institutions. For example, after the World Bank advertised the fact that entrepreneurs in Ethiopia couldn't legally start a business without paying four years' salary to publish an official notice in government newspapers, the Ethiopian government relented and decided to scrap the regulation. New business registrations jumped by almost 50 percent immediately.

Unfortunately, it is not always so easy to get corrupt governments to change their ways. Although it is becoming clearer and clearer that dysfunctional institutions are a key explanation of poverty in developing countries, most institutions cannot be described with an elegant model like Mancur Olson's, nor even with careful data-gathering from the World Bank. Most unhappy institutions are unhappy in their own way.

The world's worst library

Just such a uniquely backfiring institutional setup was responsible for the world's worst library. A few days after I arrived in Cameroon, I visited one of the country's most prestigious private schools, Cameroon's equivalent of Eton. The school is not far from the city of Bamenda. The school grounds were a mix of the familiar and the odd: low, cheaply built classrooms surrounding playing fields reminded me very much of my old school in England, but a tree-lined avenue of crazy paving (Tim Burton meets *Born Free*), along which all the teachers live, did not.

We were being shown around the school by the librarian, a volunteer for the British-based voluntary organization VSO, which aims to place skilled volunteers where they are most needed in poor countries. The school boasted two separate library buildings, but the librarian was most unhappy—and I soon understood why.

At first glance the library was very impressive. With the exception of the principal's palatial house, it was the only two-story structure on campus. Its design was adventurous: a poor man's Sydney Opera house. The sloped roof, rather than running down from a ridge, soared up in a V from a central valley like the pages of an open book on a stand.

Despite its creative design, I am sure that my memories of the spectacular new library will last far longer than the building does. Standing in the blazing sunlight of the Cameroonian dry season, it's hard to see at first what the problem is with a roof that looks like a giant open book. But that would be to forget, as the architect apparently did, that Cameroon also has a rainy season. When it rains in Cameroon, it rains for five solid months and so hard that even the most massive storm ditches quickly overflow. When that kind of rain meets not so much a guttered roof as a roof that is, essentially, a gutter that drains onto the flat-roofed entrance hall, then you know it's time to laminate the book collection.

The only reason the school's books still existed was because they'd never been near the new building; the librarian had re-

fused repeated requests from the principal to transfer them from the old library. I was tempted to conclude that the principal was in an advanced stage of denial when I stepped inside the new library to see the devastation. It was in ruins. The floor contained the stains of countless puddles. The air carried the kind of musty smell I associate with a damp cave in Europe, not a modern building on the equator. The plaster was peeling off the walls like a thousand-year-old Byzantine fresco. Yet the library is only four years old.

This is a shocking waste. Instead of building the library, the school could have bought forty thousand good books, or computers with Internet connections, or they could have funded scholarships for poor children. Any of these alternatives would have been incomparably better than an unusable new library. This leaves aside the fact that the school never needed a new library in the first place—the old library works perfectly well, could easily hold three times as many books as the school owns, and is waterproof.

The fact that the library was unnecessary goes some way to explaining its poor design. After all, nobody pays too much attention to the functionality of a building whose functions are redundant. But if the library was such a pointless endeavor, why was it built at all?

Napoleon is often credited with the statement, "Never ascribe to conspiracy that which is adequately explained by incompetence." That's the natural response: incompetence is an easy scapegoat. It's all too tempting for the visitor in Cameroon to shrug his shoulders and explain Cameroon's poverty by presuming that Cameroonians are idiots. The library looks like good evidence, but Cameroonians are no smarter or more foolish than the rest of us. Seemingly stupid mistakes are so ubiquitous in Cameroon that incompetence cannot be the adequate explanation we're looking for. There is something more systematic at work. Once again, we need to consider the incentives of the decision makers.

First, most of the senior education officials in northwest Cameroon come from the small town of Bafut. Known as the "Bafut

Mafia," these officials control considerable funds for the education system, which they hand out on the basis of personal connections rather than necessity. Not surprisingly, the principal of this prestigious private school was a senior member of the "Bafut Mafia." Wanting to convert her school into a university, the principal needed to build a library building of university size and quality. It was irrelevant to the principal that the current library was more than sufficient, and that the taxpayers' money could have been better spent in other ways or by other schools.

Second, nobody was monitoring the principal or her spending. Members of staff in the education system are not paid or promoted on merit but absolutely on the decisions of the principal. This is a prestigious school with good conditions for teachers, so staff would be particularly eager to keep their jobs, which meant keeping in good favor with the principal. In fact, the only person with the ability to defy the principal was the librarian, who was accountable only to the VSO head office in London. She turned up after the library was built but was at least in time to prevent the book collection from being transferred and destroyed. The principal was either so stupid that she did not realize that water ruins books, or she did not care very much about the books and simply wanted to demonstrate that the library had some books in it. The second explanation seems more likely.

With the money at her fingertips and nobody to object to the wastefulness of building a second library, the principal had full control over the project. She appointed a former pupil of the school to design the library, probably to demonstrate the quality of education provided by the school; she did prove a point, although perhaps not the one she intended. But no matter how incompetent the architect, the flaws in the design would have been spotted if anybody concerned had a strong interest in making sure that the library functioned as a library. But that was never the prime concern of anybody with any authority. The people in power simply cared about putting up *something* that could qualify the school as a university.

Consider the situation: money that was provided because of social networks rather than need; a project designed for prestige rather than to be used; a lack of monitoring and accountability; and an architect appointed for show by somebody with little interest in the quality of the work. The outcome is hardly surprising: a project that should never have been built was built, and built badly.

The lesson of the story might appear to be that self-interested and ambitious people in power are often the cause of wastefulness in developing countries. The truth is a little sadder than that. Self-interested and ambitious people are in positions of power, great and small, all over the world. In many places, they are restrained by the law, the press, and democratic opposition. Cameroon's tragedy is that there is nothing to hold self-interest in check.

The plot thickens—incentives and development in Nepal

The Cameroonian education system gives administrators such perverse incentives that educating children is the last thing anyone profits from doing, and hence, the last thing education officials focus on.

Other development projects involve more subtle webs of unusual incentives. One example was uncovered by the economist Elinor Ostrom, who looked in detail at the intricate irrigation designs in Nepal. In addition to older traditional systems of dams and canals, Nepal also has some modern concrete dams and canals, designed by expert engineers and funded by big international donor organizations. Which works best, and why?

When I heard about this study I thought I could guess the punch line. The obvious conclusion is that the best of modern design, materials, and engineering, with massive funding, should produce a better irrigation system than a bunch of farmers using mud and sticks, right? Wrong.

We know better now. We know that large dam projects have often been poorly suited to local conditions, and that in fact "small is beautiful"—local methods and traditional knowledge handed down over long years from generation to generation turn out to work far better. Right? Wrong again.

It turns out that the real story in Nepal is much more interesting than either of these oversimplified assumptions. Elinor Ostrom identified an apparent paradox. The first part of the paradox is that modern dams, which are professionally designed and built, seem to reduce the effectiveness of irrigation systems. But the second part of the paradox is that when donors pay to have irrigation channels built, or reinforced with modern materials, they strengthen the irrigation system, reliably delivering more water to more people.

Why can donors provide effective irrigation channels, but not effective dams? Clearly there is something more subtle going on than the tired debate between modern technical expertise and traditional wisdom. The truth is clearer to someone who tries to work out the motivations of all concerned.

Start with the obvious insight that any project is most likely to be successful if the people who benefit from its success are the same people who make it possible. That immediately explains why the existing methods of irrigation might have an advantage, not because they are full of traditional wisdom (they may be, of course) but because they're designed, built, and maintained by the farmers who use them. The modern dams and canals, by contrast, are designed by engineers who will not starve if the dams fail, commissioned by civil servants whose jobs do not rest on their success, and paid for by donor agency officials who are more likely to be judged by procedure than results. Immediately we start to see why better materials and vastly superior funding do not necessarily lead to success.

Looking deeper still, irrigation systems have to be maintained to be of any use. But who will maintain them? Neither donor agencies nor civil servants have as much interest in maintenance as they should. Nepalese civil servants are promoted mostly by

seniority and partly by being associated with "prestige" construction projects. Maintenance is a dead-end job, regardless of whether it pays dividends for the farmers. What civil servant would want to oversee an unending menial task, far from Kathmandu where his wife shops and his children go to school? On top of that, bribes are always a potential source of income for civil servants, and a large construction contract offers much greater chances of accepting backhanders than does maintenance work.

Like the civil service, donor agencies work under constraints that tend to favor large construction projects. All donor agencies need expensive projects because if they fail to spend cash, they are unlikely to raise more. In addition many bilateral aid organizations, like USAID, are tied to country-specific types of aid: USAID typically has to use equipment purchased in the United States, which tends to be heavy, high-tech machinery. Since bulldozers are of more use building a dam than maintaining it, the outcome is yet again in favor of big construction projects. Even if the donor agency has no bias toward large projects, they still have to rely on the information they receive from local staff and consultants—who will often have the same incentives as the civil service.

All of this starts to explain why those who commission construction projects do not have as much interest in building good, cost-effective systems as do the farmers. But it does not explain Ostrom's finding that donor-funded dams actually make things worse, and neither does it explain why donor-funded irrigation canals seem to work well despite the fact that the people who commission them don't much care whether they do or not. To understand why, we need to think about the farmers themselves.

Nobody except the farmers is likely to be very interested in maintaining an irrigation system once it is built. This may not be a problem. Before any major modern irrigation systems were built, the farmers had to maintain the traditional systems. If they could maintain the traditional systems, can't they maintain the modern ones, too?

Maintenance requires two big jobs: keeping the dam in one piece, and clearing the canals of obstructions. This is a lot of work. Farmers won't bother unless they see the benefits, and this potentially leads to a problem. The problem is that while all farmers need the dam to be kept in one piece, farmers near the dam don't much care what happens to the drainage canals farther down the hill. So why should they bother to help with the drainage canals? Fortunately, most farming communities in Nepal have worked out a system of cooperation; while the details differ, the general principle is that the farmers downstream help maintain the dam in exchange for assistance on the canals. So far, so good.

If a big donor pays for new, concrete canals to be installed, then things will improve—the new canals are better, carry more water, and require less maintenance. But if a big donor pays for a new dam, everything falls apart. This is not because the dam itself does: quite the reverse. Because the concrete dam needs much *less* maintenance than the traditional one, the cooperative agreement, which maintained the entire irrigation system, no longer works. The traditional bargain breaks down. Upstream farmers no longer help clear the canals in exchange for help on the dam from downstream farmers. The upstream farmers don't need help, so the downstream farmers no longer have anything to offer on their side of the deal.

Many modern irrigation systems in Nepal end in failure because although the technical properties of the system may have been understood and improved, the human properties of the system have not been addressed at all.

This Nepalese example is yet another demonstration that if a society cannot provide the right kind of incentives to behave productively, no amount of technical infrastructure can save it from poverty. Development projects are often commissioned by people with no great interest in success but a great interest in bribes and career advancement. If the effectiveness of the project is a minor consideration, then it can hardly be a surprise if the project does not deliver on the publicly announced aims, even if it has deliv-

ered on the *real* aims of enriching bureaucrats. And even if the project was one that would still have been commissioned if genuine development really was the goal, bribes and other distortions are likely to spoil things.

Is there a chance for development?

Development specialists often focus on helping poor countries become richer by improving primary education and infrastructure like roads and telephones, and that's surely sensible. Unfortunately, it's only a small part of the problem. Economists who have pulled apart the statistics, or studied unusual data such as the earnings of Cameroonians in Cameroon and the earnings of Cameroonians who emigrate to the United States, have found that education, infrastructure, and factories don't begin to explain the gap between rich and poor. Because of its lousy education system, Cameroon is perhaps twice as poor as it could be. Because of its terrible infrastructure, it's roughly twice as poor again. So we would expect Cameroon to be four times poorer than the United States, but it is fifty times poorer. More importantly, why can't the Cameroonian people seem to do anything about it? Couldn't Cameroonian communities improve their schools? Wouldn't the benefits easily outweigh the costs? Couldn't Cameroonian businessmen build factories, license technology, seek foreign partners . . . and make a fortune?

Evidently not. Mancur Olson showed that kleptocracy at the top stunts the growth of poor countries. Having a thief for president doesn't necessarily spell doom; the president might prefer to boost the economy and then take a slice of a bigger pie. But in general, looting will be widespread either because the dictator is not confident of his tenure, or because he needs to allow others to steal in order to keep their support.

Then farther down the pyramid of wealth, development is thwarted because the rules and laws of the society do not encourage projects or businesses, which would be to the common good. Entrepreneurs don't establish official businesses (too difficult)

and so don't pay taxes; officials demand ridiculous projects for their prestige or personal enrichment; schoolchildren don't bother to acquire irrelevant qualifications.

It is not news to hear that corruption and perverse incentives matter. But perhaps it is news to find out that the problem of twisted rules and institutions explains not just a little bit of the gap between Cameroon and rich countries but almost all of the gap. Countries like Cameroon fall far below their potential even considering their poor infrastructure, low investment, and minimal education. But worse than that, the web of corruption foils every effort to improve the infrastructure, attract investment, and improve educational standards.

Cameroon's education system would be better if people had an incentive to get a good education; if a meritocracy were in place, and good grades and real skills—rather than personal connections—earned jobs. Cameroon would have better technology and more working factories if the investment climate was right, either for foreign or domestic investors, and if the profits weren't eaten up in bribes and red tape.

The small amount of education and technology and infrastructure that Cameroon does have could be much better used if the society was organized to reward good, productive ideas. But it is not.

We still don't have a good word to describe what is missing in Cameroon, indeed, in poor countries across the world. But we are starting to understand what it is. Some people call it "social capital," or maybe "trust." Others call it "the rule of law," or "institutions." But these are just labels. The problem is that Cameroon, like other poor countries, is a topsy-turvy world in which it's in most people's interest to take action that directly or indirectly damages everyone else. The incentives to create wealth in any way at all are turned on their heads just as surely at the roof of the school library.

The rot starts with government but it afflicts the entire society. There's no point investing in a business because the govern-

ment will not protect you against thieves. (So, you might as well become a thief.) There's no point in paying your phone bill because nobody can successfully take you to court (so there's no point being a phone company). There's no point getting an education because jobs are not handed out on merit (and in any case, you can't borrow money for school fees because the bank cannot collect on the loan, and the government doesn't provide good schools). There's no point setting up an import business because the customs officers will be the ones to benefit (and so there is little trade, and so the customs office is underfunded and looks even harder for bribes).

Now we are starting to understand just how important this is, we can begin to put it right. But it's in the nature of the problem to resist solutions, so this is a slow and difficult process. We don't usually find it acceptable to set up democracies by force, and they usually don't last when we do. We don't like development aid to be lost in red tape, but making sure the money is well spent is very time consuming.

These problems cannot be fixed overnight. But there are some simple reforms, which—with a modicum of political will—would move poor countries like Cameroon in the right direction. One simple reform is to cut red tape, allowing small businesses to be legally established, which makes it easier for their entrepreneurs to expand and borrow money. The legal reforms necessary are often trivial; and while they still rely on sensible and benevolent government, all it takes is a single minister with his head and his heart in the right place, rather than hoping for an entire civil service to permanently reform.

Another option, and a vital one, is to enlist the world economy for help. Most poor countries are also very small economies; the entire economy of sub-Saharan Africa is about the size of Belgium's. A small African state like Chad has an economy smaller than that of a Washington suburb like Bethesda and a banking sector smaller than the Federal Credit union set up for World Bank staff. Tiny countries like Chad and Cameroon cannot possibly be self sufficient: they need access to cheap fuel, raw

materials, loans from international banks, and manufacturing equipment. But Cameroonians are trapped behind high barriers to trade—among the highest tariffs in the world at more than 60 percent. Such barriers generate revenue for the government and allow it to protect the businesses of cronies or hand out profitable import licenses. A small country cannot survive without the world economy. With it, small countries can thrive. In the next chapter we shall visit one, and find out how.

NINE

Beer, Fries,
and Globalization

Once upon a time there was a prosperous trading city called Bruges, nestling on the Zwin estuary in what is now Belgium. Bruges grew up around a castle built in the late ninth century by the founder of the Duchy of Flanders. A century later Bruges was Flanders's capital, and it began to grow wealthy as trade expanded across Northern Europe. Bruges was a center for the manufacturing of cloth, and ships sailed up the Zwin estuary to buy the fabric, bringing with them English cheese, wool, and minerals, Spanish wine, Russian furs, Danish pork, and silks and spices from the East, traded through the mighty Italian cities of Venice and Genoa. The queen of France herself visited Bruges in 1301 and is reported to have commented, "I thought I alone was queen, but I see that I have six hundred rivals here."

Bruges's wealth continued to flow in for 250 years, despite conquest by the French and the Dukes of Burgundy. Regardless of who was in charge, Bruges continued to prosper: it was the center of gravity for the Hanseatic League of trading cities, its arts scene was flourishing, it was developing new industries such as cutting diamonds from India, and its population was twice that of London. Fine goods from across the world were traded in the tavern owned by the merchant family Van der Beurs—some would have you believe that this is why, to this day, stock exchanges are

called "bourses." Tall masts and broad sails adorned the Zwin estuary.

But in the fifteenth century something strange began to happen. The Zwin began to silt up. The great ships could no longer reach the docks of Bruges. The Hanseatic League moved up the coast to Antwerp. Bruges quickly and literally became a backwater. So lifeless did it become that it was nicknamed "Bruges-La-Morte." Today it is a quaint museum piece. Perfectly preserved, it hums busily only because of the tourists eager to visit a time capsule: a beautiful and prosperous trading city of the fifteenth century whose wealth and development dried up with the river.

Meanwhile, Antwerp, still connected to the world via the Scheldt River, took over from Bruges as the greatest economic power in Western Europe. The wealth of that time is clearly visible today: Antwerp's great cathedral dominates the skyline, and more striking still to the first-time visitor are the great guild houses of the Grote Markt, which soar five, six, seven stories above the cobblestones, and appear even higher yet because of their spindly architecture of spires and pencil-thin windows. Although the appearance of air, rail, and motorized road transportation have diminished its geographical advantages, Antwerp remains an economic powerhouse. It is still the diamond capital of the world, and the mighty port on the Scheldt operates around the clock.

The contrasting stories of Bruges and Antwerp suggest a simple message: if you would like to be rich, then it is a good idea to forge close links with the rest of the world. If you prefer nothing to change, then it is best to have a harbor that silts up. If you would like to be rich *and* have nothing change, then you will be disappointed.

There are few pleasures I enjoy more than sitting in Antwerp, wolfing down hot fries smothered in mayonnaise and cooling my mouth with a heady, fizzy beer. Of course, being an economist, I am inclined to contemplate the world trading system as I do. Fries from *Frituur No. 1* simply cannot be matched anywhere in

the world. But the glass of Duvel beer to wash them down is obtained without difficulty in Washington DC. It may cost twice as much but it tastes every bit as good and is certainly just as potent. So when I am in Antwerp, sitting just off the Grote Markt and enjoying a Duvel, I cannot help but feel a little sad that this thrill has been cheapened by its ready availability in my home city. Of course, when in Washington DC—and sober—I can only praise the noble and enterprising merchants who have brought exotic beers such as Duvel, Chimay, and Maredsous 10 to my doorstep, and look forward to when they get around to importing Westmalle Trippel as well.

The most visible manifestation of the world's increasing economic interdependence is the availability of foreign products in familiar settings. It is both a blessing and a curse: a blessing because it becomes possible to enjoy a wider variety of treats without straying far from the place you were born. It is a curse because when you do travel you may find that foreign places look a little too familiar. From McDonalds in Moscow to Starbucks in Shanghai, are we not all becoming the same? The whole world seems to have become one seething mass of internationalization. The commerce with foreign lands that was once the preserve of Florence, Venice, and Bruges now appears ubiquitous.

If you spend too much time in airports, hotel chains, and capital cities it is easy to feel this way; but we live in a big and varied world. You may be able to visit Starbucks in Shanghai, but Starbucks is not the whole of Shanghai and Shanghai is not the whole of China. The world has a long way to go before it truly is "globalized," if by that odd word we mean "the same everywhere." No doubt we are on the way. Reading biologist Edward O. Wilson, I discover that in a few dozen generations all human beings will be "the same," in the sense that whether in London or Shanghai or Moscow or Lagos, the same racial mix would be found. Viewed differently, the variety of human beings would be unprecedented: as this process of racial mixing accelerates, "many more combinations of skin color, facial features, talents, and other traits influenced by genes are now arising than ever existed before."

Personally I find both predictions encouraging, although others might find them alarming.

The same is true for cultures, technology, economic systems, and the range of products available. On the one hand they will increasingly resemble each other across the world; on the other, in any one place they will display tremendous diversity and exciting new mixes, as anyone who enjoys Ethiopian stir-fry Tibbs in Washington DC, Japanese sashimi in Antwerp, or Bangladeshi curries in London will attest. Like racial intermixing, economic and cultural integration will take a long time. Furthermore, new ideas and new technologies are always arriving. Globalization will never homogenize what we have, not while new ideas are always appearing and adding fresh ingredients to the slowly turning blender of economic integration. Those who fear a terrible global sameness must remember that new ideas, welcome or unwelcome, will always arise faster than they can be mixed in.

But perhaps by commenting on culture and race I am stepping well outside the boundaries of my expertise. I shall therefore return to economics, where my "comparative advantage" lies.

Comparative advantage is the foundation of the way economists think about trade. Let's picture it this way: who is the better economics writer, me, or E. O. Wilson? Professor Wilson is "one of the twentieth century's greatest thinkers" and "considered to be one of the world's greatest living scientists" according to the jacket of his book *Consilience*. His chapter on social science was written after interviewing some of the world's greatest economists; the result was an insightful explanation, which introduced me to plenty of things I didn't know about economics. The truth is that E. O. Wilson is probably a better economist than I am.

So I know when I'm beaten. Why write a book about economics when Professor Wilson could write a better one? The answer is comparative advantage. Because of comparative advantage, Professor Wilson hasn't written a book about economics, and I'm fairly confident he never will.

We owe the idea of comparative advantage to the star of chapter one, David Ricardo. If Wilson and I shared David Ricardo as an agent, he might advise us as follows: "Tim, if you write biology books you are unlikely to get more than one sale per year of writing—the one your wife buys. But your economics is passable, and we predict sales of twenty-five thousand books for every year you spend writing. Professor Wilson, your economics books will probably sell five hundred thousand copies for every year you spend writing: but why not stick to the biology books and sell ten million?"

E. O. Wilson is twenty times as good an economics writer as I am, but, advised by David Ricardo, he sticks to writing biology, a subject at which he is ten million times more accomplished than I. On a personal level, Ricardo's advice is plain common sense: E. O. Wilson should choose his vocation not with reference to what he does better than I do, but with reference to what he does best. Meanwhile, I would be well advised to make a living as an economics writer, not because I am the best economics writer in the world but because economics writing is what *I* do best.

Ricardo's advice becomes more controversial when it comes to trading with the Chinese. "Chinese wages are so much lower than ours," cry the protectionists. "They can make televisions and toys and clothes and all kinds of things much more cheaply than we can. We should protect our domestic producers with a tax on Chinese products—or perhaps an outright ban." And so we do. The United States defends the interests of American companies (but not the American people) by blocking Chinese imports through "antidumping" laws. Dumping, according to these laws, is selling products cheaply. But the truth is that this is not dumping, but competition. Who benefits when, for example, Chinese furniture is blocked because it is "unfairly" cheap? American furniture manufacturers, perhaps. Certainly not the average American who wants to buy furniture. Many Europeans, meanwhile, cannot afford large, high-definition television screens because the European Union is trying desperately to prevent their

arrival from China. Steel, which China now produces more than the United States and Japan combined, was recently subject to illegal tariffs imposed by the United States. Agriculture is even more highly protected.

Isn't this necessary to stem what would otherwise be a flood of cheap foreign products under which our domestic industry would drown? It is not. The United States ought to produce goods and services not by asking what it does more cheaply than China but by focusing on what the United States does best.

Ricardo's insight is that trade barriers—whether they are subsidies to our farmers, regulations on textiles, or taxes on televisions—make both us and the Chinese worse off. It does not matter if the Chinese really are better than we are at making everything: they should stick to producing whatever their economy is most efficient at turning out. Meanwhile, we, despite (apparently) being worse at everything, should stick to producing what we are least bad at producing. The argument is the same as one the spirit of David Ricardo gave to me and E. O. Wilson: I may be worse at everything, but I should still produce the economics books while E. O. Wilson sticks to biology. Yet barriers to trade are also barriers to this common-sense arrangement.

An example may help to persuade the unconvinced. Let's say an American worker could produce a machine drill in half an hour, or a flat-screen TV in an hour. A Chinese worker could produce a machine drill in twenty minutes or a flat-screen TV in ten. The Chinese worker is evidently the E. O. Wilson of manufacturing. (Incidentally, the productivity numbers in this example are not only fictional but fantastical. Sadly for the Chinese, workers in developing countries are far less productive than workers in developed countries. They are able to compete only because they are paid much less; in fact, the relationship between lower wages and lower productivity is an extremely close one.)

If China and America do not trade, it takes ninety minutes work to produce a flat-screen TV and a drill to mount it on the wall in the United States. In China the TV and drill can be made

in half an hour. If the protectionists get their way, then that is how things will stay.

If there are no trade barriers, we can trade with each other and both be better off. The Chinese worker makes two televisions, which take her twenty minutes, and the American makes two drills, which take him an hour. Trade one drill for one television and both are better off than when they started, having saved a third of their time. Of course, being more efficient the Chinese worker can quit work earlier, or earn more; but that does not mean the American worker has lost because of trade. Quite the reverse.

It's true that if the Chinese worker put in a bit of overtime, she could do her own job and also do the same work as the American would have achieved all week. But why would she be so extraordinarily generous? The Chinese do not export televisions to the United States out of the goodness of their hearts; they do so because we send something in exchange—even if, as with our hypothetical machine drills, the Chinese are better at making them, too.

Contrary to popular belief, it is simply not possible for trade to destroy all of our jobs and for us to import everything from abroad and export nothing. If we did, we would have nothing to buy the imports with. For there to be trade at all, somebody in America must be making something to sell to the outside world.

This should be obvious, but somehow it isn't. Think of American workers in, say, Pittsburgh, producing those machine drills. The workers are paid in dollars. The factory is rented in dollars. The heat and light and telephone bills all come asking for payment in dollars. But the drills are exported to China and sold locally or used to make goods in the Chinese currency, the renminbi. The costs of production are in dollars, the revenues are in renminbi. Somewhere renminbi have to be "turned into" dollars to pay the Pittsburgh workers' salaries, but of course there is no process of magically turning dollars into renminbi. The only thing that will work is for an importer in the United States

to provide dollars in exchange for renminbi, which he will use to buy imports. Exports pay for imports.

Economics, surprisingly to some, is about the interconnectedness of things: goods and money do not just appear and disappear. Nobody outside the United States would accept dollars in payment if the United States was not exporting things that the dollars could be used to buy.

In a more complex world the dollars and renminbi, drills and televisions, will not be directly exchanged for each other. We sell drills to the Saudis, the Saudis sell oil to the Japanese, the Japanese sell robots to the Chinese, and the Chinese sell televisions to us. We can borrow money temporarily—the United States is currently doing this—or we can produce assets like machine drill factories and sell the factories rather than the machine drills. But the circular flow of currencies will balance out completely in the end. The United States can afford imports only if we eventually produce exports to pay for them, and the same is true for every country.

A more extreme example may clarify things further. Think of a country whose government is very keen on self-sufficiency. "We need to encourage our local economy," says the Minister for Trade and Industry. So the government bans all imports and patrols the coast to prevent smuggling. One effect will be that a lot of effort will be devoted to producing locally what was once imported: this certainly is encouragement to the local economy. But another effect is that all of the export industries will quickly shrivel and die. Why? Because who would want to spend time and money exporting goods in exchange for foreign currency, if nobody is allowed to spend the foreign currency on imports? While one part of the local economy is encouraged, another is crippled. The "no imports" policy is also a "no exports" policy. And indeed, one of the most important theorems of trade theory, the Lerner theorem, named after the economist Abba Lerner, proved in 1936 that a tax on imports is exactly equivalent to a tax on exports.

Lerner's theorem tells us that restricting imports of Chinese televisions to protect American jobs in television manufacturing makes as much sense as restricting exports of American machine drills to protect American jobs in television manufacturing. In fact, the American television manufacturing industry is not really competing against the Chinese television manufacturing industry at all; it is competing against the American machine drill industry. If the machine drill industry is more efficient, the television manufacturing industry will not survive, just as surely as E. O. Wilson's promising career as an economic journalist never got off the ground in the face of his superior skills as scientist.

This certainly makes us look at trade barriers in a new light. But it doesn't prove that trade barriers cause any harm: after all, mightn't the benefit of trade barriers to the American television manufacturing industry outweigh the harm to the American machine drill industry? David Ricardo's theory of comparative advantage tells us that the answer is no. As we know, under free trade, both Chinese and American workers can quit work earlier than they could under restricted trade, having produced the same amount as before.

The commonsense answer based on practical experience is also no: compare North Korea with South Korea, or Austria with Hungary. To take a very rough guide to how much better it is to have an open, liberal economy than a closed one, simply note that in 1990, just after the fall of the Berlin wall, the average Austrian was between two and six times richer than the average Hungarian (depending on how you measure it). The average South Korean is wealthy while the average North Korean is starving. North Korea is so isolated that it's hard to get any measurement of quite how poor the country is.

Trade barriers will always cause more harm than good, not just to the country against which the barrier is erected but also the country that erects the barriers. No matter if other countries choose to inflict trade restrictions on themselves, we're better off without. The great economist Joan Robinson once quipped that

just because others throw rocks into their harbor, that is no reason to throw rocks into our own. As the Zwin silted up, the citizens of Bruges were no doubt realizing the same truth centuries before.

None of this is to say that free trade is good for everybody. Competition from cheaper or better foreign products cannot put all of our domestic industries out of business, because otherwise we couldn't afford to buy the foreign products. But it can alter the balance of our economy. To go back to the example of machine drills and televisions, although in our example the Chinese are better at producing both machine drills and televisions, we still produce machine drills when trading with the Chinese. In fact, we produce twice as many machine drills as we did before, but our television manufacturing industry has been wiped out. Good for the machine drill industry, bad for the television manufacturing industry. People will lose their jobs. They will have to try to learn new skills and get reemployed in the machine drill sector, which may be easier said than done. Overall, the United States is better off, but some people will lose out, and the losers will curse free trade and demand restrictions on imported televisions, although we know now that they could equally demand restrictions on exported machine drills.

Even the most casual historian will be reminded of the Luddite rebellion in Britain. Luddism began in 1811 in the English midlands, a desperate response by skilled textile workers to competition from the latest technology: stocking and shearing frames. The Luddites were well-organized, destroying mills and machines ("frame-breaking") and protesting against the new economic system. Contrary to the modern stereotype of an unimaginative thug, the Luddites were responding to a real threat to their livelihoods.

So did technological change hurt some people? Without a doubt. Did it impoverish Britain as a whole? A ridiculous notion. Without minimizing the genuine suffering to those who lost their livelihoods along the way, it's obvious that technological progress made us far better off.

Trade can be thought of as another form of technology. Economist David Friedman observes, for instance, that there are two ways for the United States to produce automobiles: they can build them in Detroit, or they can grow them in Iowa. Growing them in Iowa makes use of a special technology that turns wheat into Toyotas: simply put the wheat onto ships and send them out into the Pacific ocean. The ships come back a short while later with Toyotas on them. The technology used to turn wheat into Toyotas out in the Pacific is called "Japan," but it could just as easily be a futuristic biofactory floating off the coast of Hawaii. Either way, auto workers in Detroit are in direct competition with farmers in Iowa. Import restrictions on Japanese cars will help the auto workers and hurt the farmers: they are the modern-day equivalent of "frame breaking."

The solution, in a civilized but progressive society, is not to ban new technology or to restrict trade. Neither is it to ignore the plight of those people put out of work by technology, trade, or indeed anything else. It is to allow progress to continue while helping support and retrain those who have been hurt as a result.

Perhaps that sounds callous. After all, even one person who wants a job and cannot find one is suffering a personal tragedy. Yet the interest groups who oppose free trade for their own profit have vastly overblown the effects of trade. Between 1993 and 2002, almost 310 million jobs were lost in the United States. Over the same period, more than 327 million jobs were created. Nearly 18 million more people had jobs in 2002 than in 1993. Each of the 310 million times somebody lost a job, that person was entitled to sympathy and to help, whether or not foreign competition had anything to do with it. Trade or no trade, a healthy economy loses jobs all the time, and creates them as well.

But is globalization a good thing?

It is one thing to say that trade makes countries like the United States richer. It is quite another to say that globalization is a good thing. To do justice to all the arguments about globalization would

take an entire book. In a short chapter there is time to address two common complaints about globalization. The first is that globalization is bad for the planet; the second is that globalization is bad for the world's poor.

We first need to be somewhat clearer about what globalization means, without becoming too technical. Even leaving aside noneconomic phenomena such as the spread of American television, Indian cooking, and Japanese martial arts, there is plenty to international economic integration besides trade. I would list at least five distinct issues: trade of goods and services; migration of people; the exchange of technical knowledge; "foreign direct investment," or building or buying factories and companies abroad; and cross-border investments in financial assets like shares and bonds.

Many discussions of globalization confuse all these. At the risk of oversimplification, let me set three to one side: migration, exchange of technology, and cross-border investments in financial assets. This is not because they are unimportant, but because they are not what people tend to think of when they talk about globalization. Migration is controversial for other reasons; generally, xenophobia and selfishness. On the other hand, few object to the spread of peaceful scientific and technical know-how. Cross-border investments in financial assets are the subject of considerable technical debate among economists; they are a great opportunity for both rich and poor but an opportunity that brings dangers. For the sake of space, we shall say no more about these three trends.

For most purposes, when people argue about globalization they are talking about the two trends that remain: more trade, and more direct investment by companies from rich countries, such as building factories in poor countries. A substantial proportion of foreign investment in poor countries is designed to produce goods for shipment back to rich countries; while this remains true, trade and foreign investment will be closely linked together. Foreign investment is widely recognized to be good for economic growth in poor countries: it is an excellent way for them to create

jobs, learn cutting-edge techniques, and do so without having to invest their own scarce money. Unlike investments in shares, currency, or bonds, foreign direct investment cannot quickly be reversed in a panic. As economics journalist Martin Wolf puts it, "factories do not walk."

Although trade with and investment in poor countries has risen rapidly in recent years, we should be clear that both trade and foreign investment overwhelmingly takes place between the richest countries, not between rich and poor. People look at their Nike shoes and assume, perhaps, that everything is made in Indonesia and China. However, far more money is spent importing wine from Australia, pork from Denmark, beer from Belgium, insurance from Switzerland, computer games from Britain, cars from Japan, and computers from Taiwan, all carried on ships from South Korea. These rich countries are mostly trading with each other. Mighty China, with about a quarter of the world's population, produces less than 4 percent of the world's exports. Mexico, a country of over a hundred million people, in a free trade agreement with the world's largest economy, the United States, and in a situation of rapidly expanding trade as the US economy was red hot in 2000, exported less than gallant little Belgium. Meanwhile India is nowhere at all, with a billion people producing less than 1 percent of world exports. And these figures are for physical merchandise: if you look at trade in commercial services, fuss over "offshoring" notwithstanding, developing countries participate even less.

What about the very poor countries? Sadly for them, rich countries trade very little with them—and as trade expands elsewhere in the world, the poorest countries are being left behind. North American imports from the least developed countries were only 0.6 percent of total imports in 2000, down from 0.8 percent in 1980. But 0.5 percent of Western Europe's imports in 2000 were from the least developed countries, down from 1 percent in 1980. For Japan, the figure is 0.3 percent, down from 1 percent. And for all the major world traders put together, the percentage of their imports from the least developed countries is 0.6 percent,

down from 0.9 percent twenty years before. For the really poor countries, their problem certainly isn't excessive participation in the world trading system. A similar story holds true for foreign investment.

The theory of comparative advantage, common sense, and experience all tell us that trade is good for economic growth; foreign direct investment is closely related to trade, and it, too, is good for growth. The poorest countries miss out on those benefits. This is a simplification but a fair one. In both cases, though, questions remain open: what is the effect of trade and foreign investment on the environment? And what is the effect of foreign investment in poor countries on those who have to accept so-called sweatshop jobs, poorly paid jobs in awful conditions?

Globalization is green

Take the environment first. We saw in chapter 4 that the economist's concept of externalities gives us a powerful tool to appreciate the risks of environmental damage, and externality charges give us a solution. Many—perhaps most—economists understand the risks of environmental damage and want action to preserve the environment.

But the link between trade and environmental damage just doesn't stand up to close scrutiny. There are three reasons for concern. The first concern is of a "race to the bottom": companies rush overseas to produce goods under cheaper, more lenient environmental laws, while hapless governments oblige them by creating those lenient laws. The second is that physically moving goods around inevitably consumes resources and causes pollution. The third worry is that if trade promotes economic growth, it must also harm the planet. While each has some initial plausibility, the idea that trade is bad for the environment is based on weak thinking and little evidence.

The first worry, that free trade causes environmental problems because goods produced overseas are subject to more lenient environmental standards, or no standards at all, should first

be qualified by reminding ourselves that the overwhelming majority of trade is between rich countries, who have similar environmental standards. But what about investment in poor countries? The environmentalist Vandana Shiva speaks for many when she declares that "pollution moves from the rich to the poor. The result is a global environmental apartheid." Strong words—but are they true?

In theory, they might be true. Companies that can produce goods more cheaply will be at a competitive advantage. They can also move around more easily in a world of free trade. So the "race to the bottom" is a possibility.

Then again, there are reasons to suspect that it's a fantasy. Environmental regulations are not a major cost; labor is. If American environmental standards are really so strict, why do the most pollution-intensive American firms spend only 2 percent of their revenues on dealing with pollution? Most spend much less. When companies move abroad they are seeking cheap labor, not a pollution haven. And companies do not pollute for fun; the latest manufacturing techniques are often cheaper and less polluting at the same time. Energy efficiency, for instance, saves money and reduces pollution. This is why many companies regard environmental performance as part of general quality control and good efficient manufacturing. Even if it was possible to save some costs by cutting environmental corners, many firms build factories everywhere in the world using the same latest, cleanest technology from the developed world, simply because that kind of standardization itself saves costs. As an analogy: if ten-year-old computer chips were still produced in bulk, they would be simpler and cheaper to make than modern chips, but nobody bothers any more. It's now hard to buy an old computer even if you want to. And these arguments leave aside the possibility that firms want to offer high environmental standards to please their workers and their customers.

So . . . a "race to the bottom" is possible in theory; but there are also good grounds for doubting its existence. So leaving theory to one side, what are the facts? First, that foreign investment in

rich countries is far more likely to go into polluting industries than foreign investment in poor countries. Second, foreign investment in polluting industries is the fastest growing segment of foreign investment coming into the United States. In contrast, foreign investment in clean industries is the fastest growing segment of American investments abroad. In other words, foreigners are bringing dirty industries to the United States, but American companies are bringing clean industries to the world.

You may have blinked a little when you read that last paragraph. To those brought up on a diet of environmentalist guilt, those statistics seem insane. They are not so insane when you consider that poor countries produce goods like clothes, children's toys, and coffee, while the seriously polluting industries like bulk chemical production require high levels of skill, reliable infrastructure, and—since a lot of capital investment is involved—political stability. Why jeopardize that by moving the plant to Ethiopia to save a few dollars on environmental costs?

Another indicator of the environmental performance of foreign investment in poor countries comes from measures of pollution in China, Brazil, and Mexico. Sixty percent of foreign investment in poor countries arrives in these countries. The first figure on page 217 shows how as the Chinese economy has developed, urban air pollution in China has been reduced. At the same time, foreign investment has exploded as foreign firms build factories in China, either to cater to the Chinese market or to take advantage of cheaper labor and export to the rest of the world. Brazil and Mexico have very similar patterns.

This is not to give foreign investment all the credit. As China has grown richer, the government has imposed tighter environmental restrictions at the same time that foreign investment has arrived. All the same, it is hard to reconcile tales of a "race to the bottom" with this picture. Such tales are convenient scare-stories for protectionists looking for new ways to favor privileged industries at the expense of customers and the developing world alike.

Does globalization cause pollution?
China: Urban air quality and foreign investment

Source: Wheeler 2001.

The truth is that protectionism itself can have tremendous environmental costs. The most obvious case: the splendidly "multifunctional" Common Agricultural Policy in the European Union, a package of trade barriers and subsidies designed to protect European farmers. To its defenders, multifunctionality is supposed to convey self-sufficiency, security, environmental performance, and a fair deal for poor farmers. But instead, the policy subsidizes farmers in the European Union to the tune of almost half the Union budget, with the largest quarter of the farms

Protected agriculture is intensive
Agricultural protection and use of fertilizers in agriculture

Source: FAO 1998; OECD 2000.

getting over two-thirds of this—the richest man in England, the Duke of Westminster, received £448,000 (nearly $900,000) in subsidies in 2003–4. The policy encourages intensive farming with the obvious results of poor food quality and high use of pesticides and fertilizers, and all the while dumps food on the developing world and depresses the prices received by farmers in poor countries. Into the bargain it is helping to derail the current round of world trade liberalization. As Martin Wolf commented in the *Financial Times*: "This is a multifunctional policy indeed: regressive, wasteful, damaging to food quality and the environment and an obstacle to trade liberalization everywhere."

Other rich nations, especially Japan and Korea, privilege their farmers the same way as the European Union: a third of the typical OECD farm's revenue comes from government support, and as the second figure on page 217 shows, the more agriculture is subsidized, the more fertilizers it consumes. If the Common Agricultural Policy and other examples of agricultural protectionism were abolished, there is little doubt that the world's environment would be substantially improved as the intensity of farming could be reduced. At the same time, both European consumers and third-world farmers would get a much better deal.

The United States provides less subsidy for its farmers, but it can still lay on trade protection and cause environmental damage when it has to. In 1998, domestic sugar producers enjoyed a $1 billion subsidy, half of which went to just seventeen farms. (Because of the distortions caused by protection, this cost consumers nearly $2 billion, half of which was pure waste.) The protection has damaged sugar producers in Colombia, who have turned to producing cocaine instead. Of course, the environmental lobby might still approve if the environment was benefiting, but it is not: chemical runoff from the intensive farms in South Florida is damaging the Everglades.

Intensive farming is an unusually clear-cut case. Not all environmental problems will be automatically solved by free trade. One example is the tendency to monoculture: growing only rice, only coffee, or only wheat. This lack of biodiversity renders crops more vulnerable to pests and to fluctuations in the weather.

That might seem like an argument against free trade, since increased trade encourages countries to specialize in single crops for which they have a competitive advantage. But trade barriers are a terrible way to deal with the problem of intensive farming. First, local biodiversity and global biodiversity are both important, but national biodiversity is irrelevant: environmental problems do not notice political boundaries. To the extent that lack of biodiversity is a problem, the solution is direct environmental regulation: the keyhole economics of chapter 5. Hoping that a trade barrier will fix the problem is ludicrous.

This is a special case of another important piece of trade theory. There will always (in theory) and usually (in practice) be an alternative policy, which will fix the environmental problem more directly and efficiently than any trade barrier. Jagdish Bhagwati, an eminent trade theorist, comments in this context that "You cannot kill two birds with one stone." Trade barriers are a clumsy and damaging way to pursue worthwhile objectives, like a healthy environment.

Transport costs are another instance of Bhagwati's principle. Again, it seems superficially attractive to restrict international trade to cut down on the pollution caused by container ships and freight airplanes. Yet again, direct regulation in the form of an externality charge is the solution. Trade barriers attack the transport of goods across borders: but there is nothing especially environmentally damaging about crossing a border. The transport costs of moving a CD player from Osaka harbor to the port of Los Angeles are less than the transport costs of moving it from the port of Los Angeles across to Arizona, or even into a branch of Best Buy in Los Angeles itself. The transport costs of somebody then driving to Best Buy and back home with the CD player are often higher yet, when the true environmental costs of congestion and pollution are figured in. Just because goods are moved within countries, or even quite locally, doesn't mean that the environmental costs of transporting them are small. Again, the Undercover Economist has to recommend policies that attack

the problem directly: an externality charge would encourage the use of cleaner methods of transportation, whether within or between countries.

The final concern, then, is that trade is not bad in its own right but because it leads to environmentally damaging economic growth: that is, trade makes people richer, and this will damage the environment. This claim is worth some attention.

The most deadly and certain environmental problems of today—and possibly the most serious of the future, even given the threat of climate change—are also those that afflict the very poorest people in the world. One example is domestic pollution from wood-burning stoves, which causes blindness and fatal respiratory conditions. Another example is unsafe drinking water, which kills millions. The cure for these environmental problems is economic growth, and trade can help.

Other pollutants, such as airborne particulates emitted from cars, do get worse as people get richer—for a while. Typically, this pollution becomes less serious after people earn around $5,000 a head (as in Mexico), because at this point they are rich enough to afford improved environmental standards, and they will demand them. Trade helps both indirectly, by boosting growth, and directly, because free trade in poorer countries has been associated with the end of subsidies to heavily polluting prestige industries such as petrochemicals and steel as well as the import of new, cleaner technologies.

It is true that energy consumption, and with it carbon dioxide emissions and the threat of climate change, do increase long after people reach $5,000 a head. It seems likely, although we do not know for sure, that the richest countries in the world are just reaching the point where even energy consumption per head is about to stop rising. After all, our cars and domestic appliances get more efficient every year, and when we all have two cars and a large air-conditioned house, it's hard to see where extra energy demand will come from.

If we are honest, then, the argument that trade leads to economic growth, which leads to climate change, leads us then to a stark conclusion: we should cut our trade links to make sure that the Chinese, Indians, and Africans stay poor. The question is whether any environmental catastrophe, even severe climate change, could possibly inflict the same terrible human cost as keeping three or four billion people in poverty. To ask that question is to answer it.

Does this mean that we are doomed to choose between mass starvation and environmental Armageddon? Not at all. There is plenty we can do to aid the environment without using the counterproductive method of restricting trade. Externality taxes have already cut sulfur emissions in the United States (and will do so in China, too). They could also be used to cut carbon dioxide emissions and fight climate change; if we demanded the commitment from our leaders, this could be done. It might not even be that expensive. We could make a start by stopping outright subsidies of fossil fuels; Germany, a country fond of its green credentials and a firm supporter of the Kyoto protocol on climate change, spends $86,000 per coal miner protecting its coal industry from international competition.

What, really, are we to make of the environmentalist attack on free trade? We've seen that the race to the bottom is nonexistent; that polluting industries are still based in rich countries, rather than poor countries; that environmental standards are rising in China, Brazil, and Mexico, the major destinations for foreign investment into poor countries; that protectionist measures such as those on farming, steel, and coal, which sometimes claim environmental justifications in fact are tremendously harmful to the environment; that taxes on transportation fuels are consistent with free trade and much better for the environment than trade restrictions; and that the worst environmental problems, at least of today, are caused by poverty not wealth. The environmentalist movement should be manning the barricades to demand global free trade immediately. One day, perhaps they will.

Sweatshops, or, is trade good for the poor?

Nice running shoes! But don't they make you feel a little, well, guilty?

A number of multinational companies have been accused of subjecting workers in developing countries to poor working conditions. Nike is very frequently named and is the target of a number of campaigns. To consider just one particularly splendid example, an enterprising student at MIT named Jonah Peretti took advantage of Nike's offer to create customized shoes. In his own words:

> Confronted with Nike's celebration of freedom and their statement that if you want it done right, build it yourself, I could not help but think of the people in crowded factories in Asia and South America who actually build Nike shoes. As a challenge to Nike, I ordered a pair of shoes customized with the word "sweatshop."

Even economists think this is pretty funny. Nike did not; Jonah Peretti did not get his customized shoes.

Jonah Peretti and his sympathizers have rightly drawn attention to the fact that in developing countries, workers endure terrible working conditions. Hours are long. Wages are pitiful. But sweatshops are the symptom, not the cause, of shocking global poverty. Workers go there voluntarily, which means—hard as it is to believe—that whatever their alternatives are, they are worse. They stay there, too; turnover rates of multinational-owned factories are low, because conditions and pay, while bad, are better than those in factories run by local firms. And even a local company is likely to pay better than trying to earn money without a job: running an illegal street stall, working as a prostitute, or combing reeking landfills in cities like Manila to find recyclable goods. Manila's most famous landfill, Smokey Mountain, was closed down in the 1990s because it had become such an embarrassing symbol of poverty. But other garbage dumps continue to support

scavengers who can earn up to five dollars a day. Over 130 people were killed in a landslide at Payatas, another dump in Manila, in July of 2000. Even those ways of eking out an urban living are attractive compared with scraping an existence in rural areas. In Latin America, for instance, while extreme poverty is relatively rare in cities, it is commonplace in the countryside. Anybody with a scrap of concern for other human beings should be disgusted at the situation, but they should also recognize that Nike and other multinational companies are not its cause.

The solution to this poverty is not going to come by boycotting shoes and clothes made in developing countries. On the contrary, as countries like South Korea have opened up to multinational companies, slowly but surely they have become richer. As more multinational companies have set up factories, they have competed with each other for workers with the best skills. Wages have risen, not because the companies are generous but because they have no choice if they want to attract good workers. Local firms learn the latest production techniques and become big employers, too. It becomes more and more attractive for people to work in a factory and to acquire the necessary skills: education improves. People move away from the countryside, raising rural earnings for those who remain to a more tolerable level. Formal employment is easier to tax, so government revenues rise and infrastructure, health clinics, and schools improve. Poverty falls, and wages inexorably rise. After adjusting for inflation, the typical Korean worker earns four times more than his father did twenty-five years ago. Korea is now a world technology leader and rich enough to subsidize the hell out of its agriculture like the rest of the rich countries in the world. The sweatshops have moved elsewhere.

It is difficult to be unmoved by conditions in sweatshops. The question is how to get rid of them. Most economists believe that sweatshops are good news in two ways: they are a step up from the immediate alternatives, and they are also a rung on the ladder to something better.

But plenty of people think otherwise. William Greider, a left-of-center political commentator, praised New York's city council for passing a resolution in 2001 requiring that the city refuse to buy uniforms for police and firefighters unless they were produced under "decent wages and factory conditions." Such a resolution can only harm sweatshop laborers: they'll be out of a job and—literally, for those in Manila—back on the trash heap. Of course, it will be good news for textile workers in rich countries, who'll get the business instead. I doubt it is a coincidence that the city council resolution was drafted by UNITE, the Union of Needletrades, Industrial, and Textile Employees, exactly the people who would benefit if imports of textile goods decreased. (If you find my story unconvincing and want a clear conscience when buying clothes, why not visit UNITE's website and order "union-made, sweat-free clothing" at www.uniteunion.org.)

The power of special interest groups

Harry Truman is credited with the request for a one-handed economist, who would be unable to give advice and then say, "on the other hand"; Ronald Reagan, who always had better speechwriters, once said that there should be a version of trivial pursuit for economists "with one hundred questions and three thousand answers."

True enough, economists don't always agree. But it is a rare economist who will not be enthusiastic about the merits of free trade. The near universal opinion among economists is that global free trade would be a great advance, and that even if other countries refuse to lower trade barriers we would be idiots not to lower our own.

Economists estimate that the benefits of free trade are enormous. For example, when Japan was forced by the United States to open its ports to trade in the 1850s, following decades of isolation, it began to export silk and tea to an eager world market, in exchange for cotton and woolen clothes, which were cheap in-

ternationally but expensive in Japan. As a result its national income increased by two-thirds.

More recently, the Uruguay round of trade negotiations, which reduced trade barriers across the world from 1994, is estimated to have increased world income by roughly $100 billion. If tariffs on agricultural and industrial goods, and services, were reduced by a third, there would be a further gain of $600 billion—about 2 percent of world income. Removal of all trade barriers would deliver over 6 percent of world income. These are surely underestimates of the benefits, because they include only the most straightforward gains of bringing cheaper goods from world markets into protected markets: ergo, the straightforward application of David Ricardo's theory of comparative advantage. Other advantages are likely, since, contrary to popular belief that trade is the friend of the multinational, free trade also destroys the scarcity power of big firms by subjecting them to international competition. It encourages the use of new ways of working and better technology. Some people even think it promotes peace by giving trading nations powerful reasons not to go to war with each other.

If free trade really has so many benefits, why does the world still have so many trade barriers? Why don't politicians grab easy votes by lowering trade barriers? Why did the Japanese have to be *forced* to implement a policy that almost doubled the country's income? Unfortunately, in most countries, rich and poor, special interest groups with disproportionate influence have reasons to oppose free trade.

Tariffs tend to impose a small and disguised cost on most of the country, in the form of higher prices, and a further cost on foreigners, who do not have a vote. The benefits of the tariffs are substantial for a narrowly concentrated group of people, often sectors with organized unions and large businesses. If voters are well informed and fully understand economic theory, then in a democracy the protectionists will be voted down. But if people are not well informed about the costs of tariffs imposed on them,

then given the small effect on any particular voter of any particular tariff, the tariff may not even enter their thoughts—especially if the campaign for trade restrictions is disguised as a campaign about sweatshops. Reform efforts may also be stymied by inertia and nervousness on the part of these poorly informed voters, while the special interest groups are well aware that they stand to gain from protection and find it worthwhile to devote substantial funds and lobbying effort to defend their narrow interests.

In a healthy democracy special interests should have less power than in a fragile democracy or an undemocratic country, like Cameroon. If special interest groups are part of the explanation behind trade barriers, we might expect countries with better-established democracies to have lower trade barriers.

The numbers tell us exactly that. In 1999, the United States had average tariffs of 2.8 percent. In the European Union, average tariffs were 2.7 percent. In the emerging tiger, Korea, 5.9 percent. In Argentina, allegedly a paragon of economic reform, 10.7 percent. In the giant economies of China and India, 15.7 percent and 29.5 percent respectively. We have already heard that the poverty and corruption of sad little Cameroon is not being relieved by staggering tariffs averaging 61.4 percent.

It seems that even if we are able to pressure our politicians to do the right thing for everyone by reducing tariffs, an equal responsibility lies with the governments of these poor countries. Why do they maintain tariffs, which harm their citizens? Perhaps because international isolation is good for political stability. The world's longest-serving political leader is Fidel Castro, surely president-for-life as a result of sanctions from the United States, which have had the opposite effect to that desired. Saddam Hussein's rule seemed stronger than ever after a decade of sanctions: it was external force, not internal change that removed him. Myanmar and North Korea are international pariahs with frustratingly stable governments.

This explains why the Japanese had to be forced to liberalize and vastly increase the country's income. The policy of isolation

was not designed for the good of the Japanese people but for the good of their rulers, the Tokugawa clan. Historian Janet Hunter concludes:

> Mechanisms of political control were backed up by a harsh system of regulation, which attempted to minimize all social, political and economic change among the population at large. . . . Potentially damaging foreign influences were minimized after 1640 by cutting off the country from virtually all contact with the outside world.
>
> While these careful measures succeeded in preserving Tokugawa rule for some two and a half centuries, they could never hope to prevent all social, economic and political change. . . . The reopening of foreign contacts with the United States and the imperialist powers of Europe rapidly brought matters to crisis point. . . . From 1853 [during] the crisis over US demands for formal relations . . . Tokugawa authority went rapidly downhill.

Special interest groups have tried to define the trade policy of the United States, with varying success. Tariff barriers have to be approved by Congress, and congressional representatives defend the interests of their own constituents, demanding protection of farming in Iowa, steel in Pennsylvania, sugar in Florida, or auto-manufacturing in Michigan. By trading votes with each other they could get tariff after tariff passed, and if the president came back from some trade negotiation with a treaty in his hand reducing trade barriers, they would refuse to ratify it.

Presidents tend to be more enthusiastic supporters of free trade because they need votes from the whole nation, and so would be relatively less likely to favor locally concentrated protectionism. Sure enough, after 1934, when President Roosevelt persuaded Congress to grant him and future presidents rolling preapproval for trade treaties, tariff rates in the United States fell from about 45 percent to about 10 percent in two decades. Now that the president has responsibility for trade policy, they have been falling ever since.

Of course, presidents are not totally immune from special-interest politics: the importance of Florida's vote in recent presidential elections guarantees protection of sugar producers at the expense of the nation. No political system is perfect, but democracies tend to favor trade more than others, because lowering trade barriers is good for the ordinary person.

How can we make things better for the poor?

You will have gathered by now that I am a big fan of both coffee and beer. My favorite coffee comes from Timor. My favorite beer comes from Belgium. My life is much happier because of the Timorese coffee pickers and the Belgian brewers. I hope that I have done enough to persuade you that their lives are happier because of me. A fundamental characteristic of the kinds of social interactions that economists usually study is that . . . everybody wins.

Unfortunately, some win much more than others. I am doing well, and so are the Belgians. The Timorese are not. They would be doing worse if it were not for trade, but that is not enough for us to relax and forget about them.

Coffee growers are poor because they have no scarcity power. There are many places where coffee can be grown. Growing mass-market coffee requires hard work but little skill. No individual coffee grower has any power to affect the market price. Even if countries can act in unison, they have no scarcity power: when the top coffee producers attempted to set up a cartel controlling two-thirds of world coffee production, the Association of Coffee Producing Countries, it failed and shut down. Whenever the cartel succeeded in raising prices, new farmers in new countries quickly found it attractive to start growing coffee. Vietnam is a great example. A few years ago, coffee was hardly grown in the country at all, but now it is the world's second-largest producer of

coffee. A cartel designed to exploit scarcity power can work only if new producers cannot easily enter the market.

We should not forget that one of the reasons it is so easy for poor farmers to produce coffee is that coffee does not grow in France or Florida, and so rich farmers are not interested in agitating for high tariffs. Unprocessed coffee is relatively free of trade barriers, so one further effect of trade barriers on beef and rice and grain is that farmers in poor countries are forced into niches like coffee, which cannot sustain all of them.

Because coffee is such an easy business to get into, I am willing to make a prediction: coffee farmers will never be rich until most people are rich. If coffee farmers became rich but other farmers or workers in sweatshops were poor, the others would switch to farming coffee. High coffee prices will always collapse, until workers in sweatshops become well-paid blue-collar workers in skilled manufacturing jobs, who don't find the idea of being even a prosperous coffee farmer attractive.

We need to understand that narrowly focused initiatives on "fair trade coffee" or "sweatshop-free clothes" will never make a substantial improvement to the lives of millions. Some, like the campaign to prevent New York City from buying uniforms from poor countries, will actively cause damage. Others, like the numerous brands of fair trade coffee, are likely to improve the income of a few coffee producers without causing a great deal of harm. But they cannot fix the basic problem: too much coffee is being produced. At the slightest hint that coffee farming will become an attractive profession, it will always be swamped with desperate people who have no alternative. The truth of the matter is that only broad-based development of poor countries will ever lift the living standards of the very poor, increase coffee prices, and improve wages and labor standards in shoe factories.

Can such broad-based development happen? Undoubtedly. Billions of people in the developing world are much richer than their parents were. Life expectancy and education is rising, even

in countries that are not getting richer. This is only partly because of free trade; there is far more to the story. For a developing economy to grow strongly, many different reforms have to be put in place. There is one country in the world that has done this for more people, more quickly, and from a worse starting point than any in history. It is where we shall finish our journey.

TEN

How China Grew Rich

"My God," I said.

I was standing with my wife in the "Renmin Gongyuan," the People's Park, in the middle of Shanghai. Renmin Gongyuan is the Central Park of the twenty-first century. It gave me the same dizzying rush as my first visit to Manhattan. Walking out into the space of the park allowed us to feel the full visual impact of Shanghai's skyscrapers. One was a modern-day Chrysler building, with a striking crown of four mirrored tines meeting at a perfect point; the entire tower was rotated forty-five degrees around its axis so that the top forty floors sat at a diagonal to the bottom forty. Another building boasted a vast glass atrium hanging suspended sixty floors above the city. Not every design was in the best of taste: one had a domed penthouse that looked like it had been stolen from the set of a fifties flying-saucer movie. There must have been thirty skyscrapers, half a dozen of which were on an incredible scale. All of them were brand new.

"My God," said Fran.

"When were you last in Shanghai?"

"Ten years ago."

"How many of these buildings were up ten years ago?" She thought for a moment.

"You see that one?"

"The boxy forty-story office building over there?"

"No. That one just beneath it." She was pointing to a twelve-story red-brick building, dwarfed on every side by more modern constructions.

"I see. Yes."

"That was the tallest one standing ten years ago."

"My God," I said.

The ambition of it all was simply exhilarating. In just a decade, the builders of Shanghai had put up a fair imitation of Manhattan. What New Yorkers would have made of it, I don't know. It made us Londoners feel like country bumpkins.

Yet it could all have been so different. For most of the twentieth century, China was poorer than Cameroon. In 1949, when the People's Republic of China came into being, the world's largest country was torn by civil war and ruled by a communist dictatorship. In the late 1950s, millions of people died in a famine induced by the failed policies of the government. In the 1960s, the university system was destroyed by the Cultural Revolution, when millions of educated citizens were forcibly relocated to work in the countryside. After all this, how did China become the greatest economic success story in history?

Two farming revolutions

A visit to Shanghai is enough to provoke the question. Clues to the answer can be found all over China. I picked up several of them on a train to the inland Chinese city of Zhengzhou.

The train itself was the first clue: it was more comfortable, faster, and more punctual than those back in England. China's road and rail network appeared to be in superb condition. Second, the Chinese seemed to have an excellent education system—I was soundly but politely thrashed at chess by a PhD in

economics, a young man who had never been outside China but who spoke mildly and thoughtfully in good English. Third, although the train was packed, there were few children and no large families. China's "one child family" policy has created a society where women have time to work and where the bulk of people are neither old nor young but in middle age, saving for the future. Those vast savings have provided the investment money for the roads, the trains, and more. At the minimum China clearly had the human resources, infrastructure, and financial capital required by traditional models of economic growth. Yet it did not always seem as though these resources would be well used; we already know that without the right incentives they will be wasted.

Under Mao, that waste was legendary. China's initial development efforts were two-pronged: massive investment in heavy industry such as steel, plus application of special agricultural techniques to make sure that China's vast population was fed. The policy focus was understandable. China's northern provinces are rich in high-quality coal, which logically could provide the basis of an economic revolution. Coal, steel, and heavy manufacturing had been the basis of the industrial revolution in the leading economies: the United Kingdom, the United States, and Germany. Meanwhile, agriculture had to be a priority for any Chinese government because there was barely enough fertile land to feed the country's hundreds of millions of people. From the window of the train to Zhengzhou I was looking out over Henan, China's most densely populated province. It is a freezing desert.

This two-pronged push was called the "Great Leap Forward." It seemed to make sense, but it was the greatest economic failure the world has ever seen. Mao conducted economic policy based on the hidden premise that if people tried hard, the impossible would happen. Zeal alone was sufficient. Villagers were ordered to build steel furnaces in their backyards but had no iron ore to put into them. Some villagers melted down good iron and steel—tools, even doorknobs—in order to meet the quotas demanded

by the state. Even Mao's personal doctor worried about the wisdom of a policy to "destroy knives to produce knives." The steel that emerged from the furnaces was unusable.

If industrial policy was a farce, agricultural policy was a tragedy. The Great Leap Forward had already pulled many workers off the land to labor at the furnaces or in public works like dams and roads. Mao ordered the people to kill grain-eating birds, and the population of insect pests exploded as a result. Mao personally redesigned China's agricultural techniques, specifying closer planting and deeper sowing to increase yields. Rice planted so closely together could not grow, but party officials, anxious to please Mao, staged shows of agricultural and industrial success. When Mao traveled by train to admire the fruits of his policy, local officials built furnaces in strips along the railroad and brought rice from miles away to replant, at the officially specified density, in adjacent fields. Even this charade could not be maintained without the use of electric fans, which were used to circulate air and prevent the rice from rotting.

Crop yields fell, of course, but even this would not have been disastrous without the state's insistence that the policy was working. When the defense minister raised the issue of the famine in a ministerial meeting, he was punished and ordered to write a "self-criticism." Less powerful figures who denied that there was a surplus were tortured. While crops were failing, China doubled its exports of grain from 1958 to 1961 as a symbol of its success. In Henan province, across which we were traveling in comfort just forty-five years later, state grain stores contained enough food to provide for the people but remained shut because the official government position was that there was a grain surplus. Meanwhile, people starved to death outside in the snow. Some were left unburied, others were eaten by desperate family members; neither fate was uncommon.

Estimates of the death toll from the famine range from 10 million to 60 million people, roughly the entire population of England, or of California and Texas combined. Even Chinese

government figures later acknowledged that 30 million people had died, although they blamed bad weather.

In the "world of truth" described in chapter 3, such disasters cannot happen. Mistakes, certainly, will be made—perhaps more frequently than under central planning. But the mistakes stay small; in market economies we call them "experiments." If venture capitalists back them, they do not expect many to succeed. When they succeed, they make some people rich and bring innovation to the whole economy. When they fail—which is more often than not—some people will go bankrupt, but nobody will die. Only command economies can promote experimentation on such a fatally extravagant scale and suppress informed criticism. (Mao was not alone. The Soviet president, Nikita Khrushchev, made a similar mistake following a visit to the United States, when he ordered Soviet fields to be replanted with the corn he had seen growing in Iowa. The failure was a catastrophe.) It is worth remembering that market failures, while sometimes serious, are never as tragic as the worst failures of governments like Mao's.

In 1976, after many more crimes against his own people, Mao died. After a short interregnum, he and his followers were replaced by Deng Xiaoping and his allies in December 1978. Just five years later, the change in China's economy was incredible. Agricultural output, always the headache of the Chinese planners, had grown by 40 percent. Why? Because those planners had brought the "world of truth" into China. As we discovered in Cameroon, incentives matter. Before 1978, China had some of the most perverse incentives in the world.

Before Deng took power, Chinese agriculture had been locally organized into collectives of twenty or thirty families. People were rewarded with "work points," which were awarded based on the output of the collective as a whole. There was little opportunity for personal improvement either through extra effort or ingenuity. As a result there was little of either.

The government also purchased and redistributed food from regions that produced a surplus, but did so at a severely depressed price, discouraging more fertile regions from making the most

of their agricultural land. Many rural workers were underemployed. The very system that was designed to boost China's agricultural output and make the nation self-sufficient was undermining it. China's output of grain, per person, was as low in 1978 as it had been in the mid-1950s, just before the Great Leap Forward.

Deng had little time for such folly and immediately embarked on a program of reform, announcing that "socialism does not mean poverty." To improve agriculture, he had to get the incentives right. He started by raising the price paid by the state for crops by nearly a quarter. The price paid for surplus crops rose by more than 40 percent, substantially increasing the incentive for fertile areas to produce more crops.

At the same time, a few collectives experimented with subcontracting land to individual households. Instead of clamping down, the government allowed the innovation to see whether it would work, just as a market economy allows small-scale experiments. Households who were renting land from collectives had every incentive to work hard and think of smarter ways of doing things because they were rewarded directly for their successes. Crop yields immediately increased. The experiment spread: just 1 percent of collectives had used the "household responsibility system" in 1979; by 1983 98 percent had switched to the system.

These reforms were linked with a number of other pieces of liberalization: the retail price of grain was allowed to rise, further increasing the incentive to produce what was needed. Restrictions on trade between regions were eased, so that each region could enjoy its comparative advantage. Production quotas were soon abandoned altogether.

The results were dramatic: agricultural output expanded by 10 percent a year in the first half of the 1980s. More impressively still, more than half of the increase was attributable, not to working harder or using more machinery but to more efficient farming and harvesting methods. Much of that productivity increase was directly attributable to the abandonment of the collective system. In the five years following the reforms, the average real

income of farmers doubled. It was not Mao but Deng, by using the power of markets and prices, who had achieved the great leap forward.

All these statistics are best understood by thinking back to chapter 3 and the world of truth. Partly by accident, partly by benign neglect, and partly by design, Deng introduced the world of truth to Chinese agriculture. Those who had good ideas, good luck, and who worked hard, prospered. Bad ideas were quickly abandoned. Good ones spread rapidly. Farmers grew more cash crops and devoted less effort to crops that were difficult to grow; all of this was the unsurprising result of introducing a price system. China had begun to travel along the so-called capitalist road.

Such a journey cannot be completed on rice alone. The success of the agricultural reforms created the momentum and popular support for Deng to continue. Attention needed to be turned to the rest of the economy—and to cities like Zhengzhou.

Investing for the future

Zhengzhou is not a stunning city like Shanghai. It is ugly and crowded and, despite being a major railroad intersection, somewhat insular: we spent nearly a week in the Zhengzhou area without seeing a single foreign face. In its own way, though, Zhengzhou is as impressive as Shanghai. A city the size of London far from the Western world, affectionately described by our guidebook as "a sprawling paradigm of ill-conceived town planning," Zhengzhou at least demonstrates that China's economic revolution has spread beyond the coastal provinces. Forty-story high-rises loom solidly over the enormous train station; there are plenty of modern banks, huge department stores and hotels, and brutal concrete overpasses. Advertising is everywhere.

To construct such buildings, rails, and roads requires an enormous investment. Economists have a label for the roads and factories, homes and office buildings, which result from investment: they call such constructions "capital," and all sustained development needs capital. Capital can come from private investors, both

domestic and foreign, who hope to recoup profits, or it can come from the government, either by taxing people and investing the proceeds, or by a program of compulsory saving.

Common sense suggests that if you want to be richer tomorrow than you are today, you should invest money rather than spending it on goods and services to be enjoyed immediately. You could invest it in an education, in a house, or in a bank account. Either way, if you consume less today and invest the money, you will be richer tomorrow—if the investments are good ones. (Building blast furnaces in the back garden will not do. Neither will building a library with a leaky roof.)

An unmysterious chunk of the development of countries is based on the same simple principle that saving and investing today makes you richer tomorrow. Savings rates have been very high in the fast-growing economies of the Pacific Rim. However, that is not the whole story, as we learned in chapter 8. A market economy cannot simply decide to save and invest more. Most people don't bother saving in Cameroon: they have few ways to recoup investments in basic infrastructure like roads, and little confidence that they will be allowed to do so if they build factories or shops. The few exceptions, such as the cell-phone sector, which can be funded by pay-as-you-go cards, have been the stunning successes you might expect. Many poor economies seek foreign investment but cannot even retain the confidence of their own citizens, who are eager to invest money overseas. Small wonder that savings rates are low, and the percentage of those savings invested inside Cameroon lower still. Without offering a secure environment for investment, the Cameroonian government can do little to encourage it.

China's socialist government had no problem with access to capital. While a market economy cannot simply decide to save and invest more, a socialist economy can and usually does. Capital came from government programs; almost all saving was done either by the government or by state-owned corporations. In both cases money was being taken out of the pockets of individuals

and invested on their behalf. There was plenty of capital available, too: about a third of national income was saved rather than consumed, roughly twice as much as in Cameroon.

Initially, China was able to get fairly good returns out of this capital. In the early 1950s, when the main task was to rebuild essential infrastructure and industry, every 100 yuan invested added 40 yuan to China's annual output, an impressive return. This should not be surprising. The tasks facing the Chinese government were clear enough: in particular, what had been broken during the war and the revolution needed to be fixed. All that was needed was for the government to give the orders.

The trouble came later. Even setting aside the chaos of the Great Leap Forward and the Cultural Revolution, the Chinese state found itself increasingly unable to get value out of its investments. By the time Mao died in 1976, every 100 yuan invested were adding only 18 yuan to China's annual output. This was less than half as efficient as two decades before. Given that the government and state enterprises were, between them, investing such a large chunk of the nation's income, this reduction in the efficiency of investment was a crippling waste.

A sympathetic observer might conclude that it was inevitable that after the obvious investments had been made, returns would fall. This might be true for a cutting-edge economy like Japan or the United States, but in 1976 China was still desperately poor. Few people had cars, telephones, electricity, or running water. In such a poor country, the right investments can achieve very high returns by providing such basics of modern life. There was plenty of effective investment to be made, but the state didn't know how to make it.

As long as it was obvious what to order people to make or to build or to grow, this didn't matter much. But as the population grew, technology advanced and long-demanded investments were made, the communist economies slipped farther and farther away from the memory of the price system. Real market economies change quickly. In South Korea, 80 to 90 percent of workers,

land, and capital were working or being used for different purposes in the 1970s than they had been in 1960—in 1960, agricultural output was 45 percent of the economy and manufacturing output less than 10 percent. By the early 1970s, the manufacturing sector was larger than the agricultural sector. More importantly, within those sectors, workers were training and retraining, firms were starting up and closing down. Korea's export industries used to make toys and underwear, but now they make memory chips and cars. If, in 1975, a planner for the South Korean government had tried to run the economy based on outdated information from 1960, the result would have been a catastrophe. Fortunately, nobody did. Such folly was left to the North Koreans. Command economies from North Korea to the Soviet Union to China simply lacked the information necessary to keep making the right choices.

Unlike Cameroon, where individuals and companies have little incentive to invest, Maoist China had no problem with incentives—after all, the leaders had the power of life and death over their followers. But incentives alone are not enough. Chapter 3 showed that the world of truth created by markets produces good outcomes not just because it provides incentives, but because it generates information about the costs and benefits of all kinds of goods and services through the price system. The socialist systems of the Soviet Union and China provided the strongest incentives imaginable, but not the information necessary to use them correctly. Rather than responding to demand from world markets, like the South Koreans did, the Chinese responded to demands from Mao: plant crops more closely, kill birds, melt down your tools to make new tools.

To get any value out of the vast sums of investment capital available, the Chinese government began a gradual shift to a market system. Where successful agricultural reforms had paved the way, more complex and far-reaching reforms of the whole economy were to follow. Fifteen years after Deng came to power, returns on investment had quadrupled: for every 100 yuan invested, China's annual output grew by 72 yuan: each investment

paid for itself after just 500 days. Nor was this because the government had scaled back its investment and was cherry-picking only the very best projects. Quite the reverse: investment levels were even higher than in the 1970s. It's small wonder the economy grew spectacularly. But how were the high returns to investment achieved?

Growing out of the plan

Like the Soviet bloc economies, China's industrial sector was controlled by planners. The plan specified, for instance, that a particular steel mill would produce a defined quantity of steel, that that steel would then be used for certain specified purposes, and that a standard quantity of coal (0.8 tons of coal were said to be required for each ton of steel) would be delivered to the steel mill in order to make production possible, and so on. The calculations required were tremendously complex, even presuming that junior bureaucrats were supplying honest information about costs and quality. (Everybody had an incentive to claim that the machinery and materials they had to manage were insufficient and of poor quality, and to claim that nevertheless their output was vast and excellent. Without a world of truth, the real story was impossible to uncover.) But, leaving aside Mao's fatal utopian whims, such a system could work tolerably well for a time because each year the planners had the previous year's plan to guide them.

As the economy grew and changed, the process of adjusting output requirements and making capital investments wisely became increasingly difficult: this is why the returns to capital in China were so much lower in 1976 than in the 1950s. A market system would have done much better, but it was no simple matter to create one. Markets do not work well without market-supporting institutions: in a market economy, people need banks for commercial loans, contract law to resolve disputes, and confidence that their profits will not be confiscated. Such institutions

cannot be set up overnight. Meanwhile, many workers in a so-
cialist economy are engaged in unproductive activities and might
simply starve unless the adjustment process was phased in or they
received some kind of compensation. The problems were most
acute for the industrial sector of the economy because it was most
closely tied into the plan system, was the vehicle the government
used to generate savings, and was the source of most government
investment.

Had Deng decided simply to abandon the plan and switch to a
market system overnight, the likely outcome would have been a
scramble to establish property rights, the collapse of the finan-
cial sector (because many government-run banks had made loans
that could never be repaid), and widespread unemployment, even
starvation. It is conceivable that things might have worked out
for the best quite quickly, but it is likely that they would not. (In
the former Soviet Union in the 1990s, such "shock therapy" re-
sulted in economic collapse.)

What is more, such extreme reforms would have offended so
many vested interests—including huge numbers of ordinary
people—that they might have been politically impossible. Deng,
who had been purged twice under Mao's chairmanship yet re-
turned to lead the country, well understood the value of political
credibility.

So Deng and like-minded reformers adopted a more tentative
strategy. In 1985 the size of the "plan" was frozen: the production
levels specified by the government did not grow as the economy
grew. Instead, state-owned firms were allowed to do as they wished
with any extra production. Efficient coal manufacturers would find
that efficient steel manufacturers wanted to buy extra coal to make
extra steel, which would be sold on to efficient construction firms.
Inefficient firms that tried to expand got nowhere.

This strategy turned out to work very well for several reasons.
First, it was easy to understand, and the commitment to freeze
the size of the plan was a credible one. Such a credible commit-
ment was important: if the planners had constantly tried to ex-
pand and update the plan in the light of the information emerging

from the fringe market, that market would quickly have ceased producing useful information. Plant managers, realizing that any successful changes they made would quickly be absorbed into next year's plan, would have stuck to safe choices.

Second, because the plan was kept fixed, a certain stability was guaranteed. Workers who had jobs could keep them. Things were guaranteed not to get worse—but if growth resulted, there was the possibility that they could get better. Many people grabbed that possibility, preferring long hours and poor conditions in a textile factory, even if they had to travel thousands of miles from their families, to their previous occupation of scraping a living—or failing to do so—on the most marginal, arid farmland.

Third, the market operated exactly where it needed to: at the margin. Remember that marginal costs and marginal benefits are what really matter for the efficiency of an economy. Imagine the decision of a factory manager trying to decide whether to produce one extra ton of steel, from which he can keep the profits. If he knows the marginal cost (the cost of producing one extra ton) and the price he is offered is a market price (which reflects the benefits to someone else of one extra ton), then he will make the right decision: produce if the price is higher than the marginal cost. The output of the factory will be efficient.

Decisions about what happens to the rest of the steel are not important for whether the quantity of output is efficient. Nine tons out of ten could be produced and allocated in accordance with the plan, but it is the decision about the tenth ton that matters for efficiency.

What this meant was that efficient firms expanded to meet extra demand: an eleventh ton and a twelfth followed the tenth. That demand was coming from expanding sections of the economy, which really needed supply, rather than from the planners. Managers got to keep profits and reinvest them—and had an incentive to make sure that the investments were profitable.

Inefficient firms, by contrast, did not grow. As long as the government kept subsidizing them through the plan (it gradually stopped doing so in the 1990s), they could still keep producing

forever; but since the Chinese economy was well over four times as big in 2003 as it had been when the plan was frozen in 1985, the relative importance of those firms shrank very quickly. The economy, quite literally, grew out of the plan.

Entry and scarcity power

We know that a market system limits the scarcity power of firms; most firms face competition, and sectors of the economy that are not very competitive tend to attract new competition over time. The competition and free entry of new firms, by limiting scarcity power, pushes powerfully toward efficient production, new ideas, and consumer choice.

The Chinese reformers needed to encourage entry and limit scarcity without resorting to a dangerously unpredictable strategy of rapid liberalization. They hoped to improve the performance of the state sector, introduce new public sector companies as competitors, gradually foster a private sector, and slowly open up to international competition. If one source of competition didn't work out, there was always another. The most important competitors at first were local-government-owned "township and village enterprises." Despite the name they were often huge industrial monsters. Later, privately owned and foreign companies were allowed to set up and grow, too.

As late as 1992, only 14 percent of industrial output was being produced by privately owned or foreign firms, while the state sector was responsible for nearly half of output. The output of local-government township and village enterprises made up most of the remainder. The Chinese economic miracle was not really about privatization. What mattered was not who owned the companies, but that the companies were forced to compete in a relatively free market, driving down scarcity power and bringing in the information and incentives of the world of truth.

The effects are even measurable. Remember, way back in chapter 1, we discovered that high profits were often a signal of scarcity power. If new entry and stronger competition were removing

the scarcity power of state-owned firms, we would expect their profit rates to fall.

That is indeed what happened. Chinese firms in the 1980s had very high rates of profit: many sectors had profit rates of over 50 percent (for a fairly competitive economy, you would expect not more than 20 percent and often much less). Profits also varied a lot from sector to sector depending on the arbitrary pricing of the plan: the oil refining sector had a profit rate of almost 100 percent, the iron mining sector just 7 percent. In all cases, the government confiscated the profit and reinvested it.

As the economic reforms began to bite, profits started to fall; they also started to converge, as the most profitable sectors faced the fiercest competition from local government, private, and foreign firms. During the 1990s, average profit rates fell by over a third; in the juiciest sectors they fell by at least a half. The effect of all this was to reduce waste, give Chinese customers better return for their money, and make China a potential player on world markets. Scarcity power disappeared.

China and the world

There have been times in China's history when it has been an insular place. This is not one of them. Far from the coast in the inland cities of Xi'an and Zhengzhou we had no difficulty finding Coke, McDonald's, pool rooms, and Internet cafes. In Shanghai it was almost impossible to escape from familiar brand names.

Anyone who visited China in the early 1990s could tell you that this is all very new. But it's more than an anecdotal impression: the statistics tell the same story. As recently as 1990, China was a minnow on the global trading scene. The United States and Germany exported almost ten times as much. Last year, China became the fourth largest exporter in the world, and even the United States and Germany export less than twice as much. This is no accident. The dramatic entry of China onto the world's economic stage has been one of the last acts of China's economic reform.

Why did China need the world? A country of over a billion people seems better placed than most to be self-sufficient. But China's economy was still tiny in 1978—smaller than Belgium's—and the reformers realized that engaging with the world could help. There were three advantages. First, China could tap into world markets for labor-intensive goods: toys, shoes, and clothes. Second, the foreign currency these exports earned could be spent on raw materials and on new technology to develop the economy.

Finally, by inviting foreign investors in, the Chinese could learn modern production and business techniques from them—hugely important for a country that had been communist for decades. Last year, China and Hong Kong managed to attract over 40 percent of all the foreign direct investment into the world's developing countries. (India, the other Asian giant, attracted a little over 2 percent.) As we discussed in chapter 9, one advantage of such investment is that it supplies capital to an economy that cannot be instantly withdrawn if investors get nervous. This happened to China's neighbors in the Asian currency crisis of 1997, where purely financial investments like loans were rapidly withdrawn in a mass panic. The capital investment expands the future capacity of the economy, but as we have already seen, China did not need foreigners to supply capital. It was the expertise that really counted: expertise, for example, in quality control or in logistics.

American and Japanese firms made investments in transportation and electronics, turning China into a high-technology manufacturer. You can see the effect of these investments in the statistics: China is now the largest producer of the majority of important consumer electronics; more than half the world's DVD players and digital cameras are now made in China. You can also see the effect while wandering around the country. Sitting on the buses around Zhengzhou, I was surrounded by people talking on hi-tech gizmos that I'd never seen before, and which didn't arrive back home for months. The foreign investors who made the technology possible hope for a good return on their invest-

ments, but it is obvious to anyone that plenty of the money is staying with Chinese consumers.

Foreign investment has been a major factor in keeping China's reforms on track. Not only did foreign firms bring capital, and not only did they bring expertise and connections to the world economy, they also continued the competitive process of the earlier reforms by competing with China's domestic firms, driving them to continue improving their efficiency.

If foreign investment is such a boon for the economy, how did China do it? Why didn't the money go to India? Why didn't the money go to Cameroon?

Luck plays a role. In contrast to Cameroon, the Chinese had a substantial and rapidly growing domestic market, always attractive to foreign investors. No Cameroonian leader, no matter how gifted, could copy this: fate dealt Cameroon a different hand. There was nothing lucky, however, about the Chinese commitment to education—one happy legacy of the communist years—which meant that by 1978 there was a huge reservoir of skilled and potentially productive workers, waiting to flood the economy with talent when the dam of the command economy burst. Cameroon's government wasted any opportunity it had to educate its people back in the 1970s, when the country was richer than it is today. But India also has a large and growing domestic market and a well-educated workforce, even though that education is less broadly available than in China; the statistics show popular hysteria about outsourcing notwithstanding, this has not yet been enough to attract foreign investors.

China had other natural advantages that India did not. The often-painful process of international economic engagement was made smoother and more effective because of mainland China's links with Hong Kong and Taiwan. Both were successful internationally integrated economies back in the days when China was very isolated from world markets, and despite the different economic systems there were close ties of family and friendship between businessmen in the three economies. These social ties helped compensate for problems in China's legal system in the

early years of reform. China was (and still is) striving to improve the commercial framework of property rights and contract law, which all successful economies need. Without such a framework it is hard to do business with confidence. How can you trust that your business partners will not rip you off? How can you feel safe if local government officials can confiscate your profits or your property?

For entrepreneurs from Hong Kong and Taiwan, personal connections meant that they were often able to rely on promises with no legal basis. A formal contract would have been better, but a businessman's word could be good enough if the opportunity for profit was attractive.

In this case, it certainly was. There was a perfect fit between China and Hong Kong. Chinese firms, producing cheap goods but unused to international deals, tapped into the expertise of Hong Kong traders. Chinese exports to Hong Kong grew dramatically in the 1980s, and Hong Kong re-exported them to the world. Taiwan joined in during the 1990s. As the economist Dwight Perkins observed at the time, "the formidable marketing talents of Hong Kong and Taiwan are being grafted onto the manufacturing capacity of the mainland."

India lacked Hong Kong and Taiwan, but also lacked any interest in welcoming foreigners. The noted Indian economist, Jagdish Bhagwati, described his own governments' policies from the 1960s to the 1980s as "three decades of illiberal and autarkic policies"— in other words, the government sat hard on the market and did its best to prevent trade and investment.

China, on the other hand, worked hard to attract foreign investors and to make the most of the links with Hong Kong and its other neighbors. The plan was to create "special economic zones," such as Shenzhen, where the normal rules of the command economy would not apply to foreign investors. At the same time, the infrastructure of the special economic zones could be improved quickly. That method perfectly complemented China's

connections with Hong Kong, Macao, and Taiwan: the zones were exclusively in Guandong Province, next to Hong Kong and Macao, and Fujian, next to Taiwan. Over half of all investment into China in 1990 came from the tiny country of Hong Kong, while Japan and the United States together supplied only a quarter. Further, almost half of all investment arrived in Guandong; Fujian was the second largest recipient. The city of Shenzhen, across the border from Hong Kong, was a fishing village in 1980 when it became a special economic zone. Twenty years later property developers were pulling down skyscrapers mid-construction to start building bigger skyscrapers. The Chinese say, "you'll think you're rich until you set foot in Shenzhen."

Unfair and arbitrary as they were, the special economic zones worked well at attracting investors without turning the entire Chinese mainland upside down. They also provided a toehold for reforms to spread. Whenever the rules for foreign firms seemed to be working well, administrators started applying them to domestic firms within the zones. Then they started applying them to domestic firms outside the zones. Other coastal provinces looked at the booming economies of Fujian and Guandong and started to demand similar privileges. Unfair or quirky rules were straightened out as foreign investors protested any special favors for domestic firms, while domestic firms circumvented special favors for foreign firms by laundering their money through Hong Kong and bringing it back as "foreign investment." As so often with the rest of China's reform program, good policies were copied and foolish ones died out quickly.

Epilogue: does the economy matter?

This chapter is called "How China Grew Rich." That's an exaggeration. China is not rich—yet. But it is growing richer faster than any country in history.

And yet . . . so what? With this economic growth comes tremendous upheaval. Chinese people are confused; many are unemployed or dislocated from the modern China. A group of

workers in Sichuan came to believe that Mao was running a factory in the afterlife—according to socialist principles, naturally. One account claims that some of them killed themselves with the aim of joining him.

Contemporary Chinese films also tell a story of bemusement and at times agonized searching. Many films, such as *Shower* and *Happy Times Hotel*, feature families split up after someone seeks his fortune in Shenzen. The movies show the heartache but not the riches. The message is that the new opportunities are destroying the old way of life. Another common theme is of total confusion: the hapless bike messenger of *Beijing Bicycle* discovers that property is indeed theft, and his attempt to engage with the capitalist system ends in misery and violence. In the touching farce *Happy Times Hotel*, well-meaning friends, unemployed after their factory unit has closed down, are so busy trying to look after a blind girl by faking the existence of a business that they fail to appreciate it would be easier simply to run a real business. It is only the girl, who grew up in the 1990s, who comes to see clearly that she has the ability to make a living for herself.

It is not easy to be part of a revolution. Young men and women growing up in rural China in the 1970s worked as part of a farming community, collecting "work points," doing as they were told, moving where they were told, and having basic needs provided for by the community and the state. Their sons and daughters grew up in a different China in the 1980s and 1990s. Life was still hard, but there was more money around and much more choice. Land was valuable; as farming methods improved, there was still less need for spare workers on the farm. Some people did what their fathers had been forbidden to do: sold their land and moved to the cities to look for work. Migration tore families apart. While new opportunities opened up, the old safety nets were becoming tattered as some state enterprises became obsolete.

Meanwhile, conditions in factories are terrible. Badly paid employees work long shifts under conditions of dubious safety. A BBC reporter picked up the stories of Li Chun Mei, who died in late 2001 at the end of a sixteen-hour shift; she was found by her

co-workers lying on the bathroom floor, blood oozing from her nose and mouth. Then there is Zhou Shien Pin, whose feet melted after he touched a high-voltage wire in a paint factory. Is this the price of economic growth? Is it worth paying?

Economists like Paul Krugman, Martin Wolf, and Jagdish Bhagwati have repeatedly tried to argue that Chinese sweatshops beat the alternatives. This is not a popular view. After Martin Wolf's book, *Why Globalization Works*, was reviewed in the *Guardian Weekly*, the paper published an outraged letter from a reader who fantasized with glee about Wolf himself being forced to work in a sweatshop.

This response is about as vicious as wishing that anyone who wears a "Mao" T-shirt be condemned to starvation—but less logical. Martin Wolf is correct to suggest that the sweatshops are better than the horrors that came before them, and a step on the road to something better. Mao's "Great Leap Forward" was a leap into hell.

Nor is it unfair or irrelevant to compare modern China with Mao's utopia. Countries that are rich or rapidly growing have embraced the basic lessons of economics we have learned in this book: fight scarcity power and corruption; correct externalities; try to maximize information; get the incentives right; engage with other countries; and most of all, embrace markets, which do most of these jobs at the same time. Cameroon's poverty costs lives—because poverty kills—and it also robs people of their autonomy and ability to make meaningful choices about their own lives. India, which has done better than Cameroon but fallen far behind China, remains so poor that half a million citizens are disfigured by leprosy, a disease that can be cured for the price of a beer. Meanwhile communist China and the Soviet Union killed tens of millions, often through pure economic failure. Economics matters. The contrast between Cameroon, India, or Mao's China and America, Britain, or Belgium could not be greater.

In the end, economics is about people—something that economists have done a very bad job at explaining. And economic

growth is about a better life for individuals—more choice, less fear, less toil and hardship. Like other economists, I believe that sweatshops are better than the alternatives and without a doubt better than starvation under the Great Leap Forward or in "modern" North Korea. But if I did not also believe that they were a step to something better, I would not be such an enthusiastic supporter of China's reforms.

That is why I was very cheered by the latest news from China. The wealth has not been evenly spread, but it is slowly seeping inland from the "Gold Coast" of Shanghai and Shenzhen. The inland economy of China grew very strongly—by 7.7 percent annually between 1978 and 1991. Between 1978 and 1995, two-thirds of China's provinces grew faster than any country elsewhere in the world. But most importantly, the people of China are feeling the difference. After years of paying low wages—because the supply of migrant labor from China seemed unlimited—factories on the Gold Coast are starting to run out of willing workers. Foreign-owned factories pay a bit more and enjoy easier recruitment and lower turnover. But wages will have to rise and conditions will have to improve, because inland China is catching up.

In 2003, Yang Li did what many Chinese workers have done: she left home to work in a sweatshop in the Pearl River delta. A month later, after working thirteen-hour shifts, she decided to go home and start her own business—a hair salon. "Every day at the factory was just work, work," she says. "My life here is comfortable." Yang Li's parents had to survive the Cultural Revolution; her grandparents, the Great Leap Forward. Yang Li has real choices, and she lives in a country where those choices mean something for her quality of life. She tried factory work and decided it wasn't for her. Now she says that "I can close the salon whenever I want."

Economics is about Yang Li's choice.

Notes

Introduction

The quotation is from Paul Seabright's book *The Company of Strangers* (Princeton: Princeton University Press, 2004), 15.

Chapter 1

David Ricardo's account of economic rents is in *On the Principles of Political Economy and Taxation* (London: John Murray, 1817). The book is available online at: http://www.econlib.org/library/Ricardo/ricP.html. His example of settlers farming different grades of agricultural land is in chapter 2, sections 2.3–2.5.

John Kay's application of Ricardo's theory to companies is in *Foundations of Corporate Success* (Oxford: Oxford Paperbacks, 1995).

To find out about the economics of criminal enterprise, see Steven D. Levitt and Sudhir Alladi Venkatesh, "An economic analysis of a drug-selling gang's finances," *NBER Working Paper Series 6592* (June 1998), and Thomas Schelling's *Choice and Consequence* (Cambridge, MA: Harvard University Press, 1984), chapters 7 and 8.

The underlying cost of a cup of coffee is artfully calculated by Brian McManus, "Nonlinear pricing in an oligopoly market—the case of speciality coffee" (working paper, Olin School of Business, Washington University, St. Louis, MO, 2004), http://www.olin.wustl.edu/faculty/mcmanus/coffee12-04.pdf. The effects of high rents on coffee company profits is explained by Astrid Wentlandt, "Avoiding a coffee has-been," *Financial Times*, August 7, 2002, 19.

A discussion of, and statistics about, immigration and wages come from Martin Wolf, "A Matter of More Than Economics," *Financial Times*, April 14, 2004; and George Borjas, "Economics of Migration" (working paper, Kennedy School of Government, Harvard University, Cambridge, MA, 2000).

Other sources for statistics:

The number of people passing through Waterloo station from Network Rail, http://www.networkrailstations.co.uk/index.cfm?fuseaction=retail.statistics.

Office rents from Insignia, reported in *The Economist*, April 20, 2002, 116.

Most expensive house in the world from BBC Online News, Sunday, April 11, 2004, http://news.bbc.co.uk/1/hi/england/london/3617861.stm.

Chapter 2

I worked out the premium on Fair Trade coffee using the Cafédirect website, http://www.cafedirect.co.uk/fairtrade/gold_prices.php. The exact premium depends on the type of beans and on the world price. (Cafédirect guarantees a minimum price, so when the world price is particularly low the premium rises.) For more discussion of the fair trade coffee market, see Tim Harford, "Fair Trade Coffee has a Commercial Blend," *Financial Times*, September 12, 2003, 15.

For more on Amazon.com's "money on" vouchers see "Keeping the customer satisfied," *The Economist*, July 14, 2001.

Hal Varian is always insightful on the subject of price targeting. The model of price targeting through periodic sales is detailed in Hal. R. Varian, "A Model of Sales," *American Economic Review* 70, no. 4 (September 1980): 651–59. Varian's textbook, *Intermediate Microeconomics*, 4th ed. (New York: W. W. Norton, 1997) covers the subject extensively, including the quotation about French railroads, which comes from Emile Dupuit, an eighteenth-century French economist, translated by R. B. Ekelund, "Price Discrimination and Product Differentiation in Economic Theory: An Early Analysis," *Quarterly Journal of Economics* 84 (1970): 268–78. The amazing stories of price discrimination in hi-tech goods are from Hal Varian and Carl Shapiro, *Information Rules* (Cambridge, MA: Harvard Business School Press, 1999), 59.

I learned why popcorn costs so much at the movies by reading Steven Landsburg's *Armchair Economist* (New York: Free Press, 1993), and why wine costs so much at restaurants in discussion with my former colleague Bill Sjostrom.

Chapter 3

Discussions of Washington DC's baseball stadium are not in short supply, but see for example: "Washington DC asks for private stadium funding," *Sports Illustrated*, December 23, 2004, http://sportsillustrated.cnn.com/2004/baseball/mlb/12/23/roundup.thursday.ap/; "Baseball's coming back to Washington," *Washington Post*, September 30, 2004, http://www.washingtonpost.com/wp-dyn/articles/A60095-2004Sep29.html; and Dennis Coates, "The DC Baseball Stadium Sideshow," *Washington Post*, November 7, 2004, http://www.cato.org/dailys/11-12-04.html.

The Wilt Chamberlain example is from Robert Nozick's *Anarchy, State and Utopia* (Oxford: Basil Blackwell, 1974).

Other sources for statistics:

Rockefeller being the only man to pay the top rate of tax, from Cato Policy Analysis no. 192, http://www.cato.org/pubs/pas/pa-192.html.

The number of deaths of the elderly due to cold, from *Age Concern*, press release, March 7, 2003.

Chapter 4

Many of the statistics on the costs of congestion and pollution, especially in the United Kingdom, are David Maddison, David Pearce et al., *Blueprint 5: The True Costs of Road Transport* (London: Earthscan Publications, 1996).

The impact of environmental taxes on different groups in Britain, such as the poor or rural residents, is discussed in *Blueprint 5* with figures from Johnson et al.; "The Distributional Consequences of Environmental Taxes," *Institute for Fiscal Studies Commentary* 23 (1990): 55; and S. Smith, "The Distributional Consequences of Taxes on Energy and the Carbon Content of Fuels," *European Economy Special Edition* (1992). A separate, more recent, study focused on London is Ian Crawford's *The Distributional Effects of the Proposed London Congestion Charging Scheme* (briefing note, no 11, Institute for Fiscal Studies, Oct. 2000), http://www.ifs.org.uk/consume/gla.pdf. Distributional consequences in the United States are explored by Howard Chernick and Andrew Reschovsky, "Who Pays the Gasoline Tax," in the *National Tax Journal* 50, no. 2 (June 1997): 233–59. More recent data, telling a similar story, are available for some states—for example, Texas, at http://www.window.state.tx.us/taxinfo/incidence/table33_66.html.

For a fairly technical review of estimates of the value people place on their own lives, see Kip Viscusi and Joseph Aldy, *The Value of Statistical Life: A Critical Review of Market Estimates Throughout the World* (AEI-Brookings Joint Center for Regulatory Studies, Related Publication 03-02, Jan. 2003), http://www.aei.brookings.org/publications/abstract.php?pid=305.

I learned about the Camelback houses from David Friedman, *Hidden Order* (New York: HarperBusiness, 1997), 91; and the window tax from David Smith, *Free Lunch* (London: Profile Books, 2003), 148.

On tradable permits in the United States, see Paul L. Joskow, Richard Schmalensee, and Elizabeth Bailey, "The Market for Sulfur Dioxide Emissions," *American Economic Review* 8, no. 4 (Sept. 1998): 669–85. The Chinese program is explained in "A Great Leap Forward," *The Economist*, May 9, 2002. For a design intended to work on a global level see Peter Cramton and Suzi Kerr, "Tradeable Carbon Permit Auctions" (working paper, University of Maryland, 1998), http://www.market-design.com/files/98wp-tradeable-carbon-permit-auctions.pdf. Paul Klemperer, the auction designer who features in chapter 7, helped to design an auction for the United Kingdom government to kick-start their program of tradable emission permits.

Anyone doubting my statement that "economists have long been in the forefront of analyzing environmental problems" will be surprised to hear that one of the first environmentalists was also one of the first and most famous economists, Thomas Malthus, whose study of overpopulation was published in 1798. ("An Essay on the Principle of Population" (London: Murray). Only slightly less famous is the inspiration for this entire chapter: Arthur Pigou, professor of economics at Cambridge University, whose seminal book *The Economics of Welfare* (London: Macmillan, 1920) developed the theory of externalities and the solution of externality pricing. Some readers may also doubt my claim that economists don't care much about GDP. Consider then, this quotation from Steven Landsburg's *The Armchair Economist* (New York: Free Press, 1995, 135–36), which is a characteristically elegant explanation of what most economists believe:

> The gross national product is the most frequently reported measure of general economic well-being. As such, it has some obvious deficiencies. It counts the value of all goods and services produced in the economy, but not the value of time spent relaxing on the beach. . . . Another deficiency is that

increased output of goods and services can be either a good or a bad thing. A construction boom that creates thousands of desirable new houses is a good thing; a construction boom that replaces thousands of old houses destroyed by a hurricane consists of running as fast as possible just to stay in one place. The GNP counts them equally.

Other sources for statistics:

Deaths in the United States caused by particulate matter, from EPA brochure, *Diesel Exhaust in the United States*, http://www.epa.gov/otaq/retrofit/documents/420f03022.pdf.

The tax bill paid by British drivers from D. Newbery, "Fair and Efficient Pricing and the Finance of Roads" *Proceedings of the Chartered Institute of Transport* 7, no. 3, 1998, cited in G. Roth, "Road Pricing in a Free Society," *Economic Affairs*, December 1998. The tax bill paid by American drivers from the US Department of Transportation, http://www.fhwa.dot.gov/ohim/2000hfbt.pdf.

The effect of London's congestion charge on traffic levels is described in "Congestion Charging Six Months On," *Transport for London*, October 2003.

Chapter 5

The classic article on lemons and asymmetric information is George Akerlof, "The Market for 'Lemons': Quality Uncertainty and the Market Mechanism," *Quarterly Journal of Economics* (August 1970). Akerlof's book *An Economic Theorist's Book of Tales* (Cambridge: Cambridge University Press, 1984) contains many of his most interesting papers up to that date—not only the lemons paper but, for instance, economic theories of the caste system.

In conversation, John Kay has made me realize that the explanation of bad restaurants in tourist traps is more subtle than it appears. Tourists can, of course, tell the difference between an upscale and a downscale restaurant, just as in the market for cars, buyers can tell a Ferrari from a Ford. But in both cases, the ignorant buyers cannot tell good from bad within the obvious categories: there are good burger joints and bad ones, and even Ferraris, when secondhand, are likely to be lemons.

Data on health-care spending in different countries is from David M. Cutler, "A Guide to Health Care Reform," *Journal of Economic Perspectives* 8, no. 3 (1994): 13–29; Cutler also reports on the survey of satisfaction with health-care systems carried out by Karen Donelan, Robert Blendon, Cathy Schoen, Karen David, and Katherine Binns: "The Cost of Health System Change: Public Discontent in Five Nations," *Health Affairs* 18, no. 3: 206–16. The responses are: "On the whole, the health system works pretty well, and only minor changes are necessary to make it work better" (these are the respondents I described as "content"); "There are some good things in our health-care system, but fundamental changes are needed to make it work better"; "Our health-care system has so much wrong with it that we need to completely rebuild it."

The World Health Organization website provides a rich resource on European health systems, http://www.euro.who.int/observatory/hits/20020525_1, while the WTO's *World Health Report 2000* provides detailed statistics on the cost of public and private health care across the world.

The cost of the American health-care system to taxpayers is analyzed by S. Woolhandler and D. Himmelstein, "Paying for national health insurance—and not

getting it," *Health Affairs* 21 (August 2002): 88–98, and administrative costs are from Harvard Medical School press release, *"New England Journal of Medicine* Study Shows U.S. Health Care Paperwork Cost $294.3 Billion in 1999 Far More Than in Canada," August 20, 2003, http://www.hms.harvard.edu/news/releases/ 0820woolhimmel.html. The US Census Bureau (2003) measures coverage of the American health system: http://www.census.gov/Press-Release/www/2003/cb03-154.html.

On the controversy over treatment for macular degeneration, see the RNIB's views at http://www.rnib.org.uk/campaign/agemacdegen.htm, and those of NICE at http://www.nice.org.uk/article.asp?a=37590. In September 2003, NICE eventually recommended the use of the treatment in certain circumstances, but the British government delayed implementation. At the time of writing, the treatment is still not widely available. My point is not to attack a specific ruling of NICE but to show that their methodology will inevitably produce results that make patients very unhappy.

The Leksell Gamma Knife is discussed in *Honolulu Star Bulletin*, May 25, 2001 http://starbulletin.com/2001/05/25/news/index.html; Steve Goetsch, San Diego Gamma Knife Center, http://www.medphysics.wisc.edu/medphys_docs/seminars/ goetsch.html.htm; *Hawaii Business*, http://www.hawaiibusiness.cc/hb72001/ default.cfm?articleid=26; and BBC Online News, September 8, 1998, http:// news.bbc.co.uk/1/hi/health/166993.stm. The Gamma Knife is manufactured by Elekta (www.elekta.com).

The Singaporean health system is described by T. A. Massaro and Y. Wong, *Medical Savings Accounts: The Singapore Experience*, National Centre for Policy Analysis report, no. 203 (April 1996), http://www.ncpa.org/studies/s203/ s203.html; and R. Taylor and S. Blair, "Financing Health Care: Singapore's Innovative Approach" http://rru.worldbank.org/PublicPolicyJournal/ Summary.aspx?id=261.

Chapter 6

The analysis of the balance between efficient markets that don't encourage information gathering and inefficient ones that do is by S. J. Grossman and J. E. Stiglitz, "On the Impossibility of Informationally Efficient Markets," *American Economic Review*, 70, no. 3 (June 1980): 393–408. The shopping cart analogy is David Friedman's idea, from his book *Hidden Order* (New York: HarperBusiness, 1996), 9.

Keynes's characterization of the stock market as a beauty contest is in J. M. Keynes, *General Theory of Employment, Interest and Money* (London: Macmillan, 1967), 156. Irving Fisher's misplaced optimism was recorded in *The Stock Market Crash—and After* (New York: Macmillan, 1930).

The sad story of Tony Dye is told by the *Times* (London), "Dye is cast out but strategy remains," March 3, 2000, and *The Guardian*, "Vindication for Dye as P&D fund wins top spot," July 20, 2000.

The most famous bullish book was James Glassman and Kevin Hassett's *Dow 36,000: The New Strategy for Profiting from the Coming Rise in the Stock Market* (New York: Times Books, 1999); the authors defend it in the *Wall Street Journal*, August 1, 2002, "Dow 36,000 revisited," available at http://www.aei.org/news/ filter.,newsID.14128/news_detail.asp) and http://www.techcentralstation.com/ 120504A.html. The prediction that the Dow will hit 36,000 in 3 to 5 years is made

on page 18 of "Dow 36,000," and economist Brad DeLong is extremely dismissive: http://www.j-bradford-delong.net/movable_type/2005_archives/000025.html.

How transformational is the "new economy"? Robert Gordon has given the definitive skeptical statement in "Does the 'New Economy' Measure up to the Great Inventions of the Past?" *Journal of Economic Perspectives* 4, no.14 (Fall 2000): 49–74. Paul David's argument that new technology takes time to have a real economic impact is most famously expounded in "The Dynamo and the Computer: An Historical Perspective on the Modern Productivity Paradox," *The American Economic Review Papers and Proceedings*, May 1990, 355–61. The results of my lost bet with John Kay are in the *Financial Times*, October 29, 1999, or at http://www.johnkay.com/articles/search.php?action=view&doc_id=127&date=&title=&topic=.

Although I am generally dismissive of the idea that Internet companies enjoy a first-mover advantage, I think there is at least one important exception. Online auction sites, which match buyers and sellers of every imaginable product, do have such an edge. The sellers want to go where the buyers are, and the buyers want to go where the sellers are. The first site to do a decent job of bringing them together will prove very hard to dislodge, even if a competitor has a superior technology. The auction site eBay has a dominant position in the United States for just this reason; but in Japan, they moved too late and were beaten out by Yahoo's auction service. (See the interview with eBay's Meg Whitman in *Business Week*, October 2, 2002.)

Other sources for statistics:

Amazon.com stock price data comes from the Amazon.com investor relations website and other information comes from Amazon.com's 2003 Annual Report.

Losses due to internet music piracy from "Rock profits and boogie woogie blues," May 2, 2004, BBC Online News, http://news.bbc.co.uk/1/hi/business/3622285.stm.

Data from Robert Shiller are available at his home page, http://aida.econ.yale.edu/~shiller/.

Chapter 7

See *Prisoner's Dilemma* by William Poundstone (New York: Doubleday, 1992) to find out more about Von Neumann and the use of game theory in the cold war. For an analysis of poker models by Emile Borel, Von Neumann, John Nash, and Lloyd Shapley, see chapter 12 of Ken Binmore's textbook *Fun and Games* (Lexington: D. C. Heath, 1992). This is the same Ken Binmore who later went on to lead the auction design team for the UK 3G auction.

The United States spectrum auctions are expertly discussed in John McMillan's "Selling Spectrum Rights," *Journal of Economic Perspectives* 8, no. 3 (Summer 1994): 145–62; also McAfee and McMillan's "Analysing the Airwaves Auction," *Journal of Economic Perspectives* 10, no. 1 (Winter 1996): 159–75. McMillan also draws lessons from failures in Australia and New Zealand. The collusion theory is explained in *The Economist*, "Economics Brief," May 17, 1997. Not all economists believe that this was the result of collusion—it may also have been a dramatic reevaluation of the licenses.

The design team for the UK auction was assembled by the ESCRC Centre for Economic Learning and Social Equilibrium (ELSE). See www.paulklemperer.org

and http://else.econ.ucl.ac.uk/research/spectrum.shtml for papers and contemporary press. Paul Klemperer's *Auctions: Theory and Practice* (Princeton: Princeton University Press, 2004), especially chapter 6, contains a wealth of material on the spectrum auctions. The book describes (187) analysts' forecasts of the auction revenues (£2–5bn); the auction raised five to ten times this amount. It also contains Klemperer's defense of the auctions (207), originally published as "The Wrong Culprit for Telecom Trouble," *Financial Times*, November 26, 2002.

William Vickrey's classic paper on auctions is "Counterspeculation, Auctions and Competitive Sealed Tenders," *Journal of Finance* 16 (March 1961): 8–37.

Bulow and Klemperer's paper on the merits of auctions relative to other forms of negotiations is "Auctions vs. Negotiations," *American Economic Review* (March 1996): 180–94. Also available at www.paulklemperer.org.

The UK auction history is still available at http://www.ofcom.org.uk/static/archive/spectrumauctions/3gindex.htm.

Chapter 8

Cameroon's level of corruption is rated by Transparency International at www.transparency.org.

Robert Lucas's memorable statement on the importance of economic growth is from "On the Mechanics of Economic Development," *Journal of Monetary Economics* (1988).

The legitimacy of Cameroon's electoral process is a matter for debate. At the time of talking to Sam, Biya's most recent mandate had been to win 93 percent of the votes in the 1997 presidential election, which was boycotted by the opposition. In October 2004, after I had visited Cameroon, Biya won another election with around 75 percent of the vote. Many external observers regarded the election as reasonably fair (see http://news.bbc.co.uk/1/hi/world/africa/3746686.stm). BBC reporters were skeptical; they concluded that many people were unaware of the election or did not vote because they felt their vote would not count. The BBC reported short lines at the polls despite official reports of a high turnout. The number of registered voters is only four million, with a voting-age population of eight million. http://news.bbc.co.uk/1/hi/world/africa/3732512.stm. My own pessimistic view of Cameroon's democracy was formed by talking to Cameroonian citizens who, like Sam, believe it to be a sham.

Mancur Olson's theories are expounded in his *Power and Prosperity* (New York: Basic Books, 2000). The World Bank measures red tape every year in the "Doing Business" reports, http://rru.worldbank.org/DoingBusiness/.

All you ever wanted to know about Nepalese dams is in Elinor Ostrom, "Incentives, Rules of the Game, and Development" (Annual Bank Conference of Development Economics, World Bank, May 1995); Nepal is now in a state of civil war and there are other reasons for civil servants not to leave Kathmandu. At the time of Ostrom's study, though, it was tedium rather than danger that discouraged them.

Alan Gelb of the World Bank gave me the striking comparisons to illustrate how tiny African economies are.

Other sources for statistics:

South Korea's gains from foreign investment from Bohn-Young Koo, "New Forms of Foreign Direct Investment in Korea," (working paper no. 82-02, Korean Development Institute, June 1982).

Cameroon's trade barriers from *World Development Indicators 2001*, 336. http://www.worldbank.org/data/wdi2001/pdfs/tab6_6.pdf.

Chapter 9

Globalization and trade has been the subject of some excellent books in recent years, and ideas and statistics in this chapter are drawn liberally from Martin Wolf's *Why Globalization Works* (New Haven: Yale University Press, 2004), Philippe Legrain's *Open World* (London: Abacus, 2002), Douglas Irwin's *Free Trade Under Fire* (Princeton: Princeton University Press, 2002), and Jagdish Bhagwati's *Free Trade Today* (Princeton: Princeton University Press, 2002). David Friedman's book *Hidden Order* (New York: Harpercollins, 1996, 65–77) contains an excellent chapter on trade theory.

E. O. Wilson's discussion of homogenization is from his splendid display of his comparative advantage. See Wilson's *Consilience—The Unity of Knowledge* (London: Abacus, 2003), 304.

The original paper proving that a tax on imports is a tax on exports is Abba P. Lerner's "The Symmetry Between Import and Export Taxes," *Economica* 3 (August 1936): 306–13.

I leave to one side discussion of migration, capital flows, and technological transfers. You can find out more in Martin Wolf's *Why Globalization Works* or in a speech by Stanley Fischer, "Globalization and its challenges" http://www.iie.com/fischer/pdf/fischer011903.pdf (delivered to the American Economics Association, January 3, 2003).

Vandana Shiva's view on environmental apartheid is from "On the edge: living with Global Capitalism," Will Hutton and Anthony Giddens, eds., cited in Philippe Legrain's *Open World* (London: Abacus, 2002).

Statistics on the cleanliness of US investment overseas from the American Census Bureau and from R. Repetto and J. Albrecht, both cited in Legrain, *Open World*. Figure 6 is from D. Wheeler, "Racing to the Bottom: Foreign Investment and Air Pollution in Developing Countries," *Journal of Environment and Development* 10, no. 3: 225–45, reported in an overview by Dasgupta et al., "Confronting the Environmental Kuznets Curve," *Journal of Economic Perspectives* 16, no. 1 (Winter 2001): 147–68.

On agricultural subsidies see Martin Wolf, "Weeding Out Subsidies," *Financial Times*, November 5, 2002; and Douglas Irwin, *Free Trade Under Fire*, 61–62.

Jonah Peretti tells his story in "My Nike Media Adventure," *The Nation*, March 22, 2001, http://www.thenation.com/doc.mhtml?i=20010409&s=peretti. The Smokey Mountain example is from Paul Krugman, "In Praise of Cheap Labor," *Slate*, Thursday, March 20, 1997, http://web.mit.edu/krugman/www/smokey.html. News of the landslide came from *The Economist*, July 13, 2000. William Greider explains his support of New York's rules on imported clothes in "No to Global Sweatshops," *The Nation*, April 19, 2001, http://www.thenation.com/doc.mhtml?i=20010507&s=greider. Douglas Irwin and Philippe Legrain both have good arguments and data to support the view that multinationals pay more and offer better conditions than local firms.

The political economy of trade restrictions explains the stability of Tokugawa, Japan, described by Janet E. Hunter, *The Emergence of Modern Japan* (London: Longman, 1989), 4–7; it is fully explored by Douglas Irwin in *Free Trade Under Fire*, chapter 5.

The BBC has covered the fate of the poor coffee farmers in depth: http://news.bbc.co.uk/1/hi/business/1493104.stm ("Coffee Farmers Switch to Drugs," August 15, 2001); http://news.bbc.co.uk/1/hi/business/1333204.stm ("Coffee Farmers Face Destitution," May 16, 2001); http://news.bbc.co.uk/1/hi/business/1488758.stm ("The Cappuccino Trail," 16 August 16, 2001); http://news.bbc.co.uk/1/hi/business/1608356.stm ("Coffee Cartel Shuts Up Shop," October 19, 2001).

Other sources for statistics:

Job creation and destruction in the United States, from Bureau of Labor Statistics, 2004.

The Duke of Westminster's agricultural handout, from "Oxfam calls for EU reform" http://news.bbc.co.uk/1/hi/uk_politics/4374655.stm, BBC Online News, March 23, 2005.

Various estimates of the benefits from trade are gathered from Douglas Irwin's *Free Trade Under Fire*, 30–48.

Data on trade barriers from *World Development Indicators 2001*, 336, http://www.worldbank.org/data/wdi2001/pdfs/tab6_6.pdf.

Other trade statistics from the *World Trade Overview 2000*, World Trade Organization, 2001.

Chapter 10

The effects of Mao's "great leap forward" are discussed by J. M. Roberts in *Penguin History of the World* (London: Penguin, 1995), 1013, and especially Jonathan Glover, *Humanity: A Moral History of the 20th Century* (New Haven: Yale University Press, 1999). John Kay tells the story of Khrushchev's great experiment in *The Truth about Markets* (London: Allen Lane, Penguin Press, 2003), 88.

A symposium in the *Journal of Economic Perspectives* 8, no 2 (Spring 1994) is a wonderful analysis of Deng's reforms in the 1980s. Articles include Dwight Perkins, "Completing China's move to the market"; Shahid Yusuf, "China's Macroeconomic performance and management during transition"; and Gary Jefferson and Thomas Rawski, "Enterprise reform in Chinese industry." Other invaluable resources are Barry Naughton, *Growing Out of the Plan* (Cambridge: Cambridge University Press, 1995); Justin Yifu Lin, "Rural reforms and agricultural growth in China," *American Economic Review* 82, no 1 (March 1992); and Robert F. Dernberger, "The People's Republic of China at 50: The Economy," in *The People's Republic of China After 50 Years*, ed. Richard Louis Edmonds (New York: Oxford University Press, 1999). More recent views on China come from Martin Wolf, "Asia's Awakening," *Financial Times*, September 21, 2003; and from David Hale and Lyric Hughes Hale, "China takes off," *Foreign Affairs* 86, no 6 (Nov/Dec 2003).

Jagdish Bhagwati's condemnation of Indian economic policy is from "Review of Sachs-Varshney-Bajpai and Lal," *Times Literary Supplement*, January 2000. Available at: http://www.columbia.edu/~jb38/TLS_SV.pdf. Charles Wheelan, in *Naked Economics* (New York: W.W. Norton, 2002), makes the point that leprosy can be cured for the price of a beer.

On the cult of Mao see Richard McGregor, "Mao and Forever," *Financial Times Magazine*, August 14, 2004. Lucy Ash reports on harsh working conditions in "Inside China's Sweatshops," BBC Online News, "From Our Own

Correspondent," July 20, 2002, http://news.bbc.co.uk/1/hi/programmes/from_our_own_correspondent/2139401.stm. Yang Li's choice is described in Alexandra Harney, "Migrant workers shun long hours and low pay," *Financial Times*, November 2, 2004.

Other sources for statistics:
 Statistics on Chinese growth rates and the size of the economy relative to others, such as Cameroon and Belgium, from *World Development Indicators 2002*.
 The statistics on the transformation of South Korea's economy are from Anne Krueger, "Institutions of the New Private Sector," in *The Emergence of Market Economies in Eastern Europe*, eds. Christopher Clague and Gordon Rausser (Cambridge, MA: Blackwell, 1992), cited in Mancur Olson, *Power and Prosperity* (New York: Basic Books, 2003).

Index

and government involvement, 107
and public transportation, 18
and random walk theory, 139–40
training, 67
trains, 51, 56, 232
transparency in auctions, 164–65, 172
Transparency International, 178
transportation, 18, 56, 96–98, 219–20. *See also* traffic
travel industry, 38, 51–52, 186–89
Truman, Harry, 224
trust, 117–18, 198, 248

unemployment insurance, 124
uninsured population, 121
Union of Needletrades, Industrial, and Textile Employees (UNITE), 224
unions, 25–26, 224–25
United Kingdom
 air pollution, 81
 efficiency vs. fairness, 73
 fuel prices, *88*
 health care system, 28, 120, 121, *122*, 126, 132
 immigration, 28
 industrial revolution, 233
 infrastructure, 183
 railroads, 151
 spectrum auctions, 163, 165–68, 168–73, 173–75
 taxation, 82
 unions, 26
 wealth inequality, 89
United States
 exports, 245
 fuel prices, *88*
 health care system, 113, 119–23, *122*
 industrial revolution, 233
 infrastructure, 183
 pollution, 81, 221
 and special interests, 227
 spectrum rights auctions, 159–61, 165
 taxation, 82

trade barriers, 226
wealth inequality, 89
universal health care, 120, 126
unskilled labor, 28, 29
Uruguay round of trade negotiations, 225
US Congress, 227
US Department of Transportation, 85
US Federal Reserve, 66
USAID, 195
used cars, 110–13, 116–19

vaccinations, 103–4
Varian, Hal, 254n.
Vehicle Excise Duties, 82
vehicle taxes, 82–83
Ven der Beurs family, 201–2
Venezuela, 23
Venkatesh, Sudhir, 24
Vickrey auctions, 164
Vietnam, 228–29
village enterprises, 244
viruses, 184
Visudyne, 127, 133
Vodafone, 173, 174
Voluntary Service Overseas (VSO), 190
Von Neumann, John, 156, 158, 161–62, 167, 175
vouchers, 90

wages, 24–26, 67, 94
The Wall Street Crash—And After (Fisher), 148–49
Wal-Mart, 26
waste, 192, 233
Waterloo station, 6
wealth and wealth inequality
 in China, 233, 252
 and development, 197–98
 and fairness, 75
 and nonmarket economies, 69
 and price sensitivity, 38
 and taxation, 71–72
 in the US and UK, 89

West End, London, 17
Western Europe, 213
Western society, 68
Wholefoods, 42, 43–44, 114–15
Why Globalization Works (Wolf), 251
Wilde, Oscar, 155
Wilson, Edward O., 203–6
wine, 48–49
Wolf, Martin, 213, 218, 251
Woods, Tiger, 75–76
World Bank, 182, 183, 188–89

world economy, 199
World War II, 73

xenophobia, 212
Xi'an, China, 245

Yahoo!, 153, 258n.
Yang Li, 252

Zhengzhou, China, 232, 237–41, 245–46
Zhou Shien Pin, 251